Road Traffic Accident Claims

Road Traffic Accident Claims

Second Edition

Roger Thorn, QC,
LLB (Hons)

and

Norman Airey
*I Eng (Engineering Council); AMIRTE;
Aff, IMI; AMSABT; MITAI*

© Roger Thorn and Norman Airey 1990

ISBN 0 85121 6714

First Edition 1987
(*Published as 'A Practical Guide to Road Traffic Accident Claims'*)
Second Edition 1990

Published by
Longman Law, Tax and Finance
Longman Group UK Ltd
21–27 Lamb's Conduit Street
London WC1N 3NJ

Associated Offices
Australia, Hong Kong, Malaysia, Singapore, USA

A CIP catalogue record for this book is available from the British Library

Printed and bound in Great Britain by
Biddles Ltd, Guildford and King's Lynn

The Authors

Roger Thorn QC is a member of the Honourable Society of the Middle Temple and the North Eastern Circuit.

Norman Airey is an Incorporated Engineer (Engineering Council), an Associated Member of the Institute of Road Transport Engineers, the Society of Automotive-Electrical Technicians Ltd and the Institute of Traffic Accident Investigators. He is also affiliated with the Institute of the Motor Industry and has a Certificate of Education from Leeds University. He was formerly a lecturer in Transport Studies and a Course Tutor for the City and Guilds Police Motor Vehicle Advanced Examination and Testing Course and with the Durham County Police Serious Incident Squad. He is presently an Accident Investigator and Transport and Training Consultant.

Acknowledgements

The authors would like to express their appreciation to Mrs Pat Airey for her support, patience and assistance.

The authors sought the help of many experts while drafting the second edition and although they are too numerous to mention individually, their help is remembered and appreciated.

The forms related to the testing of motor vehicles and trailers and the Ordnance Survey maps printed in this book are reproduced with the kind permission of the Controller of HMSO.

Contents

Foreword to the First Edition	xi
Foreword to the Second Edition	xiii
Table of Cases	xv
Table of Statutes	xix
Table of Statutory Instruments	xxi
Introduction	1

Part One: Gathering the Facts	5

The Immediate Steps	7
1 Witnesses	7
2 The place	8
3 The vehicles	9
4 Records	10
5 Exceptions	11

Contemporaneous Records	12
1 Tachographs	12
2 Definition of terms	14
3 Individual control books	16
4 MOT Tests	18
5 Goods vehicles' test	23
6 Local authority obligations	29
7 Police accident reports	29

Statutory Obligations to Provide Information About Drivers	32
1 Accident reports	32
2 Employer's duties	33
3 Insurance details	34

The Taking of Witness Statements	35
1 Checklist	35
2 Court powers	37
3 Examples	37

Illustrative Aids	39
1 Sketches	39

2 Scale plans   39
3 Photographs   44

Estimating Distances in Photographs   48
1 Road markings   48

Letter Before Action   52

Part Two: Expert Evidence   55

The Guiding Principles   57

Topics for the Expert   60
1 Vehicle damage related to speed on impact   60
2 Skid marks   61
3 The absence of skid marks   61
4 Braking efficiency   62
5 Formulae   62
6 Alteration to vehicle design and construction   70
7 Corrosion   73
8 Tyres   73
9 The expert report and proof of evidence   77
10 Recoverable fees in the county court   79

Part Three: Assessing Liability   81

The General Principles of Liability   83
1 Assessment of liability   83
2 Breach of legislation   84
3 Breach of the Highway Code   85
4 Previously decided cases   85
5 Contributory negligence   86
6 Apportionment of liability between parties   88
7 The judicial approach   88

Pedestrians
1 Assessing pedestrian negligence   91
2 Children as pedestrians   92
3 Drunken pedestrians   94
4 Crossings   94
5 Hazards for pedestrians   100

Seat Belts   101
1 Front seats   101
2 Rear seats   102
3 Contributory negligence   103
4 Coaches   105

Drivers and Vehicles   106
  1 The drinking driver   106
  2 The learner driver   107
  3 Motor cycles   108
  4 Public service vehicles   112

Crossing Traffic, Collision at Junctions and Speeding   117
  1 Junctions   117
  2 Speed limits   121

Lights   124
  1 Lighting-up times   124
  2 Lighting on vehicles   124
  3 Parking at night   125
  4 Conspicuity of the sides of vehicles, trailers and projecting loads 127

Miscellaneous Hazards   133
  1 Builder's skips   133
  2 Negligent opening of vehicle doors   134
  3 Drivers in convoy   135
  4 Horses and road accidents   137

Part Four: Motor Vehicle Loss or Damage   143

Damage or Loss of the Vehicle   145
  1 Compensation from criminal courts   145
  2 Calculating the loss of use   147
  3 Repairs   150
  4 Hire charges for the replacement   152

Part Five: Litigation   155

Finance   157
  1 Financial arrangements   157

Pleadings   163
  1 Procedure   163
  2 Pleaded cases   165

Appendices   169
  1 Conversion Table of Equivalent Speeds   169
  2 Distance to Stop in Feet   170
  3 Time to Stop in Seconds   173
  4 Record of Interview   175
  5 Exemptions from Tachographs   178

Foreword to the First Edition

Both of us, practising in our own separate fields over the years, came to be surprised that there was no comprehensive guide to road traffic accident claims, representing as they do each year such a bulky part of all litigation; so many millions of pounds in damages, costs and fines; the first brush with the law for ordinary folk, and so much sheer personal suffering.

Rapid changes in the law, to be found in abstruse corners of varying obscurity, may perhaps have deterred some from attempting what we may so foolishly have attempted to place in one book.

In darker moments we have even wondered if it might be thought that dissemination of what expertise we have sought to share might be seen as 'obvious' for those professionally engaged in this field who might turn to this guide, or 'threatening' to any profession whose clients might find this work of help and their service less necessary. Our experience gives us cautious optimism to the contrary.

But when the first-named author started the outline of this work on the Isle of Islay in the Summer Vacation of 1984, none of these doubts were present. Combining everyday work with this labour of love thereafter has caused too much delay, with not enough time to do it the justice we had hoped for, but if it assists in the saving of time for others, the more efficient conduct of claims, or the alleviation of some suffering and many of the uncertainties of litigation: then we may feel its imperfections will be forgiven in a field we readily acknowledge is too vast to be covered entirely other than in a book.

Every attempt has been made to ensure that this work is up-to-date and accurate. We ask forgiveness from our less cynical readers that, in a world where exemption clauses against 'any liability however arising' have to be relied upon, we find ourselves (and those associated with this work) in no different a position.

Roger E Thorn
Norman Airey
1987

Foreword to the Second Edition

We welcome the assistance of our publishers in producing this second edition. Since the first edition we have received numerous requests for assistance about matters that could have been simply answered by reference to the book. Where this was not possible we hope the second edition remedies this.

The 1988 Road Traffic Act legislation and the repeal of the 1972 Road Traffic Act in entirety, along with other changes over three years, has involved substantial alterations and additions. (Whether this consolidating measure merited three separate Acts might be doubted). Two years after the passing of that legislation, replacement statutory Forms (eg for vehicle testing) are still not being universally used.

In the main, substantial alterations to road traffic law have been effected by statutory instrument (eg, the Pelican Pedestrian Crossing Regulations and the Motor Vehicles (Wearing of Seat Belts by Children in Rear Seats) Regulations). There have also been some important developments in case law. As a result, this second edition bears substantial additions, particularly in respect of tachographs; pelican crossings; learner drivers, instructors and examiners; motor cyclists; horses; legal aid, and in respect of quantum. There are completely new sections in relation to tyres, public service vehicles and apportionment of liability.

The Lord Chancellor's welcome attempts to speed up and reform civil litigation are represented in broad outline. We remain of the view that detailed references in a book such as this to court procedure and pleadings would make it cumbersome.

We continue to be dismayed by the lack of attention to detail by the police at accident scenes and a frequently low standard of accident investigation which so often hampers civil accident claims. The unrepentant explanation offered by many forces is that the police are only concerned to investigate criminal offences.

Putting aside the question as to how the police can pre-judge at the scene of an accident what quality of investigation is required, and even accepting financial constraints, we find this blinkered stubborness and acceptance of two different standards of investigation, despite what may have been serious injuries, wholly contrary to the public interest.

Nor can it be said that civilian accident investigators show a maximum acceptable standard of competence. The formation in 1989 of The Institute of Traffic Accident Investigators, with its objectives to improve professional standards is therefore warmly welcomed.

The law is up to date as at 1 August 1990.

Roger E Thorn
Norman Airey
August 1990

Table of Cases

Aldham v United Dairies (London) Ltd [1940] KB 507 140
Andrews v Freeborough [1966] 1 QB 1; [1966] 3 WLR 342; 2 All ER 721, CA 92
Arnold v National Westminster Bank plc [1989] *The Independent*, 24 November;
  [1990] 3 All ER 977, Ch D *Affd* [1990] 1 All ER 529, CA 90
Arnold v Teno [1978] CLY 2064; 83 DLR (3d) 609, (Can Sup Ct) 100
Azzopardi v State Transport Authority [1983] CLY 2515; 30 SASR 434 (Supreme
  Court of South Australia)... 116
Bacon v Cooper [1982] 1 All ER 397 151
Baker v Market Harborough Industrial Co-operative Society [1953] 1 WLR 1477 89
Baker v Willoughby [1969] AC 467; [1970] 2 WLR 50; [1969] 2 All ER 549 91
Barkway v South Wales Transport [1950] AC 185; 1 All ER 392; 94 SJ 128, HL 136
Bartlett v Sidney Marcus [1965] 1 WLR 1013; [1965] 2 All ER 753; 109 SJ 451, CA.. 23
Bell v British Gypsum (Lawson J, Carlisle Crown Court 13 January 1983) 77, 78
Boss v Measures [1988] Crim LR 582 34
Bray v Palmer [1953] 1 WLR 1455; 97 SJ 830 89
Brown & Lynn v Western Scottish Motor Traction Co Ltd [1945] SC 31, Ct of Sess. 137
BSM v Simms [1971] 1 All ER 317; [1971] RTR 190.. 108
Burns v Ellicott (1969) 113 SJ 490 140
Burr v Ware RDC [1959] 2 All ER 688, CA.. 164
Capps v Miller [1989] 2 All ER 333, CA 104, 110
Carryfast v Hack [1981] RTR 464 .... 140, 141
Carter v Sheath [1989] *The Times*, 10 August.. 88
Chidgey v Crow [1989] CLY 1168 147
Clarke v Winchurch and Others [1969] 1 WLR 69; [1969] 1 All ER 275; 112 SJ 909,
  CA... 118, 119
Clayards v Dethick [1848] 12 QB 439.. 87
Clifford v Drymond [1976] RTR 134; 120 SJ 149, CA 96
Clippens Oil Company v Edinburgh & District Trustees [1907] AC 271 153
Condon v Condon [1978] CLY 2611; RTR 483 104
Crank v Brooks [1980] RTR 441, DC 95, 111
Crawford v Jennings [1982] CLY 516... 119
Crowther v Shannon Motor Co [1975] 1 All ER 139 23
Daily Office Cleaning Contractors v Shefford [1977] RTR 361, DC 152
Darbishire v Warran [1963] 1 WLR 1067; [1963] 3 All ER 310; [1963] 2 Lloyd's Rep
  187, CA.. 150
Davies v Journeaux [1975] 1 Lloyd's Rep 483; [1976] RTR 111, CA 93
Dexter v Ellis [1968] CA 190.. 92
Dodd Properties v Canterbury County Council [1979] 1 WLR 433; 2 All ER 118;
  [1980] 1 All ER 928, CA 153
Donn v Schater [1975] RTR 238.. 105
Donoghoe v Blundell [1986] CLY 2254 94
Drury v Camden LBC [1972] RTR 391 134
Dymond v Pearce and Others [1972] 2 WLR 633; 1 All ER 1142; 116 SJ 62, CA.... 126, 134

Eastman v South West Thames Health Authority [1990] *The Times*, 4 May 105
Elpidoforos Shipping Corporation v Furness Withy (Australia) Pty Ltd [1986] *The Times* 28 November 152
Evers v Bennet [1983] CLY 2518; 31 SASR 228, (Supreme Court of South Australia)...... 91
Fardon v Marcourt-Rivington (1932) 146 LT 391...... 86
Ferdinand Retzlaf, The [1972] 2 Lloyd's Rep 120 152
Fitzgerald v Lane & Another [1987] 2 All ER 455 89
Fitzgerald v Lane & Another [1989] 2 All ER 961 88
Foskett v Mistry [1984] RTR 1; (1983) 80 LSGaz 2683, CA 86, 93
Froom v Butcher [1975] QB 286; 3 WLR 379; 3 All ER 520 ...... 101, 104, 105
Fury v Council of the City of Cardiff [1977] CLY 2031 114
Gaunt v Nelson [1986] RTR 1; *The Times*, 21 May, DC...... 15
Gaynor v Allen [1959] 2 QB 403; 3 WLR 221; 2 All ER 644...... 121
Gazell, The 1844 2 W Rob (Adm) 279 151
Gibbons v Kahl [1955] 1 QB 59; [1955] 3 WLR 596; 3 All ER 345 94
Gibbons v Wall [1988] *The Times*, 24 February, CA...... 162
Gibbons v Priestly [1979] RTR 4...... 108
Glasgow Corporation v Sutherland [1951] WN 111; 95 SJ 204, HL...... 114
Gough v Thorne [1966] 1 WLR 1387; [1966] 2 All ER 398; 110 SJ 529, CA...... 92
Grant v Sun Shipping Co Ltd [1948] AC 549; 2 All ER 238; 92 SJ 513 87
Haimes v Watson [1981] RTR 90, CA...... 140
Hamilton v Whitelock [1987] RTR 23; [1987] 3 CMLR 190 (European Court); *The Times*, 10 June 179
Hannam v Mann [1984] RTR 252, CA...... 121, 127
Harding v Price [1948] 1 KB 695; 1 All ER 283; 92 SJ 112...... 33
Hardy v Walder [1984] RTR 312, CA 120
Hassel, The [1962] 2 Lloyd's Rep 139...... 152
Hatch v Platt [1988] CLY 1073...... 147
Hatton v London Transport Executive [1956] CLY 6032; *The Times*, May 3 114
Hill-Venning v Beszant [1950] 2 All ER 1151; 94 SJ 760; 49 LGR 12, CA...... 126
Hill v Phillips (1963) 107 SJ 890, CA...... 126
HL Motorworks v Alwahli [1977] RTR 276, CA 152
Hoadley v Dartford District Council [1979] RTR 359; CLY 2367; 123 SJ 129 105
Hollington v Hewthorn [1943] 1 KB 587...... 37
Hopwood Homes Ltd v Kennerdine 1975 RTR 82, CA...... 120
Hoy v Smith [1964] 1 WLR 1377; [1964] 2 All ER 670; 62 LGR 661, DC 99
Hunter v Wright [1938] 2 All ER 621, CA...... 61
Hyde & South Bank Housing Association v Kain [1989] *The Times*, 27 July...... 90
Jarvis v Fuller [1974] RTR 160; [1974] Crim LR 116, DC...... 137
Jones v Bristol Crown Court 1986 CLY 2904; 1986 150 JP 93, DC 125
Jones v Stroud [1988] 1 WLR 1141; 1 All ER 5; 279 EG 213...... 151
Jones v Lawrence [1969] 3 All ER 267...... 93
Jones v Maggi [1954] CA 267...... 92
Jungnickel v Laing (1966) 111 SJ 19, CA 137
Kelly v Shulman [1989] 1 All ER 106, QBD...... 14
Kenning v Eve Construction Ltd [1989] 1 WLR 1189...... 77
Kite v Nolan [1983] 126 SJ 821; [1983] RTR 253, CA 100
Kozimor v Adey (1962) 106 SJ 431; [1962] Crim LR 564 95
Lancaster v HBH Transport [1980] CLY 267...... 119
Lawrence v W M Palmer (Excavations) Ltd (1965) 109 SJ 358...... 96
Lawson v Ramsden [1980] CLY 269 93
Lee v Lever [1974] RTR 35, CA 126
Liesbosch Dredger v SS Edison [1933] AC 499 153
London Passenger Transport Board v Upson [1949] AC 155; [1949] 1 All ER 60; [1949] LJR 238...... 87
Losexis Ltd v Clarke [1984] RTR 174, DC...... 111
Luyke-Roskott v Cupocci [1989] CLY 122...... 147

Mackay *v* Jackson (1987) 3 CL 53; CLY 1128 136
Martindale *v* Duncan [1973] 1 WLR 574; [1973] 2 All ER 355; 117 SJ 168 153
Maynard *v* Rogers [1970] RTR 392; 114 SJ 320 95
Millar *v* Candy (1984) CLY 1035 147
Millensted *v* Grosvenor House (Park Lane) Ltd [1937] 1 KB 717 90
Moore *v* DER [1971] 1 WLR 1476; [1971] 3 All ER 517; 115 SJ 528 .... 150, 152
Moore *v* Maxwells [1968] 1 WLR 1077; 2 All ER 779; 112 SJ 424, CA 126
Moore *v* Poyner [1975] RTR 127, CA 100
Murray *v* Doherty [1986] CLY 2331; [1986] 2 NIJB 56 147
Nettleship *v* Weston [1971] 2 QB 691 [1971] 3 WLR 370; 3 All ER 581 107
New Brunswick Railway *v* British & French Trust Corporation [1939] AC 20; In Re
  B (minors) (1989) *The Times*, 5 October 90
North West Water Authority *v* Binnie & Partners [1989] *The Independent*, 24
  November 90
O'Connell *v* Jackson [1972] 1 QB 277 110
O'Driscoll *v* Sleigh [1985] CLY 136 161
O'Grady *v* Westminster Scaffolding Ltd [1962] 2 Lloyd's Rep 238 151
Ollett *v* Bristol Aero Jet Ltd [1979] 1 WLR 1197; [1979] 3 All ER 544; 123 SJ 705 78
Owens *v* Brimmel [1976] 3 All ER 765 106
Parkinson *v* Liverpool Corporation [1950] All ER 367; 48 LGR 331; 94 SJ 161 114
Parnell *v* MPDR [1976] RTR 201, CA 137
Pasternack *v* Poulton [1973] 1 WLR 476; [1973] 2 All ER 74; 117 SJ 225 105
Patience *v* Andrews [1982] CLY 789; [1983] RTR 447, CA 104
Payton *v* Brookes [1974] RTR 169; [1974] 1 Lloyd's Rep 241, CA 151
Phillips *v* Britannia Hygenic Laundry Co [1923] 1 KB 548 139
Pitt *v* Hunt [1990] *The Independent*, 4 May 106, 112
Pittalis *v* Sherefettin [1986] QB 868; [1986] 2 WLR 1003; [1986] 2 All ER 227 90
Powell *v* Moody (1966) 110 SJ 215, CA 118
Powney *v* Coxage [1988] *The Times*, 8 March 161
Practice Direction [1984] 3 All ER 165 166
Quinn *v* Scott [1965] 1 WLR 1394; [1969] 3 All ER 1212; 113 SJ 687, CA 122
R *v* Inwood RJ [1973] 1 WLR 647; (1973) 60 Cr App R 70 146
R *v* Mayfield Chicks Ltd [1989] 14
R *v* Worthing Justices *ex p* Waste Management [1989] RTR 131, DC 134
Rhesa Shipping Co SA *v* Edmunds [1985] 1 WLR 954 88
Richley *v* Faull [1965] 1 WLR 1454; 3 All ER 109; 109 SJ 937 61
Rubie *v* Faulkner [1940] 1 All ER 285 107
Saper *v* Hungate [1972] RTR 380 134
Saunders & Partners *v* East Glenn Ltd [1989] *The Times*, 28 July 37
Schilling *v* Lenton [1989] 6 CL 321 (Australia) 127
Schott Kem Ltd *v* Bentley & Others [1990] *The Independent*, 6 March, CA 162
Scott *v* Warren [1974] RTR 104; (1973) 117 SJ 916; [1974] Crim LR 117, DC 137
Searle *v* Wallbank [1947] AC 341; [1947] 1 All ER 12; 91 SJ 83, HL 139
Sever *v* Duffy [1977] RTR 429; [1977] Crim LR 487, DC 134
Sharp *v* Avery [1983] 4 All ER, 85 CA 136
Skolimowski *v* Haynes [1983] CLY 2525 97
Smith *v* Geraghty [1986] RTR 222, DC 106
Smith *v* Harris [1939] 3 All ER 960, CA 136
Smithers *v* H & N Transport (Oxford) Ltd (1983) CLY 2527; 133 New LJ 558 120
Snow *v* Giddins (1969) 113 SJ 229, CA 95
Stewart *v* Hancock [1940] 2 All ER 427 126
Stone *v* Fulleylove [1985] CLY 929 153
Swadding *v* Cooper [1931] AC 1 87
Thomson *v* Spedding [1973] RTR 312, CA 137
Tremayne *v* Hill [1986] RTR 131; *The Times*, 11 December 95, 96
Truscott *v* McLaren [1982] RTR 34, CA 119
Tustin *v* Arnold (1915) 84 LJKB 2214 164
Verney *v* Wilkins [1962] Crim LR 840; 106 SJ 879 107

Vulcano v Benitez [1983] CLY 2561 119
Wallace v Newton [1982] 1 WLR 375; 2 All ER 106; (1982) 126 SJ 101 141
Waller v Laughton [1982] CLY 2132.. 93
Wardell-Yearburgh v Surrey County Council [1973] RTR 462................................... 121
Watson Norrie v Shaw and Nelson [1967] 1 Lloyd's Rep 515, CA 152
Webb v Crane [1987] RTR 204; (1987) *The Times*, 14 October, DC 102
Webster v Wall [1980] RTR 284; [1980] Crim LR 186, DC... 125
Western Scottish Motor Traction Co v Allam [1943] 2 All ER 742, HL................. 114, 116
Whitehead v Chaplin [1952] CA 91 87
Wilkie v London Transport Board [1947] 1 All ER 258; LJR 864; 177 LT 71, CA..... 114
Williams v Needham [1972] RTR 387 95
Wills v Martin [1972] RTR 368; 116 SJ 145; [1972] 1 Lloyd's Rep 541 134
Wooler v LTB [1976] RTR 206, CA.. 137
Worsfold v Howe [1980] 1 WLR 1175; [1980] 1 All ER 1028; (1979) 124 SJ 646, CA
.... 118, 120

Table of Statutes

Animals Act 1971 139
  s2(2) 140
    (b) 141
  s8(2) 139
Arbitration Act 1980 165
Civil Evidence Act 1968—
  s2(2)(b) 37
County Courts Act 1984—
  s51 166
Criminal Justice Act 1988—
  s104 145
Health and Safety at Work Act 1974—
  s47 (1) 85
Highways Act 1935—
  s72 .... 138, 139
Highways Act 1980—
  s71 138
  s139 .... 133, 134
  s140 134
    (6) 134
Law Reform (Contributory
  Negligence) Act 1945—
  s1(1) 86
Legal Aid Act 1988 160
Licensing Act 1872—
  s12 141
Limitation Act 1980 157
Motor Cycle Crash Helmets
  (Religious Exemption) Act 1976 ... 110
Motor Cycle Crash Helmets
  (Restriction of Liability) Act 1985 . 110
Powers of Criminal Court Act
  1973—
  s25(4) 146
  s35 145
Public Order Act 1986 .... 113, 115
Public Passenger Vehicles Act 1981 .. 112
  s8(2) 113
  s20 112
  s29 114
Road Traffic Act 1972—
  s33(a) 101
Road Traffic Act 1988 .... 34, 141
  s8(2) 106

Road Traffic Act 1988—contd
  s11 106
  s14(4) 102, 110
  s15(1) 102
    (3) 103
  s16 110
    (2) 110
  s17(2) 111
  s18 111
    (7) 111
  s22 125
  s38(7) 85, 165
  s39 29
  s45 .... 18, 22
  s48 18
  s49 .... 23, 29
  ss54–65 70
  s75 .... 21, 71
  s76 71
  s149(2) 106
  s151 .... 34, 164
  s152(i)(a) 34
  s154 34
  s165 32
  s168 33
  s170 32
  s172 34
  s175 .... 18, 21
Road Traffic Regulation Act 1984—
  ss14–16 122
  s25 94
  s26 97
  s28(1), (2) 99
  s82 122
  s87 121
  s88 122
  s95 99
  s112(a)(i), (ii) 34
  Sched 6 121
Sale of Goods Act 1979—
  s14(2), (3) 21
Supply of Goods (Implied Terms)
  Act 1973—
  s10(2), (3) 21

Supreme Court Act 1981—
  s32A 166
Theft Act 1968 145
Third Party (Rights Against
  Insurers) Act 1930 164

Transport Act 1968—
  s97 14
Transport Act 1981 106
  s27 101

Statutory Instruments and EEC Legislation

Builders Skips (Markings) Regulations 1984 (SI No 1933) 133
Community Drivers' Hours and Recording Equipment (Exemption and
  Supplementary Provisions) Regulations 1986 (SI No 1456) 15
Community Road Transport Rules (Exemptions) Regulations 1978 (SI No 1158)..... 14
  reg 4(3)(*b*) 15
Construction and Use Regulations... 9, 71
County Court Fees (Amendment No 2) Order 1986 (SI No 2143)............................ 79
County Court Rules 1981
  Ord 12, r 1 161
  Ord 38, r 10.. 44
  Ord 38, r 14.. 79
      (2) 79
Drivers' Hours (Goods Vehicles) (Keeping of Records) Regulations 1987 (SI No
  1421) 18
Driving Licences Regulations 1981 108
EEC Directive 71/127.. 71
EEC Directive 71/320.. 71, 73
EEC Directive 85/647
  Art 2.2.1.8.. 71
EEC Regulation 543/69.. 15
  Art 14 (*a*)(2), (3).. 14
EEC Regulation 1463/70 15
  Art 3 14
  Art 15... 14
  Art 17... 14
EEC Regulation 3820/85 .... 14, 15
  sI, Art 1 14
  sV, Art 7 14
  Art 4 178
EEC Regulation 3821/85 .... 15, 16
Motor Cars (Driving Instruction) (Amendment) Regulations 1989 (SI No 1373)....... 108
Motor Cycle (Eye Protectors) Regulations 1985 111
Motor Cycle (Eye Protectors) (Amendment) Regulations 1988 (SI No 1031)............ 111
Motor Cycles (Protective Helmets) Regulations 1980 (SI No 1279)
  reg 4(2)(*b*)(*c*) 110
  reg 4(3)(*c*)... 110
  reg 5... 110
Motor Vehicles (Construction and Use) Regulations 1941 136
Motor Vehicles (Construction and Use) Regulations 1986 (SI No 1078)
  regs 24–26 73
  reg 27 .... 73, 75
  reg 46 101
  reg 47 101

Motor Vehicles (Construction and Use) Regulations 1986 (SI No 1078)—*contd*
  reg 48 101
  reg 101 125
  reg 105 134
Motor Vehicles (Driving Licenses) Regulations 1981 (SI No 952)—
  reg 8 107
Motor Vehicles (Driving Licenses) (Amendment No 2) Regulations 1982 (SI No
  230) 108
Motor Vehicles (Tests) Regulations 1981 (SI No 1694) 18
Motor Vehicles (Variation of Speed Limit) Regulations 1947 (SR&O No 2192) as
  amended by SI No 943 122
Motor Vehicles (Wearing of Seat Belts) Regulations 1982 (SI No 1203) 101
Motor Vehicles (Wearing of Seat Belts by children in rear seats) Regulations 1989
  (SI No 1219) 103
Notification of Accidents and Dangerous Occurrence Regulations 1980 ('NADOR')
  (SI No 804) 33
'Pelican' Pedestrian Crossings Regulations and General Directions 1969 (SI No
  888) as amended by SI No 401 96
Public Service Vehicles (Carrying Capacity) Regulations 1984 115
Public Service Vehicles (Conduct of Drivers, Conductors & Passengers) Regulations
  1936 115
  regs 4–8 113
  reg 5 113
  reg 6 113
  regs 9–11 114
  reg 12 .... 114, 115
Public Service Vehicles (Conduct of Drivers, Inspectors, Conductors & Passengers)
  Regulations 1990 .... 113, 115
  reg 5 114
Public Service Vehicles (Drivers' & Conductors' Licence) Regulations 1934
  reg 14 113
Reporting of Injuries and Dangerous Occurrences Regulations 1985 ('RIDOR') (SI
  No 2023) 33
  reg 3 (1) 33
  reg 3(3) 33
  reg 10(2) 33
Road Vehicle Lighting Regulations 1988 .... 124, 125
  reg 23 125
  reg 24 125
  reg 27 125
Road Vehicles Lighting Regulations 1989 (SI No 1796) 124, 127
  Sched 9 128
  Sched 17 128
  Pt I 127
  reg 21 .... 128, 129
Road Vehicles (Registration & Licensing) Regulations 1971
  reg 35 (4)(1) 179
Rules of the Supreme Court 1965 (SI No 828)—
  Ord 18 r 7 A 165
       (3) 166
  Ord 18, rr 12, 13 62
  Ord 25, r 8(1)(*b*) 77, 78
       r 28(1)(*b*) 79
  Ord 29, r 2 18
  Ord 29, r 11 161
  Ord 29, r 12 161
  Ord 37 79
  Ord 38 79

Rules of the Supreme Court 1965 (SI No 828)—*contd*
    Ord 38, r 2(A) 37
    Ord 38, r 22(2) 37
    Ord 38, r 38 78
    Ord 62/A2/58 44
    Ord 73 165
Traffic Signs Regulations (and General Directions) 1981 (SI No 859) 45, 48, 99
'Zebra' Pedestrian Crossing Regulations 1971 (SI No 1525) 94
    reg 8 .... 94, 96
    reg 8(1)(*b*) 97
    reg 8(i)(*c*) 96
    reg 8(i)(*e*) 97
    reg 8(ii) 97
    reg 9 96
    reg 9(ii)(*b*) 97
    reg 9(ii)(*c*) 97
    reg 9(iii) 97
    reg 10 95

Introduction

A road traffic accident may cause far-reaching disaster, and for more than one person. It may mean an end to a real future or a promising ambition. Even where there is no substantial personal injury, there may be long term financial consequences. At the moment there is no immediate prospect of Parliament providing for 'no fault' civil liability, even for personal injury claims (despite the recommendations of the Pearson Committee). Litigation may be the necessary result of such accidents, whether by the State in the form of criminal proceedings, and/or by the injured party in civil proceedings. This Guide is concerned with both types of proceedings.

The essential purpose of this Guide is to help reduce the risks involved in such litigation, according to the necessarily different needs of whoever is involved. This may be the person who caused the accident, or who suffered from it. It may be the investigating police or the private investigator. It may be the insurer concerned, or the loss adjuster acting on behalf of the insurer. It may be a Citizens' Advice Bureau, a law centre, or a lawyer. For each of these interested parties in any road traffic accident claim, this work is designed to increase the prospects of a successful outcome to litigation and to diminish the risks involved.

This cannot be more than a Guide; it does not seek to replace the consultation of either the appropriate professional adviser or the specialist textbook. What follows does, however, aim to provide in one book the kind of continuity of assistance, advice and comment, that may be of help from the happening of the accident to the start of any trial.

Like any Guide, it is designed to enable an informed view of not only what the claim involves, but also of the merits of the claim in question. Consequently, the appropriate decision may be to bring a halt to the claim; whether by a plea of 'Guilty', a payment into court, or an acceptance of whatever is offered in settlement by the other party. Where the appropriate decision is to press on with litigation, this Guide may help to indicate some useful steps that might be taken.

The prospects of involvement with a road traffic accident claim may be gauged from some recent statistics:

(1) 64 per cent of households in Great Britain now have the use of at least one car or van (and 16 per cent have two or more).

(2) The Central Statistical Office estimates 502 billion 'passenger kilometres' per annum, in 23 million licensed vehicles.

(3) 1.9 million driving tests are conducted in Great Britain every year, and just under half of the candidates pass; (44 per cent of women and 54 per cent of the men).

(4) In the last decade there was a steady annual average of about 300,000 vehicle accidents, of which about 62 per cent involved slight personal injury, but 81,000 people were seriously injured and 6,000 were killed.

(5) Some 1.25 million defendants are proceeded against annually in summary criminal proceedings in England and Wales.

(6) 28 per cent of the drivers killed in road accidents had exceeded the prescribed limit of alcohol in the body.

(7) About 44,000 blood or urine tests are taken annually, of which 85 per cent are positive.

The 1988 Road Traffic Accidents Great Britain Casualty Report contains statistics which show that:

(1) the number of people killed on the roads in 1988 was the lowest annual total since 1954;

(2) the 5,025 road deaths was 1.5 per cent lower than 1987;

(3) the 63,000 serious injuries were 1 per cent lower than 1987; and

(4) the 254,000 slight injuries represents a slight increase.

The report shows that despite a general improvement, there were a number of areas where the casualty rates were a cause for concern. For example:

(5) casualties per kilometre travelled had an increase by 12 per cent among pedal cyclists, in comparison to the 1981–85 average;

(6) pedestrian deaths rose to 1,753 from 1,703;

(7) 12 per cent of all deaths on the roads were either passengers or riders of motor cycles and sadly out of 84 per cent of male casualties, 64 per cent were below the age of 25; and

(8) 29 per cent of all the accidents occurred during the hours of darkness.

It is therefore hoped that whenever evidence of fact or expert opinion or other appropriate advice is sought, it will be found more readily and effectively with the assistance of this book; and when found, that it will be better understood, analysed and taken into account. Where problems may be thought to exist, it is hoped that this book will diminish them. Where the case may wrongly seem straightforward, it is hoped that this book will reveal (and perhaps diminish) any difficulties which should be recognised.

The modern motor car industry started with the perfection of the internal combustion engine by Otto in 1876. It is said that the first fatal road accident in the UK occurred only 20 years later—on 17 August 1896. Disraeli just lived to see the day. In a more general context he wrote: 'What one anticipates seldom occurs, and what one least expects generally happens.' While this statement is often appropriate with regard to road accident claims, it is hoped that this book will enable the reader seeking assistance to keep litigation risks to a minimum.

Each case invariably turns upon its own facts. But which of two contradictory factual accounts of the accident is to be accepted by the court, and how is one to assess what the court may decide? The preparations suggested here, combined with reference to previously decided cases, will assist the reader in determining the possible outcome of a trial before embarking on the expense and delay involved in litigation. Moreover, it is hoped that the prospects of a successful conclusion to any trial that does take place will be enhanced.

But witnesses will *still* say with surprising frequency in so many courts:

'I saw him, but I had right of way.'

'He came from nowhere.'

'I always leave it to my wife to look left.'

'But I can still hold my drink, and it makes me drive better,'

And even,

'Everyone knows that I turn right here.'

These remarks should only be from witnesses appearing on the other side!

This book is divided into five parts. Each part deals with various aspects of the claim in chronological order, from the occurrence of the accident to the doors of the court, as follows:

Part One: Gathering the Facts

Part Two: Expert Evidence

Part Three: Assessing Liability

Part Four: Motor Vehicle Loss or Damage

Part Five: Litigation

Part One

Gathering the Facts

Chapter 1

The Immediate Steps

Whenever court proceedings appear to be likely after a road traffic accident, certain steps should be taken at the first available opportunity. Almost inevitably, for want of knowledge, skill and experience, these steps will not have been taken by those directly involved in the accident. Therefore, the responsibility for appreciating the need for the enquiries set out here, and putting them into effect, will rest upon those professionally involved in the potential claim, be they the solicitor or the insurance investigator (that is, 'adviser') although in principle there is no reason why the potential litigant in person should not make these important enquiries on his own behalf or to assist his adviser.

Some steps have to be taken immediately, regardless of how soon (or long) after the accident the adviser is consulted or that the individual involved in the accident believes no court proceedings will arise (for the adviser need not have been consulted otherwise). The adviser has only heard one side of the story at this stage. Nor is it any good waiting to see if the other side is going to deny liability or if the police intend to prosecute: this delay serves only to give them the opportunity and advantage of making the first enquiries, when the evidence is most fresh.

The rest of the chapter deals with these necessary steps.

1   Witnesses

No-one's memory improves with time, although to the mind of the witness it might. While recollection might be improved with time (and prompting by photographs, sketches or statements of evidence might aid this), the sooner the witness provides a written statement of what he recalls, the better. Even where the statement is taken by the police shortly after the accident it may not be sufficient. The witness seen by the police may have been interviewed while still suffering from some shock, however minor, or when unaware of matters of importance with which he could assist. In such a situation the witness may not in fact appear to assist the case, but the written statement should still be taken. The trap to avoid is 'if he doesn't help us, we'll forget him'. But the opponent may take a different view, and a record is then needed of what the witness says. Such a statement may assist:

(1) the future assessment of litigation risks;
(2) the eventual cross-examination of the witness if called by the other side;
(3) the witness to refresh his memory if called by you.

Do not be content with recording merely a brief summary of what the witness says in case something said is later denied, said to be inaccurate, or even emerges as a point of particular significance later on. As with any statement, it should record the time and place it was taken and who took it. Preferably, it should be signed by both the witness and the writer. The witness may at some future date disappear, go overseas, or die; in which case, with these precautions, the statement itself may still be admissible in evidence.

Before leaving the witness, always ask if anyone else might be able to assist and, if so, how they might be traced. You cannot be sure that the attending police officer has traced all the relevant witnesses or recorded all that they wanted to say. Also check if the witness has made any statement about the accident to anyone else (and if so, to whom, on behalf of whom) and request the witness to notify any change of address hereafter. In the case of the adviser's client, he should be asked to attend with his own written account of what he thinks happened in detail. This, too, should be dated and signed by him.

Some of these essential first enquiries can be made by post, but some necessarily involve foot-slogging, painstaking enquiries and interviews. Some of this will have to be delegated to an office employee, an enquiry agent, or preferably to the expert accident investigator referred to later. Written instructions should be given to the delegatee, specifying what is required. In many cases this is easily done by the preparation of a *pro forma* document setting out the substance of a record of interview (see Chapter Four and Appendix Four).

2   The place

The place of the accident obviously needs to be identified and recorded with clarity at the first opportunity. Further, it should be photographed as soon as possible (Chapter 5). Something about the scene of the accident will have changed from the time of the accident to the date of any trial—somehow it always does. If the accident is one of several, it may suggest to the Highways Authority that a change in lay out or markings is required. Thus, it is vital to acquire evidence of the actual scene since it may be considered in a cause of action against them for not having made the changes earlier. Other changes occur because of pre-planned roadworks or the changing seasons which may have wrought a material change (the heights of hedgerows and trees, for example) which affect vision ahead. Lighting conditions may have changed meanwhile, as might the condition of a country verge or footpath (when allegations of contributory negligence have to be considered in respect of an injured pedestrian or horse rider).

3 The vehicles

For each vehicle that is (or may seem to be, or is alleged by another to be) involved in the accident in question, a separate part of the developing file should be started. The following information should be noted for every vehicle:

(1) registration number;

(2) make;

(3) its driver, his employer and the registered owner;

(4) insurers concerned;

(5) name (and classification) of the road upon which it was at the material time, and where it had come from;

(6) direction in which it was travelling (or facing) immediately before the accident;

(7) estimates of speed, given by whom, from what position, related by whom, and when;

(8) whether it was obviously involved in the causation of the events under examination or has become involved by the allegation of another; and if so, by whom, when and in what circumstances (for this may be very relevant later to the question of costs if a party has been joined but is later cleared of any liability).

The nature, place and extent of the damage to any vehicle involved in a collision is likely to be of the greatest importance. Evidence of the vehicular damage may be sought from the following:

(1) The vehicle's owner or driver. (This may, however, be the other interested party to any court proceedings from whom it is not realistically practicable to gain any assistance.)

(2) The police. The briefest details of damage should be recorded in their accident report. A full report may, however, have been prepared, whether with a view to a prosecution relating to the accident, or the condition of the vehicle being unroadworthy before the accident, and in contravention of the Construction and Use Regulations. The police may be in possession of photographs, so this may need checking.

(3) Other witnesses to the relevant accident; although their evidence may well be vague and possibly not wholly reliable.

(4) The garage, whether as storers or repairers of the vehicle.

(5) The insurance company concerned. This may easily be overlooked. But should an issue arise about the accident damage, whether on liability or the value of the claim, and the insurance company are to rely upon their inspection made with a view to litigation, any such documentary report should be disclosed.

(6) The subsequent purchaser, for instance a garage (whether or not the purpose of purchase was the vehicle's scrap value).

(7) The scrap-merchant, who may not even have paid for the wreckage (but towed away the remains for no charge.)

The purposes of the enquiry into accident damage to a vehicle may be many and varied. The liability of the driver in question, or of any other driver, or of any pedestrian, may in part be assessable from this (see Chapter 9). It may be necessary to prove or exclude the involvement in an accident of an animal, or some part of the scene of the accident with which the vehicle may have come into contact. Issues of quantum may turn upon the damage to the vehicle. Such damage is rarely irrelevant.

Even a month after an accident, a damaged vehicle may still be lying unrepaired and not significantly altered in the yard of a police station. The vehicle may remain unrepaired and in the control of a garage for a still longer period. Some basic questions need to be posed in either event.

(1) What, if any, alteration has taken place; if the extent of any corrosion is possibly relevant, has the vehicle been stored in covered premises with open or closed sides, or outside?

(2) Why, and at whose order, is the vehicle being so kept, and at whose authorised expense? (If the client has not authorised this, expressly or impliedly, no storage fees may be due.)

(3) Are any photographs of it needed that have not already been taken?

(4) Is an independent vehicular examination, and subsequent written report, needed? Should the present custodian of the vehicle be notified of this? Does any mechanic who is to do work upon it need to be instructed to prepare an appropriate report?

(5) Should the vehicle be removed from its present place, whether to enable further examination or to mitigate any loss arising?

(6) Who else, and on behalf of whom, has made any similar enquiry in respect of the above?

(7) What record has been made in respect of any of the above queries, about what exactly, on behalf of whom, when, and with what result? What record has been made by you yourself of the asking of these questions, their results, and what has been (or is to be) done about any of them? A timed and dated memorandum prepared at the time may one day prove an essential safeguard of these matters. It should record who was spoken to, and in what capacity.

4   Records

Some records are kept only for a limited period of time. However, the appropriate request should still be made, even if this period has expired by the time their relevance comes to be considered, for instance by the adviser or representative of the individual involved who did not have knowledge of their relevance until after the expiry of the limitation period.

The question of what records may exist, and what is to be deduced from them, is dealt with in later chapters in Part One. But at this stage, so far as the immediate steps to be taken are concerned, the following basic time limits after which records may be destroyed should be noted. By law:

(1) Tachograph charts (see Chapter 2) need only be kept for twelve months.

(2) An individual control book (see Chapter 2) need only be kept for twelve months.

(3) Repair and maintenance records of a vehicle subject to an 'Operator's Licence' need only be kept for 15 months.

(4) Police accident records (see Chapter 2) may only be kept for three years, being the period within which an action involving person injury must ordinarily be brought by a plaintiff.

There may, of course, be many other records, formal and informal. Whatever their formal description, much may depend upon their early discovery and preservation. The guiding rule must therefore be that all records should be sought out as soon as possible.

5 Exceptions

These urgent steps will almost inevitably incur some modest expenditure. The question of finance ought to be kept under review at all stages of litigation; for the important question of costs and the funding of these, see Chapter 18. Every possible attempt should be made to raise the necessary resources to undertake these important early enquiries. In certain situations, this will unfortunately prove impossible. Further, two occasions may arise when the initial enquiries ought to be limited anyway:

(1) where the driver to be blamed is untraced, and compensation is to be looked for from the Motor Insurers' Bureau, recoverable disbursements may be limited to obtaining the police accident report only (see Chapter 18).

(2) where one party is to be financed by legal aid, the financial assistance under this scheme will not cover expenses incurred prior to the issue of the legal aid certificate. The expenses involved for any urgent enquiries necessary to ensure successful litigation may still have to be incurred, but the solicitor ought to advise the client of both the limitations of the certificate and the desirability of gathering the vital evidence urgently. (The sort of advice that might be given in these circumstances is suggested in Chapter 18).

Chapter 2

Contemporaneous Records

The previous chapter has dealt with the urgency of obtaining contemporary records before they disappear. During litigation, much may turn upon the evidence contained in such records. There may be evidence concerning both the driving and the driver, as well as the vehicle driven. Frequently there is more than meets the inexperienced eye in these documents, or information is not recorded within them which should be there. In some instances, the documents do *not* contain the information or evidence that the layman may expect. With these observations in mind, a detailed consideration can be made of the following records:

(1) Tachograph charts;
(2) Individual Control Books;
(3) MOT Tests;
(4) Goods Vehicles' Tests.

1 Tachographs

The tachograph, dubbed 'the spy in the cab' by its opponents when first introduced, is a machine connected to a clock and the speedometer of the vehicle. The driver sets the 'mode' to record his various activities as follows:

Mode	*Symbol*
Drive	⊗
Work	☑
Rest ⎫ Break ⎭	⊢

Outside the UK the mode representing active work of the driver that does not involve driving is also recorded and this is represented by the symbol ✕. This symbol appears on the tachograph chart also (see *Fig 1*), but will rarely require attention. Once the mode has been set by the driver, the tachograph will automatically record:

(1) the times of start and finish of that mode;
(2) speeds in km per hour, (sometimes not recorded below 10 km/h (6.6 mph)

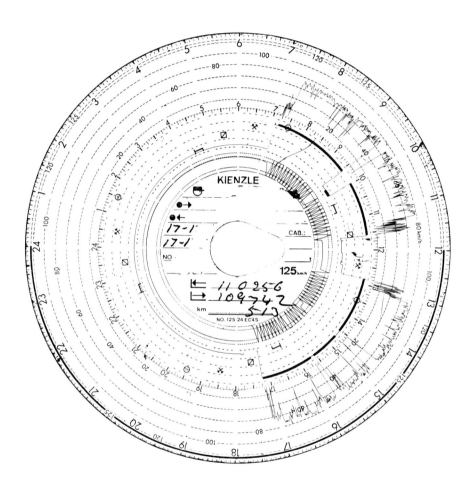

Figure 1: The Tachograph Chart

(3) distances in kilometres.

A stylus will record this information upon a waxed disc which may only be fully interpreted by a suitably qualified expert using special equipment. If the tachograph in question does not record speeds below 10 km/h its use in interpreting low speed accidents may be limited.

Section 97 of the Transport Act 1968 specifically provides that in any proceedings an entry on the chart made by a driver is evidence of the matters appearing in that entry, and that a record produced by the equipment is evidence in any proceedings under the Act.

The tachograph chart illustrated in *Fig 1* shows that the driver commenced driving at about 0705 hours and drove until 0930 hours from which time he took a break until 0955. He then drove until 1135, had a break until 1250 and drove again until 1715. Throughout the working day his periods of driving can be clearly seen as represented by the thick black line.

2   Definition of terms

According to the council regulation (EEC) No 3820/85 the following terms are defined:

(1) 'Day'. Strangely, the term 'Day' is not to be found in Section 1, Art 1, of the regulation. However, in *Kelly* v *Shulman* [1989] 1 All ER 106, it was held to be, 'Successive periods of 24 hours, commencing with the resumption of driving, after the last weekly rest period and not any 24 hour period starting at mid-night.'

(2) 'Breaks from Driving'. Provisions for such breaks are set out in Section V, Art 7, as, 'After four and half hours' driving, the driver shall observe a break of at least 45 minutes, unless he begins a rest period.' This break may be replaced by breaks of at least 15 minutes each distributed over the driving period or immediately after this period in such a way as to comply with the provisions of para 1. However, see *R* v *Mayfield Chicks Ltd* (1989) in which it was held that it was an offence to follow a period of four and half hours driving which had been split up in this way with an uninterrupted second period of four and a half hours driving since a driver would not have had a break of at least 45 minutes after a period of four and half hours' *aggregate* driving.

The tachograph must be fitted on most goods vehicles whose weight, including any trailer, exceeds 3.5 tonnes, and many public service vehicles (but not buses on regular passenger service or, for example, vehicles of the emergency services). Up to 29 September 1986, the requirements relating to the fitting of tachographs are to be found in Art 3 of EEC Regulations 1463/70, subject to the exemptions set out there and under Art 14(a)(2) and (3) of EEC Regulations 543/69, and as provided for by the Community Road Transport Rules (Exemptions) Regulations 1978 (SI No 1158). The legal requirements as to calibration and fixing are contained in great detail in Arts 15 and 17 of EEC Regulation 1463/70.

Since 29 September 1986, EEC Regulation 543/69 and 1463/70 have been repealed by Regulations 3820/85 and 3821/85, which re-enact the former provisions with amendments. In particular, some of the definitions are changed and the rest periods of crew members (other than drivers) are no longer regulated. The complementary UK subordinate legislation has been largely replaced.

Liability to install and operate tachographs is now imposed by EEC Regulation 3821/85 subject to exceptions, which include certain exceptions which may be granted under national legislation (for a list of exemptions, see Appendix 5). The burden of proving that the exceptions granted under national legislation apply to the particular circumstances which are the subject of proceedings for an offence lies with the defendant (*Gaunt* v *Nelson* (1986) *The Times*, 21 May; where under reg 4(3)(b) of the Community Road Transport Rules (Exemptions) Regulations 1978 (SI No 1158), revoked and replaced by the Community Drivers' Hours and Recording Equipment (Exemptions and Supplementary Provisions) Regulations 1986 (SI No 1456), the defendant had to show that a 'specialised vehicle' had been used for door-to-door selling; but the new provisions do not require a vehicle used for such purposes to be a 'specialised vehicle').

There should be at least one chart per driver, for each 'day's' driving. Operators who are legally required to use tachographs however, need only preserve the charts for twelve months. Due consideration must therefore be given in a road accident claim not only to whether such records are likely to have been required, but also to the fact that they may be destroyed after 12 months.

There are many accidents in which the vehicle using a tachograph has been travelling at a low speed, for example when emerging from a minor onto a major road or attempting to use a cross-over lane through a central reservation of a dual carriage-way. In such cases the use of the tachograph recording as a means of reconstructing the vehicle movements will be limited to the amount of 'cut-off', ie, the lowest possible speed which is capable of being recorded. This value may vary between 8 and 12 kilometers per hour.

Figure 2 shows an enlarged diagram of speed recording, in which the stylus does not begin to record until a speed of about 9 km/h has been attained. The base line with a value of 0 km/h is not marked on a chart but has been delineated on this diagram in order to give some idea of the difference between the stylus zero and the actual situation. The thick vertical marks are of course the time scale, with the longest representing the hours and the intervening shorter marks representing five minute intervals. In the absence of evidence of speed from the chart, other means of obtaining relative evidence may have to be used; for example a test drive in a similar vehicle. It is important to note that:

(1) charts need only be preserved for 12 months—make sure that an application for disclosure is made before the expiry of this time;

(2) the surface of a chart is wax coated and is easily damaged; take care

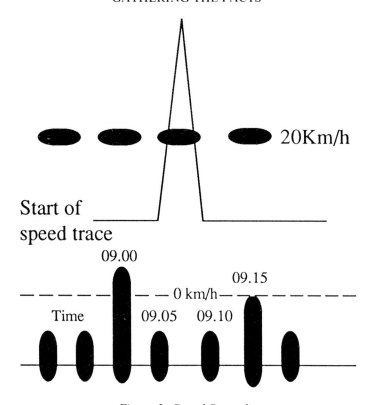

Figure 2: Speed Recording

when handling or packaging for posting.

The maximum tolerances for the distance travelled and speed and time recorded by the instrument are set out in Annex One of Council Regulation (EEC) No 3821/85. When the vehicle is in use:

(1) distance travelled is 4 per cent more or less of the real distance, where that distance is at least one kilometre;

(2) speed is six km/h more or less than the real speed; and

(3) time is plus or minus two minutes per day or plus or minus 10 minutes per seven days.

3   Individual control books

Where goods vehicles exceed 3.5 tonnes gross weight, but do not have to be fitted with a tachograph, their drivers nevertheless have to keep an 'Individual Control Book', which is almost universally referred to colloquially as the driver's 'log book'.

This record, in the format defined by EEC Regulations (see *Fig 3*), should be kept up by the driver as his day progresses. The driver is required to

2 Registration No. of Vehicle(s)	2 Registration No. of Vehicle(s)	1 DAILY SHEET	3. Day of week and Date
a)	b)		
OPERATORS LICENCE Nos.	2 Registration No. of Vehicle(s) c)	No. **6**	

	1	2	3	4	5	6	7	8	9	10	11	12
4												
5												
6												
7												

	13	14	15	16	17	18	19	20	21	22	23	24
4												
5												
6												
7												

8 PLACE OF COMING ON DUTY

9 PLACE OF GOING OFF DUTY:

10 TRANSPORT OF GOODS-PERMISSIBLE MAXIMUM WEIGHT OF COMBINATION OF VEHICLES LORRY WITH TRAILER OR ARTICULATED VEHICLES (WHERE APPLICABLE) — (a) (b) (c)

10a PASSENGER TRANSPORT SYSTEM OF DAILY REST SELECTED:

12 — Number of hours

11 Distance Recorder: (a) (b) (c) Km/miles

End of Duty: _____ _____ _____ Km/miles — 13

Beginning of Duty: _____ _____ _____ Km/miles

TOTAL DISTANCE COVERED + + = — 14

16 REMARKS AND SIGNATURE:

15 TOTAL

13 + 14

if applicable

JOURNEY DETAILS — FUEL — OIL

Figure 3: Individual Control Book

Book No.		1. Weekly Sheet No.	2. Period Covered by Sheet				
E 10074		**7**	Week Commencing (Date) _____ to Week Ending (Date) _____				

Day 3.	Registration No. of Vehicle(s) 4.	Place where Vehicle(s) Based 5.	Time of going on Duty 6	Time of going off Duty 7.	Estimated Time spent Driving 8.	Signature of Driver 9.

10.   Certification by employer (Where applicable)

I have examined the entries in this sheet.   Signature_____Date _____

Position held _____

Figure 3a: Record Book

complete one sheet (which is duplicated) for each day worked. These sheets are required by law to be kept for twelve months (but no longer, unless a court order is obtained, eg RSC Ord 29, r 2).

Where a claim is based upon the records of the driver's activities (for instance where it may be alleged he worked excessive hours leading to tiredness causing an accident), the accuracy of the records kept by the driver will be entirely dependent upon his honesty. There may, however, be other documents from which the movements of the vehicle can be reconstructed, and hence the activities of the driver. These may include consignment notes, general import entry forms, charges' advice forms*, invoices for carriage, and records kept by security officers of entry and exit to premises.   Since 29 September 1986 a new record book has been used, based upon the format shown in *Fig 3a*. This is a much simplified version, requiring the driver to make less specific entries than were required under the previous legislation. These books are issued against a signature in a register. The driver must return completed sheets within seven days and the employer must retain them for twelve months, as with the previously issued control book (see the Drivers' Hours (Goods Vehicles) (Keeping of Records) Regulations 1987 (SI No 1421)).

4   MOT tests

Section 48 of the Road Traffic Act 1988 provides for the Secretary of State to make regulations relating to the testing of motor vehicles. The current regulations are the Motor Vehicles (Tests) Regulations 1981 (SI No 1694). Section 175 of the 1988 Act makes it an offence to issue a Department of Transport test certificate ('MOT') knowing it to be false in a material particular. The test certificate must be produced each time the vehicle is licensed once three years have passed since its first registration. The test must then be passed annually. The test will be carried out at private garage premises (as opposed to state-owned premises) approved specifically for MOT testing. Contrary to what may be thought, the testing garage is entitled to test its own vehicles and those of its customers, and indeed to grant certificates to its own vehicles (the sanction for improper use would be a prosecution under s 175 above).

The certificate (Form VT20: see *Fig 4*) declares that the 43 items specified in the check list (Form VT30: see *Fig 5*) have been tested in compliance with s 45 of the Road Traffic Act 1988. The certificate is expressly stated to be of limited effect:

'WARNING: A test certificate should not be accepted as evidence of the satisfactory mechanical condition of a used vehicle offered for sale.'

On the back of VT20, (*Fig 4a*) appears an even wider warning in Note 1:

'This certificate relates only to the condition of the testable items at the time of the

---

*These forms are ones which may be used in the transport of goods. They may contain the following information: signature of driver, registration of vehicles, dates, times, particulars of load, consignor, consignee, from which the hours worked by the driver can be reconstructed.

Serial Number

JD 0182842

The motor vehicle, of which the Registration Mark * is:-

FRG 658 W _____ having been examined

under section 43 of the Road Traffic Act 1972, it is hereby certified that at the date of the examination thereof the statutory requirements prescribed by Regulations made under the said section 43 were complied with in relation to the vehicle.

Vehicle Testing Station Number 2960I

* When no registration mark is exhibited on the vehicle the chassis or serial number should be shown.

Date of issue DEC 11TH 1984 (EIGHTY FOUR)   Make DATSUN

Date of expiry DEC 10TH 1985 (EIGHTY FIVE)

Approximate year of manufacture 1981

Serial Number of immediately preceding Test Certificate N/A

Recorded mileage 52664

(To be entered when the above date of expiry is more than 12 months after the above date of issue.)

If a goods vehicle, unladen weight N/A kg

If not a goods vehicle, horse power or cylinder capacity of engine in cubic centimetres 1600

Signature of Tester/Inspector _____

Authentication Stamp

WARNING
A test certificate should not be accepted as evidence of the satisfactory mechanical condition of a used vehicle offered for sale.

CHECK carefully that the particulars quoted above are correct.
Certificates showing alterations should not be issued or accepted. They may delay the renewal of a licence.

KEEP THIS CERTIFICATE SAFELY

(See Notes overleaf)

VT20

51-4440 Dd 8819956 250,000 PADS 9 84 K·J

Figure 4: MOT Test Certificate (Form VT20)

Notes

Nature of certificate

1   This certificate relates only to the condition of the testable items at the time of the test. It should not be regarded as evidence of the condition of the items tested at any other time nor should it be taken as evidence of the general mechanical condition of the vehicle.

Need for certificates

2   It is an offence to use on a public road any vehicle which is subject to periodic test that does not have a current test certificate. Therefore a new certificate should be obtained on or before the expiry date of this certificate if the vehicle is to continue in use on roads in Great Britain.

Date of expiry

3   The date of expiry of a test certificate is 12 calendar months from the date of issue. However if you obtain a new certificate not more than one month before this certificate expires the expiry date of the new certificate may be entered as 12 months from the expiry date of the old certificate. To take advantage of this extension of expiry date the old certificate must be shown to the tester at the time the new one is issued. If you do not produce the old certificate the tester must enter the expiry date as 12 months from the date of issue. The new certificate may then only be amended if it is produced with the old one to a Traffic Area office of the Department of Transport. The address of the appropriate office can be obtained from the testing station.

Production of test certificates

4   Production of a test certificate may be required by a police officer if the vehicle concerned is subject to periodic test. If you cannot produce your certificate within 5 days you are liable to a fine. A certificate must also be sent or produced with an application for a licence for the vehicle. You are advised therefore to keep this certificate readily available while it is in force.

Loss of certificates

5   If you lose this certificate you can get a duplicate from the testing station who carried out the test provided you can give the serial number or the approximate date of issue. If the testing station is no longer testing, you may get a duplicate from the Traffic Area Head Office but you must quote the registration number of your vehicle, the name (or number) of the testing station and the approximate date of issue of the certificate. A charge is made for a duplicate certificate whether it is obtained from the testing station or Traffic Area.

Keep this certificate in a safe place and make a separate note of the particulars in case it is lost.

VT20
July 1984

Figure 4a: Reverse of MOT Test Certificate (Form VT20)

test. It should not be regarded as evidence of the condition of the items tested at any other time nor should it be taken as evidence of the general mechanical condition of the vehicle.'

However s 75 of the 1988 Act makes it an offence for vehicles to be sold in an unroadworthy condition or altered so as to be unroadworthy. As from 31 December 1986 the 'VT30' (see *Fig 5*) has served as both a checklist and a notification of refusal to issue a test certificate. The VT30 may be issued if the vehicle passes the test but the tester, wishes to draw attention to some aspect of his inspection not covered on the form and which relates to the safety of the vehicle. The new VT30 has provision to be used both for the examination of motor cycles and motor cars. Vehicles which pass the test will be issued with a VT20.

Some important and frequently over-looked matters emerge:
The test. As can be seen from VT30 (*Fig* 5), the test is limited to a simple 'pass' or 'fail' of each item. Few limits are laid down for wear or tolerance of any item. The whole test is expected to be carried out in about 45 minutes— about a minute per item, whatever type of vehicle, with each examiner bringing his own experience and judgment to bear in assessing the condition of each relevant component.
Exclusion of general mechanical condition. Few purchasers of second-hand motor cars may be aware of this warning note on the back of VT20 (*Fig 4*) but the exclusion follows from the facts that:
(1) Form VT30 makes no provision at all for the testing of such a component relating to the general mechanical condition;
(2) no testing takes place with the vehicle in motion, so that necessarily, there is not even any check that the speedometer or odometer work or are accurate; nor
(3) is there any testing of the engine.
The test is of roadworthiness, and not in any sense a test of the vehicle's performance.
Time limitation. Although the testing is required annually, thus encouraging the belief that the vehicle is likely to remain reasonably roadworthy until the next test, or at least for an appreciable time after the test, the certification is declared to be *only* of the condition of the vehicle '. . . at the time of the test'. Thus, it may be wondered how there could ever be a prosecution of the tester under s 175 in respect of corrosion, for example, unless there was cause to have the vehicle examined independently the same day the certificate was issued. Expert evidence may, however, be forthcoming that even as long as four months after the test, the extent of certain corrosion seen then must have been apparent at the time of testing.

In civil proceedings for breach of contract in respect of secondhand cars, there may arise evidence of vehicular defects having caused an accident and a claim for breach of the implied terms of merchantable quality or reasonable fitness might be made under s 14(2) and (3) of the Sale of Goods Act 1979 or s 10(2) and (3) of the Supply of Goods (Implied Terms) Act 1973. The MOT test certificate ought rarely to assist in view of the above—

Department of Transport Road Traffic Act 1988 section 45	**Customer's Copy**	Serial No. 08263700 AA
MOT Inspection Report		● Please keep this copy as your record of the inspection.

Vehicle Reg. Mark:		Make & Model:		Year of Manufacture:		Class of Vehicle i / ii / iii / iv / v
VIN or Chassis No.:		Recorded Mileage		Colour:		

A Items tested.	Manual ref.		Pass	Fail	Reasons for failure & Remarks
Lighting Equipment	Cars & LGV	Motor cycles			
Front & rear lamps	I/1				
Headlamps	I/2				
Headlamp aim	I/6				
Stop lamps	I/3				
Rear reflectors	I/4				
Direction indicators	I/5				
Steering and Suspension	Cars & LGV	Motor cycles			
Steering control	II/1	II/1			
Steering mechanism/system	II/2	II/2			
Power steering	II/3	N/A			
Transmission shafts	II/2,4,9	N/A			
Wheel bearings	II/4	II/3,4			
Front suspension	II/5-9	II/3			
Rear suspension	II/9	II/4			
Shock absorbers	II/10	II/3,4			
Wheel alignment	N/A	II/5			
Brakes	Cars & LGV	Motor cycles			
Controls	III/1,3	III/1			
Condition of service brake system	III/3,4	III/2			
Condition of parking brake system	III/1,2	N/A			
Service brake performance	III/5-8	III/3			
Parking brake performance	III/5-8	N/A			
Tyres and Wheels	Cars & LGV	Motor cycles			
Tyre type	IV/1				
Tyre condition	IV/1				
Roadwheels	IV/2				
Seatbelts	Cars & LGV	Motor cycles			
Mountings	V/1	N/A			
Condition	V/1	N/A			
Operation	V/1	N/A			
Motor Cycle Side Car	Cars & LGV	Motor cycles			
Security	N/A	V/1			
Suspension & Wheel bearings	N/A	V/2			
Wheel alignment	N/A	V/3			
General	Cars & LGV	Motor cycles			
Windscreen wipers & washers	VI/1,2	N/A			
Horn	VI/4	VI/1			
Exhaust system	VI/3	VI/2			
Vehicle structure	VI/5	VI/3			

B Test Result: ¹ ☐ Pass - No. of Test Certificate issued [＿＿＿＿]   ² ☐ Fail - see Section C

C Notice of Refusal of a Test Certificate:
¹ ☐ For the reasons shown in Section A   ● Important: read the notes overleaf
² ☐ Because the inspection could not be completed for these reasons ▶

D Warning: In my opinion, the vehicle is dangerous to drive because of these defects

Authentication Stamp

E Signed: (Tester/Inspector)   Date:

Name: (in CAPITALS)   Testing Station No.:

VT30 (Rev. Nov. 1988)

Figure 5: MOT Inspection Report (Form VT30)

and instead, regard should be had to *Crowther* v *Shannon Motor Co* [1975] 1 All ER 139 (but see *Bartlett* v *Sidney Marcus* [1965] 2 All ER 753. The extent of the defects were held to be reasonable for the type, age, mileage and price of that particular vehicle).

Since 31 December 1986, Form VT30 (*Fig 5*) replaces Forms VT21 and 22 and serves both as a check list and a notification of refusal to issue a test certificate.

5 Goods vehicles' test

Experience suggests that enquiries into the condition of goods vehicles after an accident will be more unusual than such enquiries into the condition of other motor vehicles, dealt with in the last section. Generally, however the statutory regular testing of goods vehicles (of over 1525 kgs plated/gross weight) is more strict, and in any event the operator of a goods vehicle will have a commercial interest and a tax advantage in keeping these vehicles in good repair; the same may not be so for the domestic user of a car or light van. However, where there is a defect in a goods vehicle, relevant to the occurrence of a road accident, the consequences may well be more serious (in terms of prosecution, economic loss and the extent of any injuries) and the lack of experience and knowledge about the statutory testing of such vehicles may be more extensive for those who have to consider these matters in respect of litigation. Therefore regard should be had to the following:

(1) The test certificate concerning goods vehicles is Form VTG 5 (*Figs 6 and 6a*) and it declares that the 73 items specified in the 'First and Annual' checklist (Form VTG 4A, see *Fig 7*) have been examined in compliance with s 49 of the Road Traffic Act 1988.

(2) It should be noted that there are some important differences between the examination and testing requirements of goods vehicles as compared with the more familiar 'MOT test' referred to above. Goods vehicles:

  (a) are tested annually from the start, and not just after three years;
  (b) are tested at 'HGV Testing Stations' and by Department of Transport testers—not in ordinary garages by licensed testers;
  (c) must have an up-to-date record of maintenance work which has been carried out. The record must be kept for 15 months after the last work was done (albeit no statutory form of record is provided for).

(3) Goods vehicles which pass the annual test are given a certificate which:

  (a) does not record the mileage at the time of testing (which rarely appears to be given the same significance as that of cars and light vans); but
  (b) does not have the restrictive warning and 'note 1', as does Form VT20 (*Fig 4a*).

(4) Goods vehicles, while not having to be driven and examined during the test, or having the engine tested, are examined in respect of:

DEPARTMENT OF TRANSPORT
ROAD TRAFFIC ACT 1972, Section 45

Goods Vehicle Test Certificate   K
(Motor Vehicle)

The vehicle of which the registration mark/chassis or serial number/identification mark is ...., having been examined under Section 45 of the Road Traffic Act 1972 and in accordance with the regulations and directions issued under that section, it is hereby certified that the vehicle was found to comply with the construction and use requirements prescribed under that section.

This certificate is valid from the date of issue until the last day of the month of

.... 19...................

WARNING

Certificates showing alterations should not be issued or accepted

Signature ....

(a) Date of issue
    of certificate ....

(b) Date of examination
    completed (if
    different from (a)) ....

Vehicle testing station No ....

For Notes see reverse side _____✂

VTG 5
(Rev. 1983)

Figure 6: Goods Vehicle Test Certificate (Form VTG5)

Notes

1. NATURE OF TEST CERTIFICATES

This certificate relates only to compliance with the prescribed construction and use requirements at the time of the test. It should not be regarded as evidence of compliance at any other time nor should it be taken as evidence of the general mechanical condition of the vehicle.

2. VALIDITY AND RENEWAL OF TEST CERTIFICATES

It is an offence under Section 46(2) of the Road Traffic Act 1972 to use on roads any goods vehicle which is subject to periodical test, unless a goods vehicle test certificate is in force for this vehicle. This certificate must therefore be renewed on or before its expiry date if the vehicle is to continue in use. An application for a periodical test should be made on form VTG 40L to the Goods Vehicle Centre, 91/92, The Strand, Swansea, SA1 2DH, at least one month before the certificate expires.

3. RETENTION AND PRODUCTION OF TEST CERTIFICATES

You are advised to keep this certificate readily available. It need not be carried on the vehicle but it must be produced if required by a police constable or an examiner appointed by the Secretary of State for Transport. It must also be produced (whether or not its expiry date has passed) when the vehicle is next tested.

LOSS

If this certificate is lost or defaced an application for a replacement may be made to the Goods Vehicle Centre 91/92, The Strand, Swansea, SA1 2DH. A fee will be payable.

Anyone finding this certificate is asked to send it to the Goods Vehicle Centre.

Figure 6a: Reverse of Goods Vehicle Test Certificate (Form VTG5)

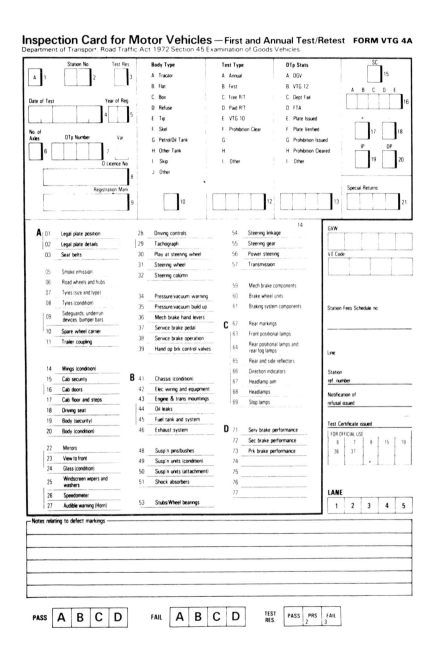

Figure 7: First and Annual Check List (Form VTG 4A)

Inspection Card for Trailers — First and Annual Tests/Retests   **FORM VTG 4B**

Department of Transport. Road Traffic Act 1972 Section 45 Examination of Goods Vehicles

Station No.   Test Res.

B | 1 | 2 · | 3

Date of Test   Year of Man.

| 4 | | 5

No. of Axles

| 6

ID Number

| 9

Body Type	Chassis	Test Type	DTp Stats
A. Flat	A. Semi	A. Annual	A. DGV
B. Box	B. D/bar	B. First	B. VTG 12
C. Skip	C. Dol	C. Free R/T	C. Dept Fail
D. Tip	D. L.Ldr	D. Paid R/T	D. FTA
E. Skel	E. 4 in L	E. VTG 10	E. Plate Issued
F. Petrol/Oil Tank		F. Prohibition Clear	F. Plate Verified
G. Other Tank		G.	G. Prohibition Issued
H. Other		H.	H. Prohibition Cleared
		I. Other	I. Other

| 10 | 11 | 12 | 13

SC | 15

A B C D E | 16

+ | 17   − | 18

IP | 19   DP | 20

Special Returns | 21

14

A | 01   Legal plate position
02   Legal plate details
06   Road wheels and hubs
07   Tyres (size and type)
08   Tyres (condition)
09   Sideguards, underrun devices and bumper bars
10   Spare wheel carrier
11   Trailer coupling (dollies)
12   Coupling on trailer
13   Trailer landing legs
14   Wings (condition)
19   Body (security)
20   Body (condition)

B 41   Chassis (condition)
44   Elec wiring and equipment
45   Fuel tank and system
48   Spring pins/bushes
49   Susp'n units (condition)
50   Susp'n units (attachment)
51   Shock absorbers
53   Stubs/Wheel bearings

54   Steering linkage
59   Mech brake components
60   Brake wheel units
61   Braking system components

C 62   Rear markings
64   Rear positional lamps and rear fog lamps
65   Rear and side reflectors
66   Direction indicators
69   Stop lamps

D 70   Trailer parking brake
71   Serv brake performance
72   Sec brake performance
73   Prk brake performance
74
75

GVW

Axle Weight

| 1 | 2 |
| 3 | 4 |

VE Code

Station Fees Schedule no:

Line:

Station ref. number

Notification of refusal issued

Test Certificate issued

FOR OFFICIAL USE

6	7	8	9	10
12	14		19	
	48	49	50	

LANE

| 1 | 2 | 3 | 4 | 5 |

Notes relating to defect markings

PASS | A | B | C | D | **FAIL** | A | B | C | D | **TEST RES.** PASS 1   PRS 2   FAIL 3

Figure 8: Test Sheet for Trailers (Form VTG 4B)

DEPARTMENT OF TRANSPORT

Road Traffic Act 1972. Section 45

NOTIFICATION OF REFUSAL OF A GOODS VEHICLE TEST CERTIFICATE

I hereby refuse a Goods Vehicle Test Certificate in respect of the vehicle described on the reverse side of this notice, which has been examined under section 45 of the Road Traffic Act 1972 and in accordance with the regulations and directions issued under that section, on the grounds that it fails to comply, to the extent shown on the reverse side of this notice, with the construction and use requirements prescribed under that section.

Signature

Date of Issue

Vehicle Testing Station No.

NOTES:

1.　Where a vehicle is found not to comply with any construction and use requirement in respect of an item shown on the reverse side of this notice, the inspecting officer will mark the space for that item and will write in the space for observations any remarks he may consider necessary to make apparent the reasons for failure to comply. In such a case a test certificate, and a plating certificate if appropriate, will not be issued.

2.　When the items with which a vehicle is found not to comply have been given the necessary attention, the vehicle may be submitted for re-test as follows:–

　(a)　at the above vehicle testing station BY PRIOR ARRANGEMENT WITH THE STATION:–
†　　(i)　on the same day as the paid examination to which this notification relates or on the next following working day, subject to the availability of test staff and station facilities: in which case no fee will be payable.

　　　(ii)　within fourteen/. . .　　　　　　days after the date of the submission of the vehicle for the examination to which this notification relates and on payment of fee of £. . .

　(b)　in any other circumstances, on an application on form VTG 40L for a re-test appointment accompanied by the fee appropriate to a full test of the vehicle. The application must be made, at least seven days prior to the date on which the re-test is required to the manager of the testing station at which it is desired to submit the vehicle.

3.　In addition to a notification of refusal of a test certificate a vehicle may be issued with a prohibition notice and in that event the vehicle may be submitted for removal of the notice at the same time as it is taken to a testing station for re-test.

4.　Any person aggrieved by a determination made on a first examination, a periodical test, or a re-test of a vehicle by the person in charge of the examination may appeal to an area mechanical engineer appointed by the Minister of Transport to act for the traffic area in which the examination was made. Any such appeal shall be lodged at the office of the traffic area not later than 10 days from the date of the determination. Information regarding the appeal procedure and the fee payable is available from traffic area offices.

　　†　delete if inapplicable.

Figure 9: Notification of Refusal of a Goods Vehicle Test Certificate

    (a) smoke emission; and

    (b) oil leaks.

If after an examination of a goods vehicle under the provision of s 49 of the Road Traffic Act 1988 (ie when it is examined for either plating or testing) the examiner is of the opinion that the vehicle does not comply with the prescribed construction and use requirements, he shall give a written notification of his refusal to issue a goods vehicle test certificate (*Fig 9*).

6 Local authority obligations

Section 39 of the Road Traffic Act 1988 requires the local authorities to propose and carry out programmes of measures designed to promote road safety. This includes the obligation to carry out studies into road accidents in their area (excluding trunk roads) and to take appropriate measures to prevent accidents. A check with the local authority responsible for the area in which an accident occurred may reveal helpful information in assessing liability. In England and Wales the appropriate local authority will be the Council of a County, Metropolitan District or London Borough or the Common Council of the City of London. In Scotland the appropriate local authority will be the Region or Islands Council.

7 Police accident reports

The request for the police accident report and statements is obviously an important step in gathering the available evidence. Frequently, it is the first step taken by or on behalf of a potential litigant. But the process of obtaining the necessary basic materials should not start here, and regard ought to be had to the previous chapters first.

    When the request is made for the records and documents of the police, enquiries should be addressed to the Chief Constable for the area where the incident occurred. Payment will usually be required in the sum notified along with delivery of the documents.

(a) Police documents

The documents to be expected from the police are:

    (1) The Accident Report Book, which will probably include information of the relevant road and weather conditions, the speed limit, the immediate oral responses of those most closely involved, and details of prosecutions arising and their result.

    (2) The statements obtained by the police.

    (3) Perhaps a separate specialist's report from an investigating police officer with particular expertise in dealing with road accidents which the patrol officer may not have. This further report may include:

        (a) additional witness statements;

        (b) the test-driving of a vehicle;

        (c) braking coefficients; (see Chapter 9)

(d) details of more elaborate examination of the scene, damage and injury; and

(e) scale plans (see Chapter 5).

ITEM	COST
	£
Police Accident Report Hort/7	34.50
Minor Accident Report Hort/1	15.30
One Statement	15.30
Two or More Statements	20.40
Sketch of Scene	15.30
One Photograph	1.40
To Interview One Police Officer	35.85
For an Abortive Search for an Accident Report	15.30

(b) Warning Observations

A number of warning observations should be noted:

(1) only an interview with the police officer in charge may reveal the details of any suspects interviewed by them, or of matters which the officer has been reluctant to put in a police document (eg 'My impression was . . .', 'The replies of the driver were inconsistent with . . .', 'There was a witness who refused to make a statement but who told me this . . . and he may be contacted at . . .').

(2) Some police forces will allow a police officer to be interviewed for the purpose of civil litigation only once, and then by the first comer. This is deeply to be deprecated as the result may be the necessary issuing of subpoenas to the police so that they may be interviewed at the doors of the court, perhaps only to find that an officer's time has been wasted.

(3) If the request to the police is for the 'police accident report and statements' alone, only those items may be delivered and photographs, plans and any secondary specialist's report prepared by the police may well be excluded. A clue to the existence of such a report and any reference to a more expert officer or accident unit being called to the scene should be looked for in the basic report. Therefore consideration should always be given to the possibility of the existence of a second report, the likelihood of which may increase with the severity of the accident.

(4) From the above it should become quite clear if, and at what stage, the officer in charge of the investigations (with or without any particular specialist skills), has concluded that there is unlikely to be sufficient evidence to lay a criminal charge, or in which way the coroner (in the event of a fatal accident) is to be led. In the light of such a conclusion, the subsequent statements may only contain the barest details and any photographs or sketches may serve only to confirm the officer's judgment.

(5) However irksome it may be to try and discern the conclusions of the

investigating police officers, they will usually indicate to a potential litigant the following important matters about the apparent evidence available:

(a) any judgment formed by the police who attended the scene, saw the damage, heard what was said, saw the demeanour of the witnesses, and felt able to form a judgment;

(b) if any judgment which appears to have been formed has been made in respect of the function of the police to detect criminal offences, and not necessarily to assist future civil claims (which, regrettably, some coroners may make only too plain during an inquest).

(c) the possibility that the other side may call a police officer or officers to give evidence whether or not there has been a preceding criminal trial. This might add to the litigation risks of your client. On the other hand, the evidence which you have collected may be better than that upon which the police have based their decision of whether or not to prosecute. It is worth bearing in mind –

(i) the higher standard of proof in criminal trials 'of beyond reasonable doubt', which the police may have been considering as compared with the lower standard of proof 'on the balance of probabilities', by which a civil litigant must prove his case, and (ii) if the urgent enquiries referred to in Chapter 1 have been undertaken.

(d) that any provisional view formed by the police about criminal proceedings may not only favour the enquirer, but may also be shown to be entirely fair and acceptable to the civil court.

Chapter 3

Statutory Obligations To Provide Information About Drivers

1   Accident reports

Under s 165 of the Road Traffic Act 1988, when requested by the police, the name and address of the owner and driver of a vehicle (other than an invalid carriage) must be given by any person driving a motor vehicle on a road at any time, or by anyone whom the police have reasonable cause to believe has either been the driver at the time when any accident occurred (because of the vehicles' presence on a road) or who has committed an offence in relation to the use on a road of a motor vehicle. If the vehicle is on hire, the obligation to provide the name and address rests on both parties to the agreement.

Under s 170 of the Road Traffic Act 1988, where owing to the presence of a motor vehicle on a road an accident occurs involving personal injury to another person, or damage is caused to any other vehicle or to an animal in or on any other vehicle or to any property forming part of the road, or adjacent to it, the driver must stop. He must, upon request, give his name and address and that of the owner of the vehicle and the vehicle's identification marks, to any person having reasonable grounds for requiring this information. If for any reason the driver does not give his name and address when so required, he must report the accident.

The accident must also be reported if personal injury has been caused to another and the driver has not at the time of the accident produced a certificate of insurance to the police or to any person having reasonable grounds for requiring this. The reporting of the accident and the producing of the certificate of insurance must be done by the driver to the police as soon as is reasonably practicable, and in any case within 24 hours of the accident. Invalid carriage drivers are exempt from this requirement.

If, however, the accident is reported in time, then the certificate of insurance may be produced within five days of the accident to any police station specified by the driver at the time the accident was reported.

If an animal is run over (for the purposes of this section, 'animal' only means horse, cow, ass, mule, sheep, pig, goat or dog) the driver must stop and, if he is not asked for his name and address or that of the owner of the vehicle at the scene, the driver must report the accident. None of these

32

provisions arise if the injury is caused to a cat. Criminal offences are committed in respect of failures to comply with the above provisions, save where the driver is unaware of an accident having happened (*Harding* v *Price* [1948] 1 All ER 283).

Under s 168 of the Road Traffic Act 1988 the name and address must be given to any person having reasonable ground to require this, by the driver of the vehicle who is alleged to have driven recklessly, carelessly or inconsiderately, or the rider of a cycle who has driven recklessly or carelessly.

2 Employer's duties

Employers have certain duties to record and report details of accidents, and this should not be overlooked when seeking documents that relate to road accidents. On 1 April 1986 the Reporting of Injuries & Dangerous Occurrence Regulations 1985 ('RIDOR') (SI No 2023) replaced the Notification of Accidents and Dangerous Occurrences Regulations 1980 ('NADOR'). Specific mention is made of those involved in road accidents.

The regulations cover some, but not all categories of accident involving vehicles moving on public roads. Those categories covered by reg 3(1) are accidents causing death or specified major injuries or conditions which involve or are connected with:

(1) exposure to any substance being conveyed by road;

(2) vehicle loading and unloading activities such as those performed by refuse collectors, brewery delivery workers, furniture removers, coal and milk deliveries;

(3) certain construction, demolition, alteration, repair or maintenance activities on or alongside public roads (see reg 10(2) for the details).

Regulation 3(1) applies in all cases where the person who dies or suffers a specified major injury or medical condition is either himself engaged in one of the listed activities or dies or is injured as a result of the work of someone else who is engaged in such activities. Thus, for example, the following would be reportable under reg 3(1).

(1) the death of an employee of a building materials supplier as a result of being struck by a passing car while unloading bricks from a lorry;

(2) major injuries suffered by a motorist as a result of being struck by an item of scaffolding falling from a building site alongside a road as he was driving past;

(3) gassing or acute illness suffered by the driver of a road tanker or by a member of the public as a result of exposure to a toxic substance spilled from the tanker.

Regulation 3(3) also covers most categories of accident but it applies only to 'over three-day' injuries to employees, self-employed people and trainees (who are at work at the time) resulting from such accidents. Dangerous occurrences on public highways are covered by the regulations, and so too are accidents and dangerous occurrences on private roads (ie those not covered by the Road Traffic Act 1988). The report may be available from (depending upon the particular circumstances) the employer, the self-employed person, the operator of the vehicle, the Health and Safety Executive or the local authority.

3   Insurance details

Under s 172 of the 1988 Act the keeper of the vehicle may be required by a police officer to give information concerning the identity of any driver of a vehicle who is alleged to be guilty of an offence listed under the 1988 Act. Under s 112(2)(a)(i) of the Road Traffic Regulation Act 1984, the keeper of a vehicle is required to give such information as to the identity of the driver of the vehicle as may be required by the chief officer of police (in respect of certain offences, a local authority is also empowered to require such information in writing, see s 112(2)(a)(ii)). Although there is no reference in s 112(2)(a)(i) such information must be provided in writing (unlike s 112(2)(a)(ii)) a chief officer of police may properly specify reasonable requirements as to whom, when, where and how such information must be supplied in written form (*Boss* v *Measures* [1988] Crim LR 582). Similarly, a requirement to provide the information within a specified time (in that case, within 21 days) is enforceable, provided that the time allowed is reasonable.

The victim of a road accident should be able to obtain details of another's insurers from the police when that information has been given to them. In any event, when a claim has been made which would ordinarily be covered by road insurance, the identity of the insurers must be given by the policy holder upon demand or a criminal offence is committed under s 154 of the Road Traffic Act 1988. Recompense will no doubt be sought from the insurer of the party at fault, and the insurer will be statutorily liable for this in accordance with the provisions of s 151 of the Road Traffic Act 1988, provided notice has been given to the insurers before or within seven days after the commencement of proceedings in accordance with s 152(i)a.

Chapter 4

The Taking of Witness Statements

The taking of witness statements is a fundamental part of all litigation, and without a doubt, the taking of a good statement may play a vital role in the conduct of proceedings. It may be the sole link between the solicitor's office, counsel, and the funder of the litigation. The witness may subsequently become untraceable, go overseas, or die before trial. All that may be available at trial from the witness is his statement.

Despite the importance of this mundane task, the taking of statements is too often left to a junior or inexperienced employee, as economics dictate. Statements taken in these circumstances may raise more questions than they answer, or may mislead rather than assist the ongoing process of assessing the litigation risks of the case. The following advice is offered, which might usefully be set out in an office *pro forma* by way of instruction and guidelines, or even as a checklist to the experienced but busy practitioner.

1 Checklist

(1) A planned approach to the order in which each witness is interviewed is desirable, where practicable. This will require careful thought, after review of the information available and the likely issues involved.

(2) The interviewer taking the statement will do well to commit to memory the advice of Rudyard Kipling:

> I kept six honest serving men
> They taught me all I knew
> Their names were WHAT, WHY and WHEN,
> HOW, WHERE and WHO.

There are perhaps few more important four lines together than these. The judge will have these six questions to hand by instinct. So ought your opponent. And so should you.

(3) A list of the items to be covered in the statement is the only sure way of making it comprehensive. In some cases, this may require a full-scale questionnaire; the questions can be typed out with spaces left for answers. Questionnaires are particularly useful when interviewing police witnesses

or when time is at a premium and accuracy is essential concerning detailed issues (see Appendix 4).

(4) If there is no prepared questionnaire, listen first to the oral account, clarify matters that seem ambiguous or obscure, and build up a mental picture of what the witness tells you. It is as well to sort out all anomalies and contradictions before attempting to commit the account to a written statement, unless the existence of those discrepancies from this witness may in fact need to be relied upon for subsequent cross-examination because it is (or becomes during the course of the interview) more likely that the witness will be called by the opponent.

(5) Be polite, but be critical. Always seek clarification of what you find doubtful or difficult to follow.

(6) While the witness may have the immediate effect of the accident uppermost in his mind, what needs to be elicited is the important evidence which he may well be able to offer concerning the events leading up to the accident, and even events thereafter (eg what was moved, by whom, or who said what to whom).

(7) Of course, no amount of skilled questioning can elicit evidence of which the witness has no knowledge. But if the answer is 'I don't know', it is important to make a note of that, too.

(8) Can this witness help identify or trace any other possibly material witness or other evidence?

(9) A note needs to be kept of who was interviewed by whom and where and when. The witness should check your record of the interview for accuracy and be invited to sign it as being accurate. (A refusal may only be because of a reluctance to sign anything, and this does not necessarily invalidate the evidential value of the record of the interview.)

(10) What about sending the witness a typed copy of the statement? There may be a danger that he will pass it on to the opponents, thus losing the privilege and confidentiality of such a statement which would ordinarily prevent the opponent seeing your proofs of evidence. But in the case of a police officer, it is suggested that this should be done as a matter of course. This is a courtesy that is not only fair, but may reap dividends in the event of more relevant evidence subsequently coming to the notice of the police which they might then share. It could also win the respect of witnesses who may have to be interviewed in other accidents and whose co-operation may be more forthcoming if your helpfulness and co-operation is already established.

(11) Any questioning, whether set out in a prepared questionnaire or otherwise, should be undertaken with questions simply framed, without hostility, and in a way that enables the most accurate conclusions to be drawn.

(12) The temptation may prove irresistible to record the witness's own opinion as to the cause of the accident, particularly when that opinion favours your client. Such an opinion from a lay witness will be (or ought to be) ruled inadmissible:

'It frequently happens that a bystander has a complete full view of an accident. It is beyond question that, while he may inform the court of everything he saw, he may not express an opinion on whether either or both of the parties were negligent. The reason commonly assigned is that this is the precise question the court has to decide, but in truth, it is because his opinion is not relevant. Any fact he can prove is relevant, but his opinion is not. The well recognised exception in the case of scientific or expert witnesses depends on considerations which, for the present purposes, are immaterial' per Goddard LJ, in *Hollington* v *Hewthorn* (1943) 1 KB at p 595.

2 Court powers

The importance of all these matters has been emphasised since 1988 with the extension of the court's powers to enable it, 'if it thinks fit for the purposes of disposing fairly and expeditiously of the cause or matter and saving costs', to direct any party to serve on the other parties, 'on such terms as the court shall think just, written statements of the oral evidence which the party intends to lead on any issues of fact to be decided at the trial' (RSC Ord 38, r 2(A)). An order for an exchange of proofs of oral evidence is now to be regarded as normal procedure (see *Richard Saunders and Partners* v *East Glenn Limited* (1989) *The Times*, 28 July).

While witness statements that have been exchanged under Ord 38, r 2(A) do not in themselves become evidence (but remain confidential until the witness makes them public by verifying it on oath in the witness box), it is obviously important that the disclosed statements should be accurate and complete. Any attempt to alter or vary a disclosed statement before trial will require leave of the court.

3 Examples

The following is an example of how an initial statement taken by the police became a detailed and complete account during the subsequent interview, with litigation in mind: 'The car came out of the junction in front of me. I didn't have a chance and my motor-cycle just hit the side and I went over the bonnet.' It did not take much astute questioning to reveal and record information which eventually proved vital; not only was it essential in the general conduct of the case, but it also obtained a full legal aid certificate and an appropriate settlement from the insurers when the subsequent statement was served upon them (under s 2(2)(b) of the Civil Evidence Act 1968 and RSC Ord 38, r 22(2)), with a view to the statement going in as evidence at the conclusion of the plaintiff's evidence-in-chief (ie at the end of his examination by his own lawyer)).

'I rode my motor-cycle around the left hand bend on the main road at about 40 miles per hour. I was riding just left of the continuous white line in the centre of the road. There was no other traffic either behind or in front of me. I first saw the car on my left on the minor road as I came round the bend. It was about two car lengths back from the 'Stop' lines across the junction. I throttled right back, reduced to third gear, and began to slow down. I covered my footbrake with my foot. I could see the car driver look towards me. The car came to a stop with the front just over the 'Stop' lines. I had my dipped beam light on. My motor cycle is fitted with a large white fairing (windshield), and my crash helmet had reflective strips upon it. The driver looked to his left, but I was sure he had seen me. Having reduced speed I was trying to change down to second with my right foot when I saw the car lurch across the 'Stop' line. The driver turned and looked towards me. I applied both my front and back brakes. The car was across, and completely blocking, my lane. I could not swerve to either side of it because I was being thrown forward off my seat. The car was still moving when my front wheel ran headlong into the front offside wheel of the car. I was thrown forward, breaking the visor on top of my fairing. I landed on the bonnet and slid off on to the road on the far side of the car.'

The effort made to obtain a detailed statement is never wasted—and the witness may very well not be aware of what he can usefully say until asked in detail. The statement thus obtained will be invaluable for any immediate criminal proceedings, or for any subsequent civil litigation, which may very well occur if there has been any personal injury or damage to property of any significance.

Chapter 5

Illustrative Aids

1 Sketches

The Police Accident Report will usually include a sketch of the scene including the position of all the relevant items. If the police sketch does not refer to a fixed point from which all the measurements should be related, is of too small a scale, or has a general lack of detail then you may need your own expert report. In any event, a separate plan of the area may also be required to illustrate from which direction people came, to highlight a reference in a statement, or to identify a position of observation (or what could have been observed).

The principle behind the production of maps, plans and photographs is to illustrate the scene. It is more than likely that those who are being asked to sit in judgment are not familiar with the locus and all its peculiarities. By utilising a mixture of maps, photographs and plans, the details can be presented with the best of evidence, short of a necessary, costly and time wasting visit to the locus.

In many cases the evidence of distances is a major element in the case. Photographs can be deceptive if attempts are made to relate them to distances which can be foreshortened by the use of a telephoto lens. There may be nothing sinister in the use of more than one lens at a locus, for a wide angle lens may have to be used to capture the best of one view, while a telephoto lens is used to show detail over a longer distance. As a safeguard against any allegations that lens changes have been made to mislead the photographer should show the positions of the camera on the plans (see *Fig 12*).

2 Scale plans

There are three main sources of scale plans.

(a) Surveyors

A surveyor may be commissioned to produce a scale plan of whatever area or specific areas are required. A gentle reminder that copies of the original may be required at some time in the distant future should ensure the preservation of the original.

(b) Digital maps

Digital maps have the advantage that when used with a computer-aided design programme they can be adapted to the specific needs of the draftsman (ie, skid marks or other related evidence can be added to the base drawing). The 1:1250 and 1:2500 scale maps cost £100 plus VAT and the department will endeavour to supply a map within ten days of receipt of the order.

(c) Ordnance survey scale plans

There are some 50,000 maps in this series. A wide range of scale plans are available, the largest of which is the 1:1250 scale on which 1 centimetre = 12.5 metres (or 50 inches to the mile). It is available for cities and most urban areas and includes such details as house numbers and height information (see *Fig 10*). Each 100 metre square = 1 hectare (2.471 acres). This scale of map is most useful when the approach to a locus must be described and identified, before a larger scale or expert's plan of the actual locus is referred to.

Figure 10 shows a section of a typical 1:1250 scale plan of an area and *Figure 11* shows a section of an enlargement of 1:500 of a section of the original. If additional information is required then the 1:500 scale plan can be used as an accurate base. Thus, in *Fig 12* the positions from which the photographs have been taken are drawn for illustrative purposes at trial. The 1:2500 maps (25 inches to the mile or 1 centimetre to 25 metres), cover most of the country except mountain and moorland areas and large urban areas.

The largest scale which covers mountains and moorland areas is the 1:10,000 at 1 centimetre to 100 metres (or 6 inches to the mile) series. For a smaller scale, the 1:50,000 (2 centimetres to the kilometer) may well be useful to show the approach to a scene, and may itself be used in conjuction with either a larger scale map or a plan especially drawn by the expert.

Whatever maps are used, as with any photograph, they should be complementary to other items of evidence. Copies of maps are usually available from the Ordnance Survey Agents (see the Yellow Pages). A catalogue of maps may be obtained from:
Information and Enquiries
Ordnance Survey
Romsey Road, Maybush
Southampton
SO9 4DH
Tel: 0703 7925584
The London Map Centre is the main agent for England and Wales at 22–24 Caxton Street, London; Tel: (071) 222 2466. One of the main agents in Scotland is Thomas Nelson & Sons Ltd, 51 York Place, Edinburgh; Tel: (031) 557 3011.

Figure 10: Large Scale Section

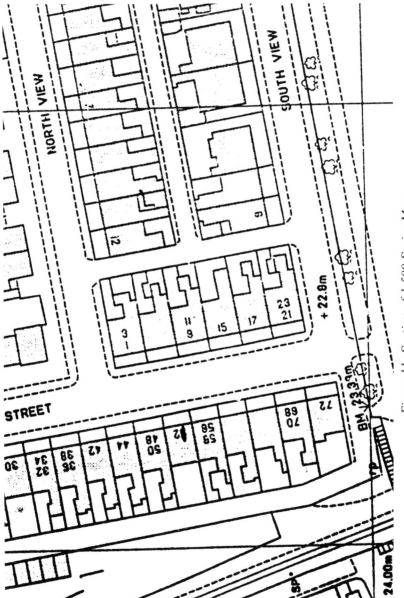

Figure 11: Section of 1:500 Series Map

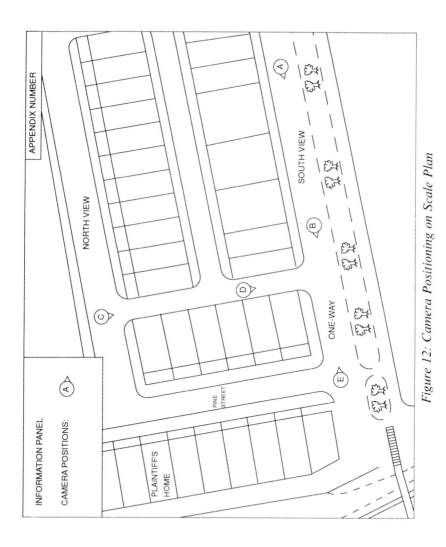

Figure 12: Camera Positioning on Scale Plan

Note: To ensure the recovery of the costs of preparing a plan (other than a sketch plan), its authorisation should be obtained from the court before the trial, or from the Taxing Officer or Registrar after trial (see RSC, Ord 62/ A2/58 and CCR Ord 38 r10).

(d) Units of measurement
If frequent reference is to be made to scale plans a multi-scale ruler is invaluable and will give an instant reading in metres from the plan. The conversion factor of metres to feet is 3.28.

CONVERSION SCALES			
Scale	*One Centimetre*	*One Inch*	*Inches To The Mile*
1:100	1 metre	2.5 metres	643.9
1:200	2 metres	5.0 metres	312.5
1:500	5 metres	12.5 metres	125.0
1:1250	12.5 metres	31.25 metres	50
1:2500	25.50 metres	62.5 metres	25
1:10,000	100.00 metres	250.0 metres	6

3   Photographs

It is paradoxical that while experience gained taking wedding or even industrial photographs may not be sufficient photographic qualification for your purposes, a Polaroid-type snap taken by an amateur, at the right time and place, may be vital. When there is a choice, however, the Polaroid-type of photograph should be avoided. The results lack definition and there is no negative available from which printed copies can be easily and cheaply prepared.

When presented with any photograph, there are two important features to note.

(a) Distances
Distances are often deceptive. When looking from foreground to background it does not follow that an object 'X' one-third of the way into the photograph, say, is the same distance away from a second object 'Y' two-thirds of the way into the photograph. There are many factors which influence distances, eg the height of the camera, its angle to the road, and the focal length of the lens. Nevertheless, there is often internal evidence from which distances can be calculated fairly accurately. For example, kerbstones are almost universally three feet long, telegraph poles and street lights are likely to be evenly spaced and a house brick is likely to be, with one half mortar joint each side, $9'' \times 4\frac{1}{2}'' \times 3''$. The Traffic Signs Regulations

1981 specify the dimensions of road markings and some fairly accurate estimates may be made by reference to these (see Chapter Seven).

(b) Lighting conditions

An object may seem clearly visible on a police photograph, eg of a night-time scene, but it is simply not possible to reproduce the same lighting conditions (except by chance) in a subsequent photograph. Variations of the time-exposure, and its processing may make a world of difference as to what the camera has or has not recorded.

Consider *Photograph 1* and *Photograph 2*. Both are views of a typical urban road taken with the same street lighting. *Photograph 1* was given a 20 second exposure, and *Photograph 2* a 40 second exposure. *Photograph 1* could be submitted to corroborate a claim that the visibility on the road was poor, while *Photograph 2* could be offered as evidence that the visibility was, in fact, quite good. Street lighting tends to create areas of light and dark. It can be seen that even this phenomenon can be altered by a manipulation of the exposure times.

Any photographs taken for you should have one set signed on the back by the photographer with the date they were taken. When preparing bundles of photographs for the court, each photograph should be *lettered* in the same sequence, (for numbers will be used to identify each separate exhibit). The letter of each photograph should be marked on its face (not the back) for ease of reference in proceedings (sticky labels will suffice). With each set of photographs the photographer should submit a signed statement to identify and detail the significance of each photograph and the time at which it was taken, to avoid the expense and inconvenience of being called as a witness. Naturally, the plans and the photographs should be complementary and ordered to follow the series of events as they occurred. To ensure this, the photographer will need specific instructions from you. The photographs should appear in an order in the bundle that helps tell the story. Thus, the first series of photographs should represent your client's approach, followed by the views of any other relevant party. Photographs across the road, and of the scene generally, may also be appropriate.

If aerial photographs of the scene are required, then assistance may be available from the local aero-club, or even from a crop-sprayer. The Ordnance Survey (see p 40) hold extensive aerial photographic coverage of England, Scotland and Wales, mainly at 1:7500 and 1:24000 scales. Photographs can be supplied as:

(1) contact prints, $9'' \times 9''$;
(2) enlargements of up to four times above; and
(3) diapositives (eg slides) or negatives, to those licensed to copy.

(c) Camera positions

Consideration should be given to the position of the camera lens when taking a photograph which purports to show what the witness could or should have been able to see. In the vertical plane, car drivers' eye levels are

Photograph 1

Photograph 2

usually about 1.07 metres (3 feet, 6 inches) to about 1.3 metres (4 feet, 3 inches) above the level of the road. Goods' vehicle and public service drivers' eye levels are generally at a higher level. When attempting to assess the view that should have been afforded to a driver, the height of his eyes must be taken into account and if neccessary the height from which a photograph is taken.

In the horizontal plane, the position of the eyes at a road junction which has obstructions on either side will affect the length of the sight lines of an emerging driver. In a long-bonneted vehicle the driver will be farther from the junction than a bus or goods vehicle driver seated in a forward control type of cab.

Consideration should also be given to the position occupied by the camera in the lanes if the view is to be representative of the driver's view along the sight line around the curvature of the road.

(d) Sunlight

Photographs of scenes may look better when taken on a sunny day against a background of blue sky rather than a dark grey pall. However, consideration should be given to the time of day when a photograph is taken and the direction in which the sun is shining. It is not unusual for one side of a street to be well-lit by the sun while the other side is blacked out in shadow, with a corresponding loss of detail. Thus, in order to photograph both sides it may be necessary to visit the scene at different times of the day. This may also be necessary when the view which has to be taken is directly into the sun.

(e) Background to photographs

The private investigator has little control over the conditions prevailing at a scene and must complete his investigation without interfering with any other road user and certainly with due regard for his own safety. Yet within these constraints and with some patience it is possible to take photographs which are free from irrelevant background details.

Where smaller individual items of evidence have to be photographed, for example vehicle components which have been removed from the vehicle, it is better to do this against a contrasting background such as a white cloth. This has the effect of eliminating, for example, the sight of a workshop surrounding an unscreened subject, which may only detract a witnesses' attention from the real issue in question.

Chapter 6

Estimating Distances in Photographs

Judging distances from photographs can be very deceptive since a two-dimensional lens will create an image that foreshortens distances and may mislead the inexperienced eye (see Chapter 5). However, almost all photographs taken in respect of road accidents will contain internal evidence from which the experienced eye may be able to assess the third dimension—depth (meaning here the depth into the photograph and therefore the distance of one object in the photograph in relation to another). The question of 'depth' (or distance) may be fundamental to assessing liability, the application of any formulae relating to the calculation of speeds, braking distances, and the avoidability of collisions. Thus a great deal of relevant information needs to be extracted from internal evidence within the photograph.

1 Road markings

In this regard road markings can be helpful since:

(1) the length of road markings is prescribed by statutory requirement, namely, the Traffic Signs Regulations and General Directions 1981; and

(2) one can make a legal presumption that the road markings will in fact comply with those Regulations (*omnia praesumuntur rite et solemniter esse acta*), until the contrary is proved.

In *Fig 13*, diagrams 'A' and 'B' are used to warn traffic when approaching or negotiating a hazard. They should not be crossed or straddled by a vehicle unless it is safe to do so. Diagrams 'C' and 'D' merely divide the carriageway into traffic lanes. In the following situations these markings are used:

'E' indicates the division between *opposing flows* on a carriageway that has four or more lanes or is 10 metres or more wide.

'F' indicates the edge of a carriageway at a road junction.

'G' indicates the edges of a carriageway at a road junction or layby.

In *Photograph 3*, distances may be estimated from the dimensions of the road markings. On the left, there are 600 mm marks with 300 mm gaps ('F'), indicating edge of the carriageway at a road junction. Beyond them is the 'give way' marking, with its 600 mm marks and 300 mm gaps. ('F'). The central carriageway hazard marking is made up of 4000 mm lines and 2000

48

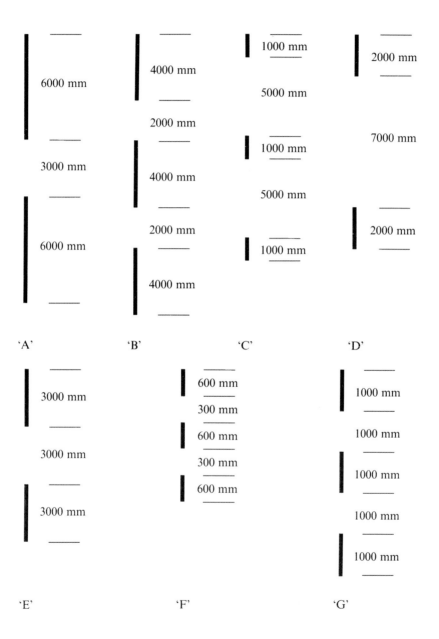

Figure 13: Road Markings

Photograph 3

Photograph 4

Photograph 5

mm gaps, ('B'). On the right, the markings are 1000 mm long with 1000 mm gaps, ('G').

Photograph 4 shows 1000 mm markings, with 5000 mm gaps, ('C'). It gives some indication of the difficulties involved when attempts are made to estimate the distances between foreground and background without the aid of such known distances.

The 'give way' markings at the junction in *Photograph 5* with their 600 mm marks and 300 mm ('F') gaps should be of some assistance in estimating distances across the width of the junction.

Where Imperial units of length are used, the conversion factor is 1 metre = 3.28 feet. While it must be remembered that these marks are made with either a rather imprecise spray or a crude mould, it is important to know that sometimes a photograph can hold a key to questions of distances—if one knows where to look.

Chapter 7

Letter Before Action

The correspondence referred to here will more usually be relevant to civil proceedings than a criminal trial, but the following observations could be relevant to both. In civil actions, it is customary to think of the appropriate letter as being sent by the plaintiff. However, where both parties claim in respect of their own loss and damage it may only be matter of who sends a letter first as to who is the actual plaintiff. In any event, both parties have much to gain from the matters that follow and which are addressed to whoever may be party to the litigation.

First, the 'Contents' list to this Guide should be consulted concerning all that has been covered so far, to make sure that all relevant matters have been considered. Check to ensure that all relevant details have been obtained concerning witnesses, the place of the accident, those involved as potential parties, the details of insurers involved, the police accident report and statements as well as any other records or necessary statements, sketches, plans and photographs. If so, a reliable preliminary assessment of the party's case and prospects of success can now be made, advice given, and correspondence entered into with impressive argument and detail. The letter before action, or in response, should now have some considerable effect upon the recipient, and perhaps equally or more importantly, upon the court.

There is, however, a school of thought and practice that advises that such correspondence should be limited to mere generalities such as: 'It is alleged that the accident was caused by your negligence'; or 'Our client denies liability and claims it was your client who was at fault'. There may be good reason for this approach in complicated cases where initial enquiries are limited because adequate access to the necessary witnesses and documents is limited to one of the litigants (eg factory accidents, where it is only *after* the close of pleadings that discovery of important documents necessarily held by the other side can usually be obtained, from which essential facts and perhaps the identity of some witnesses may be apparent). But this practice can become a thoughtless habit if applied to all litigation. In road traffic litigation, there is rarely any justification for such guardedness, commonplace as it may be in some quarters. Indeed, in road traffic claims, the general practice should always be to set out the case with both force and detail:

(1) Litigation and costs may be avoidable, but not by making bland, unsupported allegations.

(2) The immediate recipient of the detailed letter may be blind to the voice of reason, but subsequent readers of it who have to deal with the claim and who have greater objectivity, may be more impressed.

(3) If none of the readers on the other side of litigation are convinced, the judge may be, since an early opportunity has been taken both at the start and thereafter to assert a consistently detailed case.

(4) To do otherwise may only signal weakness which may be entirely inappropriate, or suggest a lack of detailed enquiries to date, or a party who wishes to keep all options open so that he may backtrack later. Vague correspondence may only indicate laziness or a reluctance to pursue the issues involved; but it may later be interpreted as sinister prevarication.

Only rarely will lack of finance (see Chapter 18) truly prevent detailed early enquiries, so beware the pressure of false economies. It may be that the first round of correspondence is justifiably brief and simple, but not thereafter. Cases are not unusual where detailed correspondence has also had the advantage of preventing the other party obtaining legal aid (or its extension) or preventing an application to strike out for want of subsequent prosecution of the claim (because the other party cannot prove the requisite prejudice from the delay by reason of early notice of the material allegations to be met).

By the time initial correspondence has begun, especially in a dubious claim or defence, there ought to be an awareness of the pitfalls to be avoided in a letter that deals with the substance of the claim (since the above detailed enquiries should already have been made). The Lord Chancellor's plans to speed up civil litigation of road accidents, including the trial of some cases on the documents alone, have given added impetus to these observations.

Part Two

Expert Evidence

Chapter 8

The Guiding Principles

Certain aspects of road accident claims necessarily require expert assistance. Some factual evidence will require expert interpretation and opinion which a court cannot or will not allow a layman to undertake, other than perhaps the advocate by way of submission at the end of the case (when it may become plain that in reality he is seeking improperly to give evidence himself of an expert nature). The court may well be persuaded to take 'judicial notice' of certain matters, such as lighting-up times (see Chapter 2) where the issue is not likely to be in doubt, and minimum braking distances set out in the Highway Code. Judicial notice will also be taken of basic mathematical propositions, such as:

speed = distance travelled ÷ by the time taken to travel it

However, this basic formula only applies where the speed is constant, so that there has been no braking or any speed loss due to a collision. Of course the use of this formula at all requires the evidence of two assessable factors; the application of the correct units of measurement can only be applied where the speed is a constant and there has been no braking (see Chapter 9).

The following are set out as tentative guiding principles in respect of expert evidence.

(a) The choice of expert

The choice of expert is extremely important. Ideally, the witness will have previous experience of what is expected in court, and will be known to be reliable. However, even where a suitable expert is known, they may be unavailable because they have taken instructions from the other side (hence the importance, in part, of instructing the witness sooner rather than later). Moreover, the evidence upon which the expert will advise will be both available and reasonably fresh. Similarly, the accident scene may be too far from their place of practice to make a visit and enquiries practicable, or the enquiry may even be too urgent for it to be possible to be able to assist in time.

A list of suitable experts is available from The Secretary, The Forensic Science Society, Clarke House, 18A Mount Parade, Harrogate, HG1 1AX.

The Society will need an indication of the sort of expert required, eg for accident reconstruction, a report on tyres (ie, at what stage it is likely they failed), the analysis of a tachograph, or the significance of the failure to wear a seatbelt. Help may also be available from the local Law Society, or even the police officer who attended the accident, by reason of the officer's particular training and qualification in the relevant field of expertise.

The Institute of Road Transport Engineers (1 Cromwell Place, Kennsington, London; Telephone (071) 589 3544 or Fax (071) 225 0494) has also built up a unique data bank of knowledge on the problem of the detachment of road wheels. While in the past it was an accepted assumption that road wheel detachment was the fault of the owner (ie, failure to maintain the vehicle) their research has shown that there are other causes of wheel detachment, such as inherent design or metalurgy faults. An enquiry to the Institute may yield some help in the preparation of a defence to a prosecution for such an alleged offence.

(b) Qualifications

The qualifications of the expert must be made plain. The evidence and conclusions of the expert are generally going to have to be based upon 'opinion evidence'. For this evidence to be admissible it must satisfy the court that the author is qualified to give such expert evidence. These need not necessarily be 'paper' or examination qualifications, for length and depth of experience can be more important.

(c) The facts

The facts upon which the expert bases an opinion must be set out first, and with clarity. If those facts are not clear (and inevitably they may not be), at least the reasoning for choosing those facts as a base must be stated. Certain assumptions may be unavoidable before the expert opinion can be given so it is important that the bases for them are made plain.

(d) The use of formulae

The use of formulae and the expression of the opinions based upon them must be set out with discretion and fairness. There will have to be sensitivity to the difficulties that may be experienced both by the advocates and the court in respect of methods of accident investigation and reconstruction, which the expert regards as traditionally acceptable.

(e) Professional independence

The expert is giving evidence not just because of personal expertise, but also by reason of his professional independence. As a witness the expert is not just there to advance the case of the client on whose behalf he is called but also to answer fairly and fully any questions put in cross-examination and by the court with a view to assisting the court impartially. What impresses the court by way of fairness and accuracy during the case in hand will make the expert a more valuable witness in subsequent cases.

Neither the disclosed report, nor the evidence of the expert, should purport to decide what is, in fact, the job of the court. The expert may assist, but not trespass, on what is in practice the final decision of the court. The witness may advance reasons why any specific allegations may be correct, but the expert should not then assert what the court has to decide—who is liable, and in what proportion. True, the witness may advise the court as to the basis upon which someone was at fault, but not that 'someone is liable'. An expert may express an opinion as to why one party was more at fault than another, but not the proportion of liability. Difficult as it may be to state the boundaries beyond which is to trespass, ultimately it may be regarded simply as a question of good manners. (Of course, what the expert chooses to say, and how it is expressed (either in a privileged proof of evidence (see Chapter 11)), or in open court in response to a direct question, is another matter).

Finally, there is a paradox with which the expert must come to terms, which faces not only any witness but also any advocate: keep the evidence simple, but do not treat your audience as such.

Chapter 9

Topics for the Expert

Each case produces its own problems upon which expert advice may be required. This chapter seeks to do no more than set out examples of such problems. Other sections of this book deal in passing with other features that call for special help, but can conveniently be dealt with separately, such as preparing appropriate photographs or plans, interpreting relevant documents, the significance of the failure to wear a seatbelt, or the calculation of the loss of use of a vehicle. Some aspects of expert evidence are too specialised for a work of this nature or are subect to continuing research projects, for instance the effect of a specific quantity of alcohol in the body, certain effects of overloading vehicles, or a specialised area of research such as might concern tyres and their performance. What follows is related to matters of more general application and occurrence, or is by way of introduction to matters of more general interest.

1 Vehicle damage related to speed on impact

The structural damage suffered by a vehicle in collision with another object (of any kind) is frequently important. It may prove involvement of the vehicle in question where this is disputed, the direction of travel in certain circumstances, and (on occasions) the place or point of impact.

However, vehicle damage is not always a reliable base upon which to estimate accurately the relative speed(s) on impact (and careful scrutiny may be required of any suggestion to the contrary). Usually, the evidence of damage is only one of a number of items of information which will have to be considered before speeds are estimated with the desired accuracy.

In pedestrian/vehicular collisions, detailed medical reports will be of great help to the expert and should be sent along with the instructions to advise. The expert may be able to relate injury and vehicular damage to show what part of the vehicle struck the pedestrian. This is particularly helpful in determining just what distance the pedestrian had covered before the impact. There is some research which tends to show that most cars (and the frontal shape is one factor) must run into a pedestrian at a speed of over 8 mph before the pedestrian will be scooped over the bonnet. The height of the pedestrian is another factor.

2 Skid marks

If, during a brake-to-stop action by a driver, a wheel is prevented from rotating by the braking force then a mark will usually be left upon a dry road. Such a mark is made by small pieces of rubber being scraped off the tyre tread by the coarse microfinish of the road surface. In some instances, if the length of that mark is recorded and the coefficient of friction is determined which existed at the time the mark was made, then the minimum speed of the vehicle at the time the wheel locked can be calculated.

Because the coefficent of friction which exists between the tyre and the road surface can change by the hour (and indeed sooner), it follows that tests ought to be made as soon as possible after the collision. These can be done by driving (preferably the same vehicle or, if that is not possible, a similar vehicle) at a known speed and measuring the length of the skid mark produced by a full application of the brakes.

If it is the police who have established the coefficient of friction of the road at the time, then only their technique may be challenged, for any later tests might be done upon a road surface which has altered radically for one reason or another. However, skid marks provide other useful information from which certain deductions can be made. They can:

(1) delineate the position of the vehicle on the road;

(2) show where lock up began and ended; and

(3) identify which wheels locked up.

Skidding in itself may not necessarily, but will usually, imply fault (see *Hunter* v *Wright* [1938] 2 All ER 621, CA; cp *Richley* v *Faull* [1965] 3 All ER 109). The possibility of fault will depend upon the information which was available to the driver, and whether or not the driver recognised the changing conditions and modified his driving to suit the new situation.

In any skidding accident, it may also be necessary to consider the liability of the Highways Authority, in failing to heed weather reports properly and failing in good time to lay salt or grit.

3 The absence of skid marks

Where there is good evidence that there were no skid marks at the scene, one of the following explanations must apply:

(1) There was no braking, either because the brakes were not applied or if they were they did not lock the wheels to create a skid mark. This may indicate a maintenance fault.

(2) There was a high coefficient of friction. If the coefficient of friction between the road and the tyre was sufficiently high (and there are some proprietary road surface dressings which are sometimes laid over short distances on approaches to dangerous stretches of roads, which have much higher 'grip' properties than the normal surface), then the braking force might not be sufficient to lock the wheel. This condition is not necessarily

indicative of a vehicle maintenance fault.

(3) The vehicle was fitted with an anti-locking device. While anti-locking brakes are not yet a legal requirement, some vehicles have various devices to prevent the driver from locking some or all of the wheels (eg ABS 'anti-locking system'). The expert must ensure that the absence of a skid mark is not attributable to such a design feature of the vehicle.

(4) If there was only one brake mark instead of a pair it may mean imbalanced braking forces at the wheels and therefore the possibility of a defective braking system. There may, however, have been a difference in the road surface between the nearside and offside of the vehicle.

(5) The surface condition was of such a nature as to be incapable of bringing about a transfer of rubber to the surface. Nevertheless there may be surface marks apparent on the water, snow or ice laid upon the road surface. Such marks would be eliminated by the weather or other traffic unless the scene of the accident was protected.

If none of the above can reasonably be accounted for there must have been excessive speed and/or late braking by the driver in question. If skidding is to be pleaded as a defence in a civil action, namely 'inevitable accident', full particulars of the matters relied upon will have to be pleaded (RSC Ord 18, rr 12, 13).

4   Braking efficiency

Appendix 2 shows the relationship between the braking efficiency and the speed of a vehicle to both the distance in which it can brake to a stop and the time it will take. The braking efficiency of a vehicle can be calculated by expressing its rate of retardation as a percentage either of 32.2 feet per second per second or 9.8 metres per second per second. For example, a 50 per cent braking efficiency is the equivalent to a retardation rate of either 16.1 feet per second per second or 4.9 metres per second per second. The retardation rate is dependent upon the coefficient of friction between the tyres and the road surface. If the coefficient is, say 0.5, the highest rate of retardation will be about 16.1 feet per second per second and the efficiency about 50 per cent.

The Highway Code assumes that a dry road surface in good condition should have a coefficient of friction of 0.68 which, in turn, should sustain a retardation rate of 22 feet per second per second and an efficiency of 68 per cent. The table shows that the vehicle will come to a stop in about 45 feet and in a time of two seconds.

5   Formulae

Many lawyers in the United States apparently study for an extra qualification in mathematics in order to understand better the application of formulae used in road traffic claims. However, even if the first perusal of formulae tends to bring back memories of fifth-form homework, endless thumbing through log tables, or even differential calculus; in their simplest form, analyses of accidents only require an appreciation of three fundamental components:

(1) distance—which is expressed in feet (or metres);

(2) time—expressed in seconds; and

(3) speed—expressed in feet (or metres) per second.

The expert will use the term 'velocity'. It may be said that there is a difference between the terms 'speed' and 'velocity' but for the present context, velocity need only be considered as speed in a given direction. (In the German language the same word is used for both—geschwindigkeit.) The expert will choose 'feet per second' or 'metres per second' rather than 'miles per hour' before attempting any calculations, and a rough and ready 'feet per second' mental conversion can be done by halving the mph and adding half to the original (ie adding 50 per cent). So that 20 mph halved is 10 mph and $20 + 10 = 30$ feet per second. The true conversion factor is however 1.46 and when used, 20mph $\times$ 1.46 = 29.2 feet per second and *pro rata*.

This section deals with the gentle introduction to the most mathematically blind, of the formulae of:

$$s = ut \text{ (and transpositions)};$$

$$s = \frac{u + v}{2}t;$$

and $v_2 - u_2 = 2as$

(a) The emerging vehicle collision

In this typical accident, an emerging vehicle 'E' (see *Fig 14*) strikes a passing vehicle 'P' where the driver of the emerging vehicle 'E' claims that at the time he began to emerge, 'P' was not in sight. *Photographs 6 and 7* show views available to two different emerging drivers. *Photograph 6* shows a fairly long sight line, whereas *Photograph 7* shows a short sight line. Consideration should be given to the amount of foliage and its effect upon the length of the sight line. This is of particular importance when the scene is visited in a different season to that in which the accident occurred.

In a worked example of an accident involving the emerging and approaching vehicle (see *Fig 14*), the following data is to be established or assumed:

(1) The distance from 'a' to 'c', say 3 metres (9.84 feet).

(2) The time taken for vehicle 'E' to drive from 'a' to 'c'. This value can be established by three test drives from a standing start, say 2.4, 2.8 and 2.7 seconds, with an average of 2.6 seconds.

(3) The time taken for the vehicle 'P' to drive from, 'b' to 'c', a distance of say 140 feet. This can be established from the evidence of the average approach speed, from whatever source that may have come (see p 68). It will not be a constant if the vehicle braked or slowed before the collision, but adjustments can be made to suit the evidence and to try to reach a

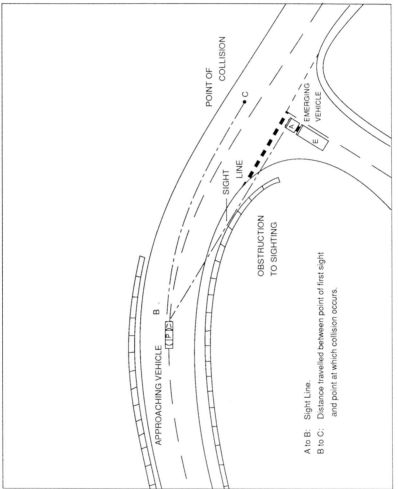

Figure 14: Emerging Vehicle Collision

Photograph 6

Photograph 7

meaningful value. Reference to a tachograph chart might show the precise speed of approach, if indeed the vehicle was fitted with such a device.

(4) Assuming that the vehicle approached at an average speed of 30 miles per hour (44 feet per second) then the time taken to drive the 140 feet would have been some 3.2 seconds.

(5) Based upon these values, vehicle 'P' would have been 3.2 seconds from point 'c' when vehicle 'E' began to move out and was 2.6 seconds from point 'c'. Thus vehicle 'P' would not have been visible to the driver of vehicle 'E' when he began to move out.

It follows therefore, that the general rule for all work done in the course of a reconstruction is that the more accurate the evidence, the more accurate will be the results of the reconstruction.

(b) Collision with a pedestrian

In a situation where a pedestrian attempts to cross a road and is struck by a vehicle the important factor is the time the pedestrian spent on the road. The distance traversed by the pedestrian can usually be determined by measuring the distance from the kerb to the point of impact. The determination of the second component, speed, is less easy. At what speed does a pedestrian move? Speed cannot always be related accurately to the age of the pedestrian, but there are generally three categories:

(1) the young, who tend to move quickly to a point of impact at about eight feet per second;

(2) the old, who move slowly, at about two feet per second; and

(3) a group between the two, who, for many reasons (and one is drink), move into the path of a vehicle at various speeds.

All the expert can do is to note the descriptions of the movements (eg 'ran fast', 'darted', 'ambled', 'strolled', 'walked normally'); and then try to simulate that manner, using a similar person. Perhaps the tests may produce a maximum/minimum time which can be agreed by both parties. Remember, however, that the pedestrian may out-accelerate a vehicle from a standing start, and can change direction quicker than any vehicle. Consideration should be given to the preservation of the clothes (or their description) worn by the pedestrian, especially if they were of a light colour and the accident occurred at night.

Reference must now be made to the speed of a vehicle. It is not generally appreciated that to brake a vehicle to a halt from 30 mph (within the Highway Code braking distance of 45 feet) takes only 2 seconds. The total stopping time is calculated by adding the thinking time of 0.68 seconds (see generally the scales at r 51 and on the back of the Highway Code).

Photographs 8 and 9 show pedestrians crossing the road into the path of a vehicle. In *Photograph 8* the pedestrian has walked a relatively short distance, whereas in *Photograph 9* the pedestrians have approached from the offside of the vehicle which usually means the driver has had more time to become aware of the danger. In both cases an essential component of the reconstruction work is to establish the point of contact upon the vehicle.

Photograph 8

Photograph 9

This, in turn, usually determines how far the pedestrian has walked before the collision.

On that basis it follows that in many circumstances (and each accident has its own peculiarities), where it can be shown that a pedestrian has been on the road for more than three seconds, the onus is upon the driver on a road with a 30 mph speed limit to offer an explanation of why he failed to stop before the collision.

(c) Calculating speed

It is important to note that in an accident the vehicle's speed will rarely be constant and as a result, two velocites are considered: the *initial* velocity (u) and the *final* velocity (v).

The analysis may involve the determination of an unknown factor, which can easily be done by the application and transposition of certain formulae. A much clearer application of the formulae may be had if they are represented pictorially:

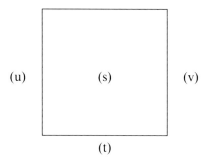

This diagram represents a vehicle travelling at a *constant* velocity for a given time (t), because the initial velocity (u) = the final velocity (v). The shape is either a square or a rectangle and its area equals u × t. That area (s) represents the distance covered by the vehicle at that velocity in that time. The basic equation is therefore s = ut. Simple transposition will enable an unknown component to be found; so,

$$t = \frac{s}{u} \text{ or } u = \frac{s}{t}$$

In the more likely event that the velocity has *not* been constant and that the vehicle has braked, the pictorial representation will be:

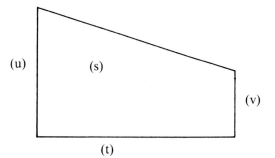

The average velocity will be $\frac{u+v}{2}$ and the distance (s) will be

$$s = \frac{u+v}{2} t$$

Where a vehicle is braked to a stop, this may then be represented by a triangle.

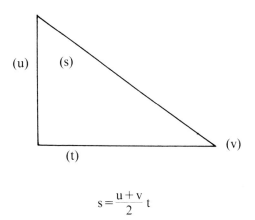

$$s = \frac{u+v}{2} t$$

When the deceleration rate of a vehicle must be taken into account the appropriate equation is

$$v^2 - u^2 = 2as$$

The term (a) means accleration (ie the rate of increase in the velocity of a body). For deceleration (ie the rate of decrease in the velocity of a body), the term $(-a)$ is used.

The equation $v^2 - u^2 = 2as$ is usually used when skid marks are left on the road. The expert will be trying to establish the minimum initial speed of the vehicle at which the wheels or wheel locked. If the vehicle came to a stop at the end of the skid marks he knows v^2 will be equal to zero. Having measured the length of the skid marks, he can determine the value of (s).

Once he can determine the value of $(-a)$, that is the rate of deceleration, he can easily calculate the minimum initial speed. By using the technique described in Chapter 9.2, he can successfully establish the coefficient of friction between the tyre and the road and from it the highest rate of deceleration. He can then complete the information for that half of the equation and from that deduce the minimum initial speed of the vehicle at the time of wheel lock.

(d) Conspicuity of pedestrians

Many drivers complain that a pedestrian had not been visible to them until the pedestrian had walked into the path of their vehicle. In these cases consideration should be given to an investigation into the conspicuity of the pedestrian. Rule 4 of the Highway Code advises pedestrians to try to make themselves conspicuous when walking on the roads in the dark. Very often, a pedestrian is only conspicuous to a driver of a car or to the rider of a motor cycle when the pedestrian is within the range of the vehicle's lights.

Wherever possible the original outer garments should be preserved and taken to the scene where they may be hung on a frame to have their conspicuity examined against the background. Mr Graham Greatrix of Teeside Polytechnic has carried out research into the effects of certain types of street lighting upon the colour of materials. For example under certain conditions blue may appear as black or grey. Because the actual colour may be critical in the assessment, in the event that the originals have not been preserved, care must be taken to ensure that the same colour of material is tested. The examination at the scene is important as the contrast afforded by the background against which the pedestrian is crossing is often a significant factor in the overall actual conspicuity.

Consideration should also be given to the position of the observer's eyes when carrying out the tests. They should be at the same height as those of the driver or rider. Similarly, because street lighting creates an uneven distribution of light (whether on a carriageway, a foot path or a verge) the degree of conspicuity of the pedestrian will depend upon whether or not he would have approached and crossed in either a lighted part or an unlit area.

6   Alteration to vehicle design and construction

Sometimes an accident may occur because there has been some alteration to the design and construction of the vehicle since it left the manufacturers, or because of some alteration to a specified material used in the course of construction. Regard may then have to be had to the following matters:

(a) Type approval and fitness of vehicles

Section 63 of the Road Traffic Act 1988 creates an offence of allowing a vehicle on the road that does not comply with type approval requirements in respect of design, construction, equipment and the marking of vehicles, as maybe required by regulations made under ss 54 to 65 of the 1988 Act.

Section 75 of the Road Traffic Act 1988 also makes it an offence to supply a motor vehicle or trailer in an unroadworthy condition. Similarly, s 76 of the Road Traffic Act 1988 makes it an offence to allow a vehicle to be fitted with a part so that the use of the vehicle on a road would breach the Construction and Use requirements as to the suitability of vehicle parts.

In an attempt to establish some kind of uniformity to the design and construction of both cars and goods vehicles, EEC working parties have produced Directives and Regulations which closely specify the parameters for the design and construction and performance of vehicles and their equipment.

For example, the design and performance requirements of whole braking systems are set out in the EEC Directive 71/320, as amended by the EEC Directive 85/647. EEC Directive 71/127 sets out the requirements for rear view mirrors, eg their angles of vision and the force at which the head should break off at the stem. Individual components, such as mirrors, are marked with EEC mark 'e' and given a number. Manufacturers must submit their whole vehicle and these individual components to the competent authority of their member state. In the UK the Department of Transport carries out the tests and issues a type approval certificate.

Problems may arise when changes are made to the vehicle so that a component (or the vehicle) no longer complies with the requirements of the Directive. This could be contrary to the relevant Construction and Use Regulation. Thus, if a mirror that was not legibly and indelibly marked with the designated marking 'e' was fitted to a type approved car, it would constitute the offence of fitting a non-approved mirror and possibly the sale or supply of a non-approved mirror.

(b) Braking systems

A more complex problem arises when alterations are made to a type approved braking system so that the system no longer complies with the requirements of the Directive. Thus, Art 2.2.1.8 requires that '. . . the action of the service brake must be appropriately distributed among the axles'. There are a number of ways in which the designer can achieve this, the object being to ensure that the vehicle will brake in a straight line and not slew to one side or the other, as could happen if the rear brakes locked. Anti-locking braking systems are an expensive way of complying with the object of the Article, but there are cheaper ways, such as the fitting of valves which control the air or hydraulic pressure to the rear axle when it is lightly laden under the effects of load transfer when braking is taking place.

On some vehicles the proper distribution of braking forces is achieved by the basic design of the system, ie by the fitting of powerful disc brakes on the front and less effective drum brakes on the rear. The substances used for the friction materials can be a critical factor in determining how the vehicle will react under braking forces. The important part played by the friction material is not always properly understood, particularly by the fringe element of the vehicle repair industry. In many cases, the cost of

Photograph 10

replacements is the determining factor as to what type of material replaces the original. Accident investigators should always be aware of the possibility that instability which has occurred during an accident might be directly attributable to a braking system which has been altered in some way, so that it no longer conforms to the original requirements.

The identification of such faults requires a detailed description of the instability which occurred, followed by a thorough examination of the vehicle. If necessary, the parts should be preserved for evidence.

Photograph 10 shows a light-vehicle brake-shoe to which is affixed a brake lining. The number on the lining identifies the vehicles upon which it can be used. In practice, however, as the lining wears down it becomes more difficult for the vehicle examiner to read the number with any degree of certainty and assistance may have to be sought from a manufacturer.

(c) Jacked up suspension

One other means of interfering with the overall inherent stability of a vehicle can occur when rear suspensions are 'jacked up'. There are a number of problems which might arise from this common practice. First, the materials used to make the shackle plate extensions may not be of suitable material and may fail in use and second, raising the body at the rear moves the centre of gravity forward which, in turn, reduces the weight on the rear axle and increases the weight on the front axle. On some vehicles this may promote the premature locking of the rear wheels.

(d) Brake fade

Brake materials are carefully selected after much testing to ensure that not only does the vehicle comply with the stability requirements, but also it has the ability to cope with repeated braking, known as the 'fade test'. Fade is the phenomenon which occurs when the friction material becomes so hot that it suffers a reduction in coefficient of friction at the point where it is in contact with the drum or disc. In effect, the heat alters its chemical composition. The 71/320 EEC Directive requires that before a vehicle is given a Type Approval Certificate it must be put through a fade test. Cars are taken up to at least 80 per cent of their maximum speed then braked to half of that initial speed. This must be done for 15 cycles, not one of which must exceed 45 seconds. Trucks must undergo a 20 cycle test sequence.

If, when brake materials are replaced, the replacements are not able to meet the test requirements, then that amounts to fitting unsuitable parts and quite possibly the attendant offence of supplying such parts.

7 Corrosion

Photographs 11 and *12* show the undersides of chassis which have become so corroded that the continuity of the load bearing structures has been destroyed. An expert may have to give an opinion as to whether or not the corrosion was in a dangerous condition at the time in question (see Chapter 2). He may seek corroboration from photographs and a description of the use of the vehicle.

8 Tyres

Regulations 24 to 27 of the Motor Vehicles (Construction and Use) Regulations 1986 provide for the legal requirements for tyres.

(a) Tyre loads and speed ratings

The smooth outer covering of rubber and a patterned tread hide the complex construction of the tyre casing, which is made up of an interwoven cord fabric. The strength of the tyre is in the cords, which may be of nylon, rayon, polyester or steel, or a combination of these materials. If the loads imposed upon a tyre are higher than the strength of the chords and the chords are broken the ability of the tyre to continue to function is impaired and continued use may result in a catastrophic failure.

Apart from shock loads which are imposed by driving the tyre into obstructions like kerbs, overloading can be imposed by speed and a static load, and of course by a combination of the two. It is a reasonable supposition that a lightly loaded tyre may withstand high speeds without suffering damage and that a highly loaded tyre may withstand low speeds without being damaged.

To prevent tyres being driven at excessive speeds and having excessive

Photograph 11

Photograph 12

loads imposed upon them, tyre manufacturers have rated tyres to their maximum speeds and loads. The tyres have been marked with a 'speed symbol' and a 'load index'. Tables 1 and 2 set out the speed and load ratings respectively. The symbol and load index number is positioned on the wall of the tyre near to the size designation eg, 155R12 76S, where the number 155 signifies the section width in millimetres, R represents that the tyre is of radial construction, 12 is the rim diameter in inches, '76' is load index (see Table 2) and 'S' is the speed symbol (see Table 1).

In the event of an accident in which the failure of a tyre is suspected of being the causative factor, efforts must be made to preserve the tyre and its wheel for a later examination by an expert.

(b) Tyre defects

The most common tyre defects are wear and inflation. With regard to wear Regulation 27 sets out the nature of the defects for which offences may be committed. The Highway Code (p 67) advises that tyres 'should be properly inflated, the tread must be at least one millimetre deep, and the tyre must be free of cuts and other defects.

Research into tyre inflation by RW Lowne of the Transport and Road Research Laboratory, Crowthorne, Berkshire showed that:

(1) under-inflation was more common than over-inflation;

(2) a pressure difference of 4 psi probably does not have a large effect on vehicle handling characteristics;

(3) differences of over 8 psi would certainly have an appreciable effect on the feel of a vehicle and a measurable effect on the handling characteristics of some vehicles (the proportion of cars with such errors in one or more tyres was 13 per cent in the survey);

(4) each 4 psi pressure drop means a reduction of about 10 per cent in the recommended maximum load, which means that on many cars an 8 psi drop in the recommended pressure could bring tyres into the 'overloaded' condition; with sufficient overload the tyre may overheat to such an extent that a failure will result;

(5) under-inflation tends to lower the maximum speeds at which specific manoeuvres can be made;

(6) if the pressures in the front tyres are high and those in the rear tyres are low the same type of instability can arise as with a combination of radial tyres on the front and cross-ply tyres on the rear; this is a condition known as over-steer, in which the front of the car tends to turn into a bend, a reaction which is not always easy to correct or control; and

(7) if there is a pressure differential between the tyres on one side and the other of the car, the car will behave differently in left and right hand turns, which will make the driver's task more difficult.

(c) Repaired tyres

Repairs to car tyres and tubes must be carried out in accordance with the current British Standard AU 159 which requires that punctured or damaged tyres must be removed from the wheel and examined internally and externally for hidden damage which could cause a later failure. Investigations into tyre failures should start with an enquiry into the history of the tyre. The Forensic Science Society (see page 57) should be able to supply the names of tyre experts.

Table 1
Tyre Speed Marking Table

Speed Symbol	Maximum car speed for which tyre is suitable	
	km/h	mph
L	120	75
M	130	81
N	140	87
P	150	95
Q	160	100
R	170	105
S	180	113
T	190	118
U	200	125
H	210	130
V	240	150
VR*	over 210	over 130
ZR†	over 240	over 150

*Where the letters VR appear within the size designation (e.g. 205/60 VR 15), the tyre is suitable for speeds over 210km/h (130mph). This form of marking is obsolescent.
†The letters ZR appear within the size designation (e.g. 205/60 ZR 15).

Table 2
Tyre Load Indices and Related Maximum Loads

Load Index	Load KG	Load Index	Load KG	Load Index	Load KG	Load Index	Load KG	Load Index	Load KG
60	250	71	345	82	475	93	650	104	900
61	257	72	355	83	487	94	670	105	925
62	265	73	365	84	500	95	690	106	950
63	272	74	375	85	515	96	710	107	975
64	280	75	387	86	530	97	730	108	1000
65	290	76	400	87	545	98	750	109	1030
66	300	77	412	88	560	99	775	110	1060
67	307	78	425	89	580	100	800	111	1090
68	315	79	437	90	600	101	825	112	1120
69	325	80	450	91	615	102	850	113	1150
70	335	81	462	92	630	103	875	114	1180

(d) Wheel detachment

The Institute of Road Transport Engineers, 1 Cromwell Place, Kensington, London, telephone (071) 589 3744 or Fax (071) 225 0494, has built up a unique data bank on the problem of the detachment of road wheels. In the past, it was an accepted assumption that this fault was a result of a failure to maintain the vehicle. However, their research has shown that there are other causes of wheel detachment, such as inherent design or metallurgy faults. An enquiry to the Institute may yield some help in the preparation of the defence to a prosecution for such an alleged offence.

9   The expert report and proof of evidence

It is essential to bear in mind the difference between the 'expert report' which is disclosable to the other side (and must in civil actions set out the substance of the case to be argued for), and the 'proof of evidence' of the expert, which is privileged from disclosure.

In the 'expert report' the basic facts relied upon must be set out, followed by the basic 'opinion evidence' from which the eventual conclusions are to be drawn as well as the 'conclusions' relating to liability which support the case to be argued in court. In the privileged 'proof of evidence' of the expert there may appear anything else which the author wishes to comment upon, eg his impressions of the accuracy or reliability of a witness, the nature and extent of the litigation risks for the party he advises, and even frank criticism of the client in question!

There is some legal debate as to whether *all* expert conclusions/opinions, favourable and unfavourable to the client, must be disclosed (assuming that there is mutual discovery of expert reports by Consent or Order of the Civil Court).

Order 25, r 8(1)(*b*) of the RSC provides: '. . . where any party intends to place reliance at the trial on expert evidence, he shall, within 10 weeks disclose the substance of that evidence to the other parties in the form of a written report which shall be agreed if possible'. Does this mean that the party need only disclose the substance of the expert evidence upon which that party relies or the substance of all of his evidence, 'warts and all', both favourable and unfavourable to his case? In *Bell* v *British Gypsum* (Carlisle Crown Court, 13 January 1983), Lawson J upheld on appeal disclosure limited to the evidence relied upon by that party alone (this excluded a covering letter containing extracts from some of the privileged witness statements, his observations as to what sort of witnesses they might make, and what the litigation risks might be, depending upon what facts might be found).

However, in *Kenning* v *Eve Construction Limited* [1989] 1 WLR 1189, Mr Michael Wright QC, sitting as a Deputy High Court Judge held otherwise. The defendants had accidentally disclosed not only their expert engineer's report, but also a covering letter indicating that the accident might not have occurred as the plaintiff had thought, in which case the defendants might be in difficulty. The plaintiff sought leave to amend the statement of claim based on that covering letter, and the defendants applied to debar the plaintiff from amending. It was held that since the points raised in the expert's letter were fairly obvious the plaintiff would have sought leave to amend the statement of claim anyway. Therefore, leave to amend should be granted. Arguably *Obiter* (and therefore, not necessarily of binding affect), and without any detailed reference to previously decided cases the judge held:

'It seems to me that the solicitor who instructs him only complies with the requirement of Ord 25, r 8(1)(*b*) if the whole of that expert's opinion is disclosed, because only if the whole of the opinion is disclosed can the substance of his evidence have been communicated to the other parties . . . (the solicitor) must make up his mind whether he wishes to rely upon that expert having balanced the good parts of the report against the bad parts. If he decides that on balance the expert is worth calling then he must call him on the basis of all the evidence that he can give, not merely the evidence that he can give under examination-in-chief, taking the good with the bad together. If, on the other hand, the view that the solicitor forms is that it is too dangerous to call that expert, and he does not wish to disclose that part of his report, then the proper course is that that expert cannot be called at all.'

It is submitted that the law has not yet been satisfactorily developed here, drawing a proper distinction between the disclosure of the full, genuine independent view of the expert as to how the plaintiff says the accident occurred as against what the defendant might aver (which ought to be disclosed); as compared with the legitimate privileged observations of the expert by way of speculation or comment, for instance on the quality of the witnesses he has seen, or how a judge might regard a feature of the case (which it is submitted ought not to be the subject of obligatory disclosure). However, the preparation by the expert of the disclosable 'expert report', separate from the privileged 'proof of evidence', enables this matter of privilege to be argued in interlocutory proceedings in the Civil Court (and, if necessary, by clearly claiming privilege in the List of Documents for 'privileged correspondence to and from the expert').

The relevant extract from the judgement of Lawson J in *Bell* v *British Gypsum* is as follows:

'(The expert) In addition to making his report with his opinion. . . also wrote a covering letter to the plaintiff's solicitors . . . it is clear from the covering letter that this is based upon information which (the expert) obtained from the plaintiff and other people in the form of verbal communications and documents, and it is also obvious that there is nothing in that covering letter which expands the plaintiff's case or makes any difference in the case against the defendant in the case which is supported by the disclosed report . . . I am referred (by the defendant) . . . to the case decided by Mr Justice Ackner, as he then was, of *Ollett* v *Bristol Aero Jet Limited* [1979] 1 WLR 1197. My attention has been drawn to the observations made by Mr Justice Ackner that tendencies seem to have grown up to limit the effect of Ord 38, r 38 that the substance of experts' reports be exchanged, so that the Order is satisfied by the expert merely setting out the factual restrictions of the circumstances and leaving out any conclusions as to the defects in the machine, the system of work or other relevant information and evidence.

Mr Justice Ackner, as he then was, goes on to say: 'This seems to me to be a total misconception of the meaning of the ordinary meaning of the word "substance". It is also a misconception of the function of an "expert". Then he expresses the view: 'When the substance of the expert's report is to be provided, that means precisely what it says, both the substance of the factual description of the machine and/or the circumstances of the accident and his expert opinion in relation to that accident, which is the very justification for calling him'. The whole purpose of Ord 38 is, in relation to expert evidence, to save expense by dispensing with the calling of experts when there is, in reality, no dispute and where there is a dispute, by avoiding parties being taken by surprise as to the true nature of the dispute and thereby being obliged to seek adjournments.

I should have said that Mr Justice Ackner, as he then was, is dealing with Ord 38, rr 37 and 38, but the observations he makes in my judgment are quite appropriately applicable to the automatic direction which results under Ord 25, r 28(1)(b).

In all the circumstances of this case (having regard to the nature and contents of the covering letter) in my opinion the covering letter does not deal with the substance of the plaintiff's case at all; it deals with other matters; it in no way enlarges or adds additional material to the case pleaded by the plaintiff against the defendant.

In my judgment, therefore, the Order of the District Registrar was wrong in principle and wrong in law, and I therefore allow this appeal". (From the court transcript).

10 Recoverable fees in the county court

Specific reference needs to be made to the standard fees recoverable of an expert witness attending county court proceedings. Order 38, r 14 of the County Court Rules 1981 ordinarily applies.

(a) Expert witness's fees (Order 38, rule 14)

'(1) Subject to para (2) and (3), the fees allowable in respect of an expert witness shall be in accordance with the following table (based on County Court Fees (Amendment No 2) Order 1986, (SI No 2143)).

(2) Where in any proceedings the judge is satisfied that any of the fees specified in para (1) ought not to be limited as therein mentioned, he may give a certificate under this rule.

(3) Rule 9(2), (4) and (5) shall apply, with the necessary modifications, in relation to a certificate under this rule as they apply in relation to a certificate under 4.9.'

These scales will frequently be inadequate. A certificate may therefore have to be sought from the judge under Ord 38, r 14(2), see below.

(b) Allowance of increased sums on taxation (Order 38, rule 9)

'(1) Where in any proceedings in which the costs are to be taxed, the judge is satisfied from the nature of the case or the conduct of the proceedings that the costs which may be allowed on taxation may be inadequate in the circumstances, he may give a certificate under this rule.

(2) Where a certificate is given under this rule, the registrar may, if he thinks fit, allow on taxation such larger sum as he thinks reasonable in respect of all or any of the items in the relevant scale except item 5.

	Amount allowable
For attending court	not less than £22.50 nor more than £42.50 (or £89.50 on scale 3)
For qualifying to give evidence if the judge thinks fit to allow such a fee and the witness has attended court, or the judge thinks that the fee should be allowed notwithstanding that the witness did not attend court	not more than £22.50 (or £45.50 on scale 3)
For a report in writing from an expert who is not allowed a qualifying fee, if the judge thinks the report was reasonably necessary	not more than £22.50 (or £45.50 on scale 3)

(3) If he decides to exercise his powers under para (2), the registrar, in determining the sum to be allowed in respect of any item, shall have regard to, but shall not be limited by, the amount allowable in respect of that item in the next higher scale, if any.

(4) Subject to para (5), an application for a certificate under this rule may be made at the trial or hearing of the action or matter or on notice to be served on the party by whom the costs are payable within 14 days after the making of the order or direction for their payment.

Provided that where an application which could have been made at the trial or hearing is made subsequently, the judge may refuse the application on the ground that it ought to have been made at the hearing.

(5) Where no direction has been given by the judge that this paragraph shall not apply, the registrar may, if satisfied as to the matters mentioned in para (1), exercise on taxation the powers conferred by para (2) as if a certificate had been given under this rule.'

Part Three

Assessing Liability

Chapter 10

The General Principles of Liability

1 Assessment of liability

The assessment of liability is an assessment of the likely result of litigation: will it be won or lost? This assessment is therefore the product of the first two parts of this book and all that has gone before. Like the preparation of one's favourite meal, one must ask whether the best raw materials have been gathered, and has the appropriate expert assistance been obtained where necessary?

In litigation (as in cooking) experience is invaluable, but the result may depend upon the vagaries of the consumer, ie the tribunal. Accordingly, wherever counsel is to be instructed at trial, counsel should be given the opportunity of not only advising on the evidence gathered (and what more may need to be done or what evidence should not be disclosed), but also advising on liability.

The assessment of liability and the litigation risks associated with it is, however, an ongoing process, forever to be kept under review. So uncertain is litigation that even during the course of evidence in court, the process of assessing the likely outcome should be continuing.

Policy reasons may, and frequently do, determine that a trial takes place, and once started, continues. The longer the case has gone on, the more intransigent may be the party in whose power a possible settlement may rest. Moreover, the prospect of success at first instance may blind that party to the daunting and expensive prospect of an appeal which could be successful.

Ultimately, however, litigation is about money; not just the legal costs (and even for the winning party these may not be inconsiderable), but also the penalty/damages to be awarded. Litigation is therefore an investment in which either a modest outlay reaps substantial rewards, or good money is thrown after bad. It should never be entirely a gamble, but rather a continuing series of business decisions to be kept under review, of weighing the evidence and assessing the likely outcome as the case progresses.

Because each case turns upon its own facts, the general observations that might usefully be made here on liability are kept to a minimum. For the main part, this book concentrates on specific, readily identifiable and frequently occurring situations which resolve into four basic questions:

(1) Has there been any breach of statute or statutory regulations?
(2) Has there been any breach of the Highway Code?
(3) Is there any previously decided case that will act as a guide?
(4) What of any contributory negligence?

2   Breach of legislation

There may be a statute, or a regulation made under a statute, which has
some bearing on liability and applies to the facts of the case in question. If
so, this will not necessarily have occurred to the police and if it has, this will
not necessarily be apparent (for they may have decided to do nothing about
it). The relevant questions here are therefore:
   (a) Has there been any breach of statutory duty?
   (b) If so, is it in any way causative of the accident?
   (c) If so, does its breach give rise to a claim for damages as a cause of
action in itself?
   (d) Is it otherwise relevant to the claim as evidence of negligence?

(a) Breach of statutory duty

If there has been a statutory duty that has been breached, so much the better
for the plaintiff in a civil action for damages. A specific duty of care may
have been provided for by Parliament which can be relied upon to
supplement the common law duty of care. If so, and there has been a
conviction, care will be required with regard to what must be pleaded by the
party in reliance on it, or in reply to such a reliance (see the following and
Chapter 19 on 'Pleadings') in any subsequent civil litigation.

(b) Causation

Whether or not the breach of statutory duty is in any way *prima facie*
relevant to the cause of the accident should be reasonably obvious. A
defendant may be driving a car with defective brakes, but this would be
irrelevant in an accident where the driver turns right across the immediate
path of an oncoming vehicle. The defective brakes would be as irrelevant in
such a case as they would be relevant to an accident where the driver did not
stop but should have stopped in time.
   But an accident may have several causes. In the example above, the driver
of the car that could not brake in time may also have been driving with
alcohol in excess of the statutory limit in his body (see hereafter) and
convicted accordingly. If the plaintiff is the occupant of the vehicle in front,
he may wish to plead both convictions, namely that the defendant was
driving with defective brakes and with an excessive proportion of alcohol in
his body (whether gauged by the measurement of breath, blood or urine).
But if the plaintiff is the passenger travelling with the defendant, and he is at
risk of an allegation of contributory negligence that he travelled with a
driver whom he knew or ought to have known was adversely affected by
alcohol, consideration may have to be given to pleading only the conviction

relating to the defective brakes. If he also pleads reliance upon the alcohol conviction, he may be taken to admit the relevance of that to the happening of the accident, and therefore the relevance of the allegation of contributory negligence that, as a passenger, he knowingly travelled with a driver adversely affected by drink.

(c) Cause of action

Some breaches of statutory duty may give rise to a separate cause of action where other breaches do not do so and only give support for a claim in negligence (see below). The law is not always clear, but broadly it can be stated that if the main purpose of an Act or Regulation is to provide for a penalty upon its breach (ie prosecution with a fine and/or imprisonment), there does not also arise a separate civil cause of action for damages unless public policy requires otherwise. Where a breach of statutory duty does give rise to a cause of action in civil proceedings, that separate cause of action must be pleaded if it is relied upon. When in doubt, the claim should be pleaded in 'negligence and breach of duty'.

(d) Evidence of negligence

The legislation may leave in doubt whether there is a civil claim for breach of statutory duty, or even expressly provide otherwise (eg s 47(1) of the Health and Safety at Work Act 1974). Nevertheless, a conviction here may still be evidence of the facts that resulted in the conviction, and consequently evidence of negligence.

3   Breach of the Highway Code

The Highway Code provides for an almost complete code of correct behaviour for those using the highway. The latest revision was published in March 1987. Section 38(7) of the Road Traffic Act 1988 expressly provides that a failure to comply with the Highway Code may be relied upon by any party to civil or criminal proceedings as tending to establish or negate any liability which is in question.

There has been a slow but steady revision over the years of the Highway Code, and this can be expected to continue. There may be substantial future variation. (If one compares our Highway Code with the much more detailed (and better illustrated) French equivalent, *Le Code de la Route*, the authors take the view that there is room for improvement.)

4   Previously decided cases

Case law is, of course, the bedrock of the common law, applying where statute law may not, or in interpretation where necessary of the statute law. However, previously decided cases relevant to road traffic accidents only rarely purport to lay down any generally applicable rule. Previous cases are

then an important guide (but rarely more) as to what a court might decide
on the facts in question.

The assessment of the prospects of success in a case will necessarily take
into account what previously decided case law has been reported. Indeed, in
the specific circumstances set out later, there is extensive reference to such
cases with the inclusion of both what have been regarded as the leading
cases, as well as some of the latest cases by way of examples. In some cases,
their result may appear to be at odds with another case. This may be
because the full implications of the individual facts do not appear from the
case report, because the one case was not cited in the subsequent,
apparently conflicting, reported case; or even because this may sometimes
be the inevitable result of case law. Accordingly, it needs to be emphasised
that the use of these previous cases must be treated with care and intelligent
discretion. Indeed, in *Foskett* v *Mistry* [1984] RTR 1, Lord Donaldson MR
expressly deprecated the citing of such authorities (at least in the Court of
Appeal) in simple running-down cases.

5   Contributory negligence

In civil proceeding there may be little difficulty in proving the primary
liability of the defendant but the contributory negligence of the plaintiff and
the apportionment of liability between the parties will still have to be
established.

By s 1(1) of the Law Reform (Contributory Negligence) Act 1945,
liability is to be apportioned between the parties, reducing the plaintiff's
damages 'to such an extent as the court thinks just and equitable having
regard to the claimant's share in the responsibility for the damage'. This
involves balancing the fault of the defendant against the blameworthiness
of the plaintiff and assessing their causative effects in relation to the
accident in question.

In the end, most cases will turn upon their own individual facts.
However, previously decided cases in which liability has been apportioned
between the parties may so closely resemble the facts of the case to be
considered that there may be no proper distinction of the facts, so that the
result of previously decided cases may be a most important guideline. In
such cases, a matter of general principle has been laid down which must be
taken into account irrespective of the specific facts of the case in question.
In others, it has to be said that no discernible distinction of the facts appears
as to why the results have not been consistent with other apparently similar
previously decided cases!

It is now settled law that road users must not assume that other road
users will act with all appropriate care. If this assumption is wrongly and
unreasonably made by a plaintiff, damages may be reduced accordingly.
The four following cases need to be seen together as settling the law to be
applied:

(1) In *Fardon* v *Harcourt-Rivington* [1932] 146 LT at p 392, Lord

Dunedin held: 'If the possibility of the danger emerging is reasonably apparent, then to take no precautions is negligent; but if the possibility of danger emerging is only a mere possibility which would never occur to the mind of a reasonable man, then there is no negligence in not having taken extraordinary precautions'.

(2) In *Grant* v *Sun Shipping Co Limited* [1948] AC 549, it was held that: 'A prudent man will guard against the possible negligence of others when experience shows such negligence to be common'.

(3) In *London Passenger Transport Board* v *Upson* [1949] AC at p 173, Lord Uthwait stated: 'A driver is not of course bound to anticipate folly in all its forms; but he is not, in my opinion, entitled to put out of consideration the teachings of experience as to the form those follies commonly take'.

(4) In *Whitehead* v *Chaplin* [1952] CA91, Somervell LJ commented: 'Since *Upson's Case*, it has been very clearly stated that he is not entitled to assume that people will not do foolish things and that they will act reasonably. I should have thought that any motorist of experience, having regard to his experience on the road, would never assume that any pedestrian was going to act reasonably. I should have thought the presumption was almost the other way.'

It may be that the negligence of a defendant creates a predicament for the plaintiff who then takes a risk. If the risk taken is one which a reasonably prudent man in the plaintiff's position would take, this does not amount to contributory negligence (*Clayards* v *Dethick* [1848] 12 QB 439).

A plaintiff who acts in the agony of the moment created by the defendant is not to be judged with the benefit of hindsight, unless he failed to take a step which a reasonably careful man would fairly be expected to take in the circumstances (*Swadling* v *Cooper* [1931] AC at p 9). Where contributory negligence is alleged, the burden of proving this is upon the defendant, who must raise the issue in the pleadings (see Chapter 19) to enable the plaintiff to deal with it.

The costs of the case are not, however, awarded to the parties in accordance with the degree of responsibility attributed to each. The costs are ordinarily to follow the event, namely whether or not the plaintiff succeeds in proving some damages (or, where there is a payment into court, he succeeds in proving damages in excess of that payment in).

Where the trial judge apportions liability as between the parties by reason of contributory negligence, an Appeal Court is unlikely to interfere, unless there is an error of law, substantial misjudgment of the factual basis found by the trial judge, or the result is clearly seen to have been wrong. If there is more than one defendant, a blameless plaintiff is entitled to full damages against the defendants jointly and severally, with the damages between the defendants being decided in accordance with the apportionment of liability. Thus, where the plaintiff succeeds wholly and apportionment is divided as to 90 per cent against one defendant who is insolvent, the plaintiff will recover in full against the other defendant, who may have been found to be only 10 per cent at fault as between the two defendants.

Aspects of contributory negligence in particular cases are dealt with in Chapters 11–16.

6 Apportionment of liability between parties

Liability is apportioned only as between parties to the action. If in the course of evidence the fault of another is established who is not a party to the proceedings, the defendant cannot rely on that fault to diminish his own liability without having that other person made a party to the proceedings.

Where a plaintiff is proceeding against two or more defendants and the judge finds all parties equally to blame it is instructive to examine *Fitzgerald* v *Lane and Another* [1989] 2 All ER 961 in which the trial judge found the plaintiff pedestrian and both drivers equally to blame. He ordered each of the two drivers to pay one third of the value of the claim to the plaintiff so that the plaintiff recovered two-thirds of the value of the claim. The House of Lords upheld the Court of Appeal's decision that the correct approach was to apportion liability equally as between the plaintiff, and the defendants collectively, so that the plaintiff only recovered 50 per cent of the total damages awarded.

The apportionment of liability in a case of contributory negligence between plaintiff and defendants must be kept separate from the apportionment of the contribution between the defendants.

7 The judicial approach

(a) The duty to decide

In some cases there may be a straight conflict of fact between the parties with little difference in credibility between the two. Where the unfortunate judge in this situation has merely said that he cannot decide, the claim will fail, an aggrieved party may complain that the judge has failed in his duty to make a decision. However:

(1) No appeal will arise where the judge expresses the difficulty of making a decision on the basis that the plaintiff has failed to discharge the burden of proof. Thus, per Lord Brandon in *Rhesa Shipping Co SA* v *Edmunds* [1985] 1 WLR at p 954:

'The judge is not bound always to make a finding one way or the other with regard to facts averred by the parties. He has open to him the further alternative of saying that the party on whom the burden of proof lies in relation to any averment made by him has failed to discharge that burden.'

(2) In *Carter* v *Sheath* (1989) *The Times*, 10 August, while the plaintiff pedestrian could prove that the driver had not seen him before the collision the Court of Appeal upheld the dismissal of the plaintiff's claim on the basis that the plaintiff had nevertheless not proven on the balance of probabilities

that the driver was negligent. The court held that there was inadequate evidence established to prove this.

(b) One of several parties liable, but which?

A slightly different situation might arise where a judge concludes that while one or other of several defendants must have been at fault (because the accident could not have happened otherwise) it is not established on the balance of probabilities which of the several was at fault. Because the plaintiff has overcome the burden of proof of establishing the negligence of a defendant (but not which one), liability may be apportioned equally between the defendants.

In *Baker* v *Market Harborough Industrial Co-operative Society* [1953] 1 WLR 1477, a lorry and a van collided in the middle of a long straight section of road and both drivers were killed. The two vehicles had collided whilst the offside front wheel of one or the other, or perhaps both, was over the centre line, but that was the extent of the evidence. Had there been an 'innocent' passenger in one of the vehicles, such a person would have proved that the accident must have been occasioned by some negligence. Denning, LJ held:

'Now take this case where there is no passenger, but both drivers are killed. The natural inference, again, is that one or the other was, or both were, to blame. The court will not wash its hands of the case simply because it cannot say whether it was only one vehicle which was to blame or both. In the absence of any evidence enabling the court to draw a distinction between them, it should hold them both to blame, and equally to blame'.

In the absence of any avoiding action by either vehicle, both drivers must have been to blame and with no means of distinguishing between them, the blame was apportioned equally.

However, in a case which the plaintiff can establish that one or other of two parties was at fault, but clearly both cannot be, liability will not then be apportioned (see *Baker's Case* [1953] 1 WLR at p 1477). The judge must then act in accordance with his duty to decide, and make that decision (see *Bray* v *Palmer* [1953] 1 WLR 1455).

(c) Plaintiff run over by two vehicles

Not infrequently a pedestrian may be stuck by the first car, and then run over again by the following car. It may not be clear what injuries were occasioned by each driver and liability may be apportioned between them equally. For example, in *Fitzgerald* v *Lane and Another* [1987] 2 All ER 455 the plaintiff was run over by two vehicles, having walked briskly onto a pelican crossing when the lights were against him. The plaintiff suffered quadrapalgia but the extent of each driver's contribution to this condition could not be established and their liability was therefore apportioned equally.

If the plaintiff does not establish that there was clearly a risk that the second vehicle caused or contributed to the serious injury (in the above case, to the neck) the need to apportion liability equally may not arise.

(d) Alterations to a judgment

A judge, having made a decision and announced it, may then have second thoughts. He might, for instance, conclude over the weekend that a witness he relied on had not in fact been accurate. A judge can alter his judgment at any time before it is drawn up and perfected (see *Millensted* v *Grosvenor House (Park Lane) Limited* [1937] 1 KB 717). This applies in civil proceedings whether in the High Court or the County Court (see *Pittalis* v *Sherefettin* [1986] 2 All ER 227 and *Hyde and South Bank Housing Association* v *Kain* (1989) *The Times*, 27 July).

(e) Facts already determined by another judge

One accident may give rise to many claimants and it is highly desirable that these cases should be consolidated so as to be heard and decided at the same time or heard one after the other, by the same judge. It may, however, be that one case is heard before and quite separately from others arising out of the same accident. If an issue of fact has been raised and decided in an earlier action in which both parties are the same, the subsequent judge will be bound by those facts (see *New Brunswick Railway* v *British and French Trust Corporation* [1939] AC at p 20, and *In Re B (Minors)* (1989) *The Times*, 5 October). Only in special circumstances will the court depart from the previous finding and consider that it was decided wrongly in either fact or in law (see *Arnold* v *Nat West Bank* (1989) *The Independent*, 24 November).

The greater likelihood is that the subsequent litigation will involve at least one different party from the earlier litigation, usually a different plaintiff. In *North West Water Authority* v *Binnie & Partners* (1989) *The Independent*, 24 November, the issue of negligence of the designers arising out of the Abbeystead disaster in 1984 had already been litigated by others. They had been found 100 per cent liable in litigation where the Water Authority had themselves been the defendants. Drake J, held that the designers were prevented from defending this second action and that for all practical purposes the party seeking to put forward the issue had already had that issue determined against them by a court of competent jurisdiction, even if the parties to the two actions were different.

Chapter 11

Pedestrians

1 Assessing pedestrian negligence

Rules 1–7 of the Highway Code and the Green Cross Code apply generally to the pedestrian road user while rr 8 to 25 concern specific circumstances. As to motorists and their duties towards pedestrians, see rr 56–57.

In assessing the contributory negligence of the pedestrian the important House of Lords decision in *Baker* v *Willoughby* [1969] 3 All ER 1528 should be examined. In this case both the pedestrian and the motorist had a clear view for 200 yards but both failed to take evasive action. The House of Lords reversed the Court of Appeal and upheld the apportionment of the trial judge that the pedestrian was 25 per cent to blame and the motorist was 75 per cent to blame. They were not equally liable because the duties of pedestrians and motorists with regard to keeping a proper lookout were different, and the potential danger of each to other road users was very different. Lord Reid (at p 1530) said:

'A pedestrian has to look to both sides as well as forwards. He is going at perhaps 3 mph and at that speed he is rarely a danger to anyone else. The motorist has not got to look sideways, although he may have to observe over a wide angle ahead; and if he is going at a considerable speed he must not relax his observation, for the consequences may be disastrous, and it sometimes happens that he sees the pedestrian is not looking his way and takes a chance that the pedestrian will not stop and that he can safely pass behind him. In my opinion, it is quite possible that the motorist may be very much more to blame than the pedestrian.'

The case of *Baker* v *Willoughby* is a rare example of an Appeal Court being willing to vary the apportionment of contributory negligence assessed by the trial judge. Successful appeals on the apportionment of liability are most unusual whatever the nature of the accident, and seemingly all the more so in road traffic accidents. The importance of assisting the court to get it right the first time round is therefore paramount. Detailed research into the facts as well as the law must therefore be done from the beginning.

In *Evers* v *Bennet* (1983) CLY 2518, The Supreme Court of South Australia found that a pedestrian walking on the wrong side of the road in a country town was 30 per cent contributorily negligent when she was struck by a car whose driver's vision was obscured by moisture on the windscreen and the bright sun.

2   Children as pedestrians

Very often cases involving children are both tragic and worrying. Quite apart from anything else, in most cases a child's actions are to be assessed by an adult, who must question whether the folly was no more than to be expected of a child of that age. Importantly, the Highway Code refers to children as in need of special protection (see rr 57–59).

A frequent problem in cases involving children is the age at which contributory negligence may arise and hence the appropriate apportionment of the contributory negligence. A useful start is r 7 of the Highway Code. This sets out the Green Cross Code which states: 'Many children under *seven* cannot fully understand and apply those parts of the Code requiring judgment of the speed and distance of approaching vehicles.' Even so, many local authorities have in recent times issued to all *five to nine* year olds 'Lessons for Life', along with the Green Cross Code; and it may be worth checking as to whether the relevant local authority has done this in your case.

Regard to previously decided cases must take into account the particular evidence before the court concerning the child, and the following are given by way of example only. They are set out in chronological order of each case, rather than in order of the age of the child involved. To do otherwise might obscure what is at least arguable since the duty of care owed by a child to take reasonable care of its own safety may have changed over the last 20 years, with increased media coverage of road safety campaigns, particularly on television. Judicial trends in the assessment of culpability of children are said by some to be discernible but varied over the years. Thus, in light of the cases cited below it is rather doubtful if culpability can be said to have increased.

(1) In *Jones* v *Maggi* [1954] CA 267 a ten year old child in charge of an eight and-a-half year old child, stepped into a busy street together with the younger child. The older child was held to be 75 per cent to blame. The younger child was acquitted of any negligence.

(2) In *Andrews* v *Freeborough* [1966] 2 All ER 721, the Court of Appeal was inclined to find generally that an eight year old girl was too young to be found liable for contributory negligence.

(3) In *Gough* v *Thorne* [1966] 3 All ER 398, a thirteen and-a-half year old girl was beckoned across the road by a lorry driver who had put his right hand out to warn the other traffic. As she passed just beyond the lorry, a car driven by the defendant came past the lorry at speed and collided with the plaintiff. The Court of Appeal held in these circumstances that she should be acquitted of any negligence since she could not be expected to do more than she did.

(4) In *Dexter* v *Ellis* [1968] CA 190, a boy of 13 ran across a 25 feet wide

street in a heavily built-up area when a few feet from the far kerb, he was struck down by a car travelling too fast. The boy's contributory negligence was assessed at 35 per cent.

(5) In *Jones* v *Lawrence* [1969] 3 All ER 267, Cumming-Bruce J acquitted a seven year boy of contributory negligence in running across the road from behind a parked van, when the defendant motor cyclist was travelling at about 50 mph in a 30 mph speed limit.

(6) In *Davies* v *Journeaux* [1975] 1 Lloyd's Rep 483, CA, an eleven and-a-half year old girl ran down some steps, paused momentarily on the pavement, and dashed across the road into collision with the front offside of a nearby passing car. The driver did not see her until she was in the act of dashing across and he was then 50 to 60 feet away, travelling at 20 to 25 mph. He braked heavily but did not sound his horn. The driver was acquitted of any negligence (compare with *Foskett* v *Mistry* below).

(7) In *Lawson* v *Ramsden* [1980] CLY 269, a five and-a-half year old girl suddenly ran into the road from a grassed area, known by the defendant driver to be much used by the local children for play. The Court of Appeal upheld the liability of the defendant even though he had slowed down from 45 to 35 mph ready to brake, and the plaintiff had run out at the last moment.

(8) In *Waller* v *Laughton* [1982] CLY 2132, a boy aged nearly eleven stood at the kerbside and then dashed across the road into collision with the defendant, who was driving his car at 40 mph in a 60 mph restricted area. The boy's contributory negligence was assessed at 40 per cent, with the defendant driver being held 60 per cent liable both for assuming that the boy had seen him, and for not sounding the horn.

(9) In *Foskett* v *Mistry* [1984] RTR 1, the plaintiff, aged fifteen and-a-half, ran from parkland across a ten feet wide pavement into the nearside of the car driven by the defendant who had not seen him. The defendant was held to be 25 per cent liable for failing to anticipate the danger, to observe the plaintiff coming from the park, and to sound the horn and brake.

The authors have recently undertaken a series of tests with *seven* year old children selected at random in order to determine how long it would take them to run 9.2 metres (30 feet) from a standing start. The fastest time was 2.1 seconds which is 14.3 feet per second (4.4 metres per second) and the slowest 2.5 seconds or 12 feet per second (3.7 metres per second). Using these values as a starting point it may be possible to establish the opportunity a driver might have been given to avoid a child once the child leaves the kerb. In assessing the negligence on the part of the driver consideration must be given to the opportunity he would have had of seeing the potential danger from the presence of children ahead of him and his reaction to that situation by either sounding his horn or reducing speed. An accurate reconstruction may show that the driver would have had time to avoid the child if he had been using all of the range of vision that would have been available to him as he approached the scene.

3   Drunken pedestrians

In *Donoghoe* v *Blundell* (1986) CLY 2254 Judge Lewis Hawser QC assessed contributory negligence at two-thirds for a drunken pedestrian. A male aged 22 was run over by a car as he lay in the road, drunk. Because he was so drunk he did not even realise he had been hit, despite a fractured pelvis, concussion, an injury to his lower spine, and several other injuries (assessed at £6,000 on full liability). It is perhaps difficult to imagine a more extreme case and it may set a useful guideline to other less serious cases.

4   Crossings

There are four kinds of pedestrian crossings: the zebra (an uncontrolled crossing), the pelican (a controlled crossing), school crossings and level crossings. Each kind of crossing is regulated by certain regulations but often it is necessary to look to the statutory regulations which created the type of crossing in question, rather than merely to rr 10–17 and 186–189 of the Highway Code. For instance, the zebra and pelican crossings are the creations of statute by regulations made under s 25 of the Road Traffic Regulation Act 1984 and s 28 of that Act lays down the circumstances under which vehicles can be required to stop and to remain stationary by the school crossing patrol. Level crossings, however, are subject to more complex statutory provisions.

(a) Zebra crossings

Zebra crossings are regulated by the Zebra Pedestrian Crossing Regulations 1971 (SI No 1525). They are otherwise referred to as 'uncontrolled' crossings. In addition to the familiar black and white stripes across the road, the regulations also require the crossings to be indicated by 'Belisha beacons'. If criminal proceedings for failing to accord precedence to pedestrians are to be taken against a driver, at least one of the beacons must be illuminated. However, the failure of the illumination of both beacons in a civil case for negligence is unlikely to assist any defendant driver (save possibly at night where the driver is a stranger to the area). The regulations apply to drivers of all types of vehicles, including fire engines, ambulances, and police cars (but not to equestrians).

The limits of a zebra crossing for traffic are defined by the studs across the road on each side of the black and white stripes and indicate to the motorist where he should stop to accord precedence to the pedestrian (referred to in the Regulations as a foot passenger) although the pedestrian is only granted protection if crossing upon the black and white stripes themselves. If, however, the pedestrian was on the carriageway within the limits of the crossing before the vehicle or any part of it entered the protected area he is accorded precedence by reg 8 of the 1971 Regulations (see below). This is confirmed in case law. For example, in *Gibbons* v *Kahl* [1955] 3 All ER 345, the court held it was the duty of a driver to be able to stop before the pedestrian gets to the crossing unless he can see there is no one on it. If he cannot see if there is anybody on it, he must drive in such a way that he can stop if there is a person on it masked from him by other traffic. Similarly, in *Kozimor* v *Adey* [1962] Crim LR 564, a civil case, Megaw J held that the only way a motorist can be certain to avoid a breach of the regulations is to approach the crossing at such a low speed that he can stop in the event of any conceivable use of the crossing by any pedestrian (except a suicidal one who deliberately walks in front of a car). Here, the 40 year old female plaintiff, after a glance to her right, ran out on to the zebra crossing. The defendant was 15 yards away and travelling at about 25 mph. As soon as he saw the plaintiff he braked and swerved. The judge found the defendant not negligent, but in breach of the absolute duty under the regulations. The plaintiff's contributory negligence was assessed at 75 per cent. In *Crank* v *Brooks* (1980) RTR 441 a child on roller-skates was held not to be a pedestrian.

Overtaking a moving vehicle within the zig-zig lines on both sides of, but before, the actual crossing, is an offence (reg 10). In *Snow* v *Giddins* (1969) 113 SJ 229 CA, a plaintiff who failed to use a pedestrian crossing which was nearby was held not to be negligent for this alone, but was held to be negligent in taking on himself the hazard of being marooned in the centre of the road at the mercy of oncoming traffic. Contributory negligence was then assessed at 25 per cent. However, the revised Highway Codes of 1978 and 1987 now provide:

'If there is a zebra crossing near, always use it. It is very dangerous to cross the road a short distance away from a zebra crossing. The most dangerous area is usually marked with zig-zag lines—do not cross on them.'

It is also to be noted that many Police Accident Report Books now require a section to be completed as to whether there was a pedestrian crossing within 50 metres of the scene of an accident and this may then form a useful guideline as to whether a pedestrian should have used the crossing. (Nevertheless, in *Tremayne* v *Hill* (1986) *The Times*, 11 December the Court of Appeal held that there was no duty in law to use an available light-controlled crossing: a pedestrian may cross where he likes providing he takes reasonable care of his own safety).

A pedestrian is under a duty first to satisfy himself that it is reasonably safe to step on to a crossing before doing so, and second to keep a good lookout during the journey across it for vehicles close enough and travelling at such speed as to raise a reasonable doubt whether precedence will be accorded to him. In *Maynard* v *Rogers* [1970] RTR 392, a 19 year old plaintiff who stepped on to a pedestrian crossing without looking to her right first (shortly after midnight in a not very well lit street) was held to be two-thirds contributorily negligent, while the driver who ran into her was held to be one-third liable, even though the defendant had very little opportunity of avoiding the accident, save perhaps by sounding his horn (see also *Williams* v *Needham* [1972] RTR 387 where the pedestrian was held two-thirds liable for failing to look before crossing).

These proportions of liability were reversed in *Lawrence* v *WM Palmer (Excavations) Ltd* (1965) 109 SJ 358, where a 77 year old deaf plaintiff was struck while on a pedestrian crossing and found to be 11 feet from the pavement she had left, and where the injuries indicated a considerable impact. The driver was held to be two-thirds to blame and the pedestrian one-third. Similarly, the plaintiff's contributory negligence was reduced to 20 per cent in *Clifford* v *Drymond* [1976] RTR 134, CA when she had travelled some ten feet into the crossing but was thrown or carried 45 feet from it by the defendant's vehicle which had been some 75 feet from the crossing at the time the plaintiff stepped onto it.

Regulation 8 of the 1971 Regulations provides that:

'Every foot passenger on the carriageway within the limits of an uncontrolled zebra crossing shall have precedence within those limits over any vehicle and the driver of the vehicle shall accord such precedence to the foot passenger, if the foot passenger is on the carriageway within those limits before the vehicle or any part thereof has come on the carriageway within those limits.'

Regulation 9 reinforces this by providing:

'the driver of the vehicle shall not cause the vehicle or any part thereof to stop within the limits of the zebra crossing unless either he is prevented from proceeding by circumstances beyond his control or it is necessary for him to stop in order to avoid an accident.'

However, it should be noted that reg 9 forbids pedestrians to loiter on the crossing:

'No foot passenger shall remain on the carriageway within the limits of the zebra crossing longer than is necessary for the purpose of passing over the crossing with reasonable despatch.'

If a police officer or traffic warden is controlling traffic upon a zebra crossing, reg 8 above will not apply, and traffic must obey the signals of the police officer or warden.

(b) Pelican crossings

Pelican crossings are also referred to as 'controlled crossings' being a crossing controlled by lights both for motorists and pedestrians. Until 18 February 1987 these crossings were subjected to the Pelican Pedestrian Crossing Regulations and General Directions 1969 (SI No 888 as ammended by 1979 regs (SI No 401). Thereafter the law was ammended by the Regulations of the same title of 1987 (SI No 16).

For motorists the red light prohibits the driver of the vehicle from crossing the stop line, or if the stop line is not visible, beyond the post of the traffic light (reg 8(i)(c)). Vehicles being used by the fire brigade, ambulance or for police purposes are exempt provided precedence is accorded to any pedestrian on the carriageway and danger is not caused to any other vehicle approaching or waiting at the crossing. In *Tremayne* v *Hill* (1986) *The Times*, 11 December the Court of Appeal held that when a pedestrian crosses a multiple road junction he is not under duty to keep a lookout for motorists entering the junction against red traffic lights. This particular accident occurred at night and the driver was found 100 per cent liable.

The amber light prohibits vehicular traffic from proceeding beyond the stop line, or if the stop line is not visible, beyond the post of the traffic light, except in the case of a vehicle so close to the stop line when the steady amber light is first shown that it cannot safely be stopped before passing it (reg 8(1)(b)). Vehicles used by the fire brigade, ambulance or police are exempt from obeying the amber light in the same circumstances as for the red light. However, the flashing amber light gives precedence to pedestrians on the carriageway before any part of the vehicle has entered the crossing (reg 8(i) (e)). In any event the traffic must proceed with due regard to the safety of other users of the road and subject to the direction of any police constable in uniform or traffic warden engaged in the regulation of traffic (reg 8 (ii)).

The pedestrians' green and red lights show respectively when they should and should not, in the interests of safety, use the crossing (reg 9 (ii)(b) and (a)). The illumination of the word 'Wait' shown by the indicator for pedestrians has the same meaning as that of the red light (reg 9(iii)). The pedestrians' flashing green light gives precedence to a pedestrian who is already on the crossing when the flashing green light is first shown but it gives a warning to a pedestrian who is not already on the crossing when the flashing green light is first shown that he should not in the interests of safety start to cross the carriageway (reg 9(ii)(c)).

Before the 1987 Regulations there was no statutory prohibition against vehicles overtaking on the approach. There was however civil liability. In *Skolimowski* v *Haynes* (1983) CLY 2525, Cantley J found the driver in the outside third lane two-thirds liable when a foreign pedestrian who was slightly disabled started to cross while the 'Green Man' was lit but was still on the crossing when the light changed in favour of the traffic. Traffic in the first two lanes slowed down, but obscured the defendant's view. The defendant owed the pedestrian a high duty of care when a pedestrian's presence was foreseeable. The plaintiff was one-third liable for failing to see the change in the lights and looking away from the traffic. When about to become trapped it was held that she should have stood still between the lines since under the 1987 Regulations, overtaking within a pelican-controlled area is an offence.

Photograph 13 shows the control box which is situated at each side of the crossing. A bleeper may also be incorporated to sound when the 'steady green man' is displayed for the assistance of poorly sighted pedestrians. Bleepers are not incorporated when two such crossings are placed close to each other and where a poorly-sighted person may be confused and begin to cross against his own lights on hearing the noise from the adjacent crossing.

(c) School crossings

County councils (or the Commissioner of Police, in the metropolis) are empowered by s 26 of the Road Traffic Regulation Act 1984 to arrange the patrolling of crossings used by children either on their way to or from

Photograph 13

Photograph 14

school or on their way from one part of the school to another.

There will not necessarily be any road markings indicating a school crossing, and the prohibition is provided by 'A school crossing patrol wearing a uniform approved by the Secretary of State . . . exhibiting a prescribed sign . . .' (s 28(1) of the 1984 Act). The words on the sign will be 'STOP: Children'. The sign must be exhibited by the 'patrol' so that the words on the sign can be seen by the driver, although they do not need to be full face to oncoming traffic (*Hoy* v *Smith* [1963] 3 All ER 670).

Upon the 'prescribed sign' (or 'lollipop') being exhibited' by s 28(2) of the 1984 Act:

He shall cause the vehicle to stop before reaching the place where the children are crossing or seeking to cross and so as not to stop or impede their crossing, and the vehicle shall not be put in motion again so as to reach the place in question so long as the sign continues to be exhibited.'

The showing of the 'prescribed sign' is mandatory, but the provision of advance warning lights is discretionary (and they are then governed by reg 37(2) of the Traffic Signs Regulations and General Directions 1981 (SI No 859)).

Appointed traffic wardens (s 95 of the Road Traffic Regulations Act 1984) may act as a 'school crossing patrol'. Section 28 of the 1984 Act does not apply to vehicles and persons in the public service of the Crown. However, under the criminal law, a prosecution for careless driving or reckless driving could still be considered, and in civil proceedings it is submitted that this would not alter the duty of care of either the public or Crown servant to an injured school child.

Photograph 14 shows a typical school crossing patrol with the prescribed sign being exhibited in a positive and correct manner. The signs have two inherent unpleasant characteristics: they are difficult to handle in the wind and they are cold to handle in the winter.

(d) Level crossings

Rules 186–197 of the Highway Code should be referred to in respect of railway level crossings and the provision of the basic duties of care required of those driving vehicles over them, or (by inference unless the contrary is apparent), of pedestrians using them.

The criminal law makes specific provisions for level crossings, according to the particular nature of the crossing involved, eg whether it is a public or private crossing. In either case by-laws of the locality may apply, and as with private crossings, special considerations may be relevant, depending upon whether the owner or operator is the NCB, a quarry, a dock or harbour board, or a local authority.

The injured party may be a member of the public, or an employee going about the business of his employer who operates or controls the crossing or the traffic upon it, to whom statutory protection may apply. In any of these circumstances, the claimant or his adviser will need to obtain and refer to the statutory source authorising the crossing, and the provisions relating to it (the varying details of which must necessarily require reference to appropriate publications of a more detailed nature than this). The fact of a breach of the criminal law may well be excellent evidence of a breach of the common law duty of care by the injured party seeking damages for resulting personal injury or loss.

5   Hazards for pedestrians

Food vans and other lures for pedestrians, especially for children, will typically involve ice-cream vans. Rule 59 of the Highway Code requires a driver to exercise care near a parked ice-cream van, with the express warning that children are more interested in ice-cream than in traffic. This is illustrated by one (of the four) photographs in the Highway Code.

In *Moore* v *Poyner* [1975] RTR 127 CA, the parked vehicle by which children were playing on the nearside was a coach, rather than an ice-cream van, but the defendant, knowing that children played in the area, did not slow down from about 30 mph and collided with a child who ran out from in front of the coach. It was held that in all of the circumstances the speed was reasonable and he could not have been expected to slow down or sound his horn.

In *Arnold* v *Teno* [1978] CLY 2064, the Canadian Supreme Court found liable an untrained 19 year old student driver of an ice-cream van from which the infant plaintiff, having brought an ice-cream, dashed into the street and was struck by the passing vehicle. The student was held liable for his failure to warn the children before they started to cross the road of the danger from cars, and his failure to take the precaution of looking through his windows. The child's mother was found not liable, having specifically reminded the child on this occasion to watch out for cars. The standard of care put on her was that of mothers in the area where an ice-cream van stopped in order to attract young children.

In *Kite* v *Nolan* [1983] RTR 253 CA, the Court of Appeal declined to interfere with a finding of fact by the trial judge that the defendant driver was not negligent in driving along the road at about 15 mph when the five-year-old infant plaintiff ran out into the road from a line of parked cars in order to get to an ice-cream van parked on the opposite side of the road.

Chapter 12

Seat Belts

Seat belts were first patented in 1902 (by a Frenchman) but the provision for seat belts in cars was not required by our Parliament until 1965, when vehicles registered after that date had to have them fitted. In 1973 and 1974 attempts in Parliament failed to make their being worn obligatory. By 1975 the wearing of seat belts was compulsory in Australia, New Zealand, Sweden, Finland, Brazil, Poland, Spain and Czechoslovakia and in this year it was little surprise that the Court of Appeal in London, with the leading judgment of Lord Denning, MR in *Froom* v *Butcher* [1975] 3 All ER 520, stepped in to lay down authoritive guidelines over a mass of inconsistent decisions. At the time of that decision the only requirement to wear a fitted seat belt was contained in the Highway Code.

1 Front seats

The vehicles that are required to have seat belts and anchorage points as set out in regs 46 to 48 of the Motor Vehicle (Construction and Use) Regulations 1986 include:

(1) vehicles constructed to carry up to 12 passengers, first used on or after 1 January 1965; and

(2) goods vehicles whose gross weight determines the date of first use from which the obligation is required.

Since 31 January 1983 it has been a criminal offence for drivers and front seat passengers in vehicles which are required to have a seat belt not to wear the fitted seat belt (by reason of s 27 of the Transport Act 1981, amending s 33A of the Road Traffic Act 1972 and the Motor Vehicles (Wearing of Seat Belts) Regulations 1982). Initially for a three-year experimental period, the order was made permanent in January 1986 upon Parliament receiving a report published by the Department of Transport and the London School of Economics showing that the compulsory wearing of seat belts prevented an estimated 200 deaths and 7,000 injuries each year. Rules 35 and 36 of the Highway Code apply.

Regulation 47 of the Construction and Use Regulations provides that in vehicles such as a mini bus where there is a middle front seat between what would be the 'specified passenger's seat' and the driver's seat (where seat belts must be provided and fitted), a passenger in the middle seat need not wear a seat belt to avoid prosecution if the far passenger seat is occupied (but must wear one if it is unoccupied). Nevertheless, for all cars and vans manufactured since October 1986 or first registered from April 1987, belts must be fitted for the centre seat.

It is the responsibility of the individual to wear a seat belt but the responsibility rests upon the driver when a child under the age of 14 is being carried in the front seat. It is an offence for someone without reasonable excuse to drive a vehicle on a road with a child under the age of 14 years in the front seat who is not wearing a seat belt (s 15(1) of the Road Traffic Act 1988). While it is the driver who commits the offence, a child passenger between the ages of ten and 14 might be guilty of aiding and abetting the offence.

There are exceptions from the seat belt regulations. For instance, if a *vehicle* does not fall within the statutory provisions set out above, the vehicle does not have to be fitted with a seat belt. Some vehicles are presently exempt from the requirements of a fitted seat belt and anchorage points such as: tractors and pedestrian-controlled vehicles, a vehicle incapable by reason of its construction from exceeding 16 mph on the level under its own power, a vehicle brought temporarily into this country by a resident abroad and a vehicle being tested for an MOT Certificate (unless seat belts are in fact fitted).

Some *persons* are also exempt from wearing fitted front seat belts. These include persons engaged in reversing a vehicle, those holding a certificate of medical exemption or a constable or prison officer protecting or escorting another person. Also exempt are firemen putting on operational clothing or equipment, a taxi driver on duty, those riding in a vehicle under trade licences (trade plates) investigating a mechanical fault, or those using a vehicle constructed or adapted and used in the local delivery of goods or mail. However, it should be noted that to be exempted on medical grounds a certificate must be produced at the time to a constable or within seven days or as soon as reasonably practicable to a police station specified by the police if it is to provide a defence to a criminal offence (s 14(4) of the Road Traffic Act 1988). Similarly, tradespersons should be aware that in *Webb* v *Crane* (1987) *The Times*, 14 October, it was held that a newsagent who made a daily journey from a point of delivery to the point of sale was not making local deliveries or collections (so as to fall within the statutory exception) and he was found guilty of failing to wear a seat belt. It was held that a 'round' meant a series of visits or calls and that the appellant's return journey to one point of call did not qualify as an exemption to the general requirement. Regard was had to the obvious intention of Parliament that the wearing of a seat belt was a general requirement and that any exceptions to that were of a limited nature.

2   Rear seats

Since 1981, the inclusion of rear seat belt mountings (but not belts) has been mandatory in new cars. In 1984, 368 rear seat occupants were killed and

4,633 were seriously injured. The accident rate statistics since 1985 show that children were three times more likely to be injured in the rear of a car, and adults were twice as likely to be injured. The view of Dr Murray McKay (Head of Birmingham University's Accident Research Unit) was that the loads on the front seat occupants roughly double when struck by an unrestricted rear passenger. In 1990 the Transport Road and Research Laboratory was reported as concluding that if all rear passengers wore a seat belt there would be 9,000 fewer injuries and 150 fewer deaths every year.

Accordingly all cars manufactured from 1 October 1986 and first registered from 1 April 1987 have been required to be fitted with a rear seat belt.

There is not yet any general statutory requirement to wear a fitted seat belt, save for children under the age of 14. However, in April 1990 the Parliamentary Advisory Council for Transport Safety published a survey indicating that compulsory rear seat belts for all passengers could reduce fatal accidents and serious injuries by two-thirds. The estimates were that 20,000 people are injured in the rear of vehicles because passengers failed to wear rear seat belts, 4,000 of which are serious, resulting in more than 300 fatalities. A Gallup Survey conducted in early 1990 among a representative sample of 1,000 motorists showed that 82 per cent supported the extension of compulsory seat belt wearing to all passengers. This reform of the law has the backing of the AA, the RAC, the British Medical Association, Police Forces and the Society of Motor Manufacturers and Traders. The Department of Transport is reported as saying that they await at least 50 per cent of vehicles already being fitted with rear seatbelts before introducing new Regulations. There is dispute as to whether this 50 per cent has not already been reached. In 1987, nearly 8,400 children, from babies to 12 year olds, were injured in crashes when riding unrestricted in the rear of cars. Since 1 September 1989 it has been an offence for someone without reasonable excuse to drive a vehicle on a road with a child under the age of 14 years in the rear without wearing a seat belt where one is fitted (s 15(3) of the Road Traffic Act 1988 and the Motor Vehicles (Wearing of Seat Belts by Children in Rear Seats) Regulations 1989). During the passage of the Bill through Parliament a number of concessions had to be made so that the law only applies to vehicles already fitted with rear seat belts (possibly less than half).

In addition to the defence of 'reasonable excuse', there are exceptions to the requirements to wear a seat belt (including exemption by reason of a medical certificate) as described in the Motor Vehicles (Wearing of Seat Belts by Children in Rear Seats) Regulations 1989 (SI No 1219).

3 Contributory negligence

The failure to wear a fitted seat belt was held to amount to contributory negligence long before the statutory requirement was imposed. Before the statutory requirement, the appropriate maximum reduction for contributory negligence for front seat travellers was 25 per cent (see *Froom* v *Butcher* [1975] 3 WLR 379. An authoritive reported decision as to whether this maximum should be increased from 25 per cent where there has also been a breach of a statutory requirement, is still awaited. However, in *Capps* v *Miller* [1989] 2 All ER 333, where the plaintiff failed to comply with the statutory requirement in respect of fastening a chin strap, his contributory negligence does not appear to have been assessed at anything more than would have been the case before the statutory requirement came into effect. The appropriate maximum reduction for contributory negligence of 25 per cent ought presumably to apply equally to front and rear passengers who fail to wear a fitted seat belt, but again one awaits an authoritive reported decision.

Where there is a failure to wear a seat belt and therefore contributory negligence is an issue, the burden of proving that the wearing of a seat belt would have been of any effect is upon the defendant. The burden of proving contributory negligence also rests upon the defendant and to establish this evidence must be called by the defendant concerning the relevance of failure to wear a seat belt (see *Condon* v *Condon* (1978) CLY 2611).

Where the issue arises as to whether the wearing of a fitted seat belt would have prevented or diminished the injuries received, the expert evidence required will almost certainly have to come from a Consultant Surgeon, or a suitably qualified or experienced Consultant Engineer.

In either event, the published results of MS Christianson contained in the British Medical Journal of 27 November 1976 at p 1313 are of great assistance. While it should be noted that this is a study of patients treated in hospital, so that the car occupant, (whether belted or not) had to be injured to be included in the study, (and the reported results in this paper should not be interpreted as a description of an overall performance of seat belts), the paper provides a description of those cases where seat belts have given only partial protection. The results are as summarised below.

The evidence suggests that the wearing of seat belts *reduces* the number of:
(1) serious chest injuries;
(2) the number and severity of rib injuries;
(3) arm injuries;
(4) severe head injuries; and
(5) facial mutilation.

However, seat belts appear to *contribute* to the number of:
(1) fractured clavicles;
(2) injuries to the abdomen; and
(3) whiplash injuries to the neck.

Regardless of this evidence, in assessing damages no allowance can be made because a seat belt, if worn, may have caused other more serious injuries (see *Patience* v *Andrews* [1982] CLY 789). However, given sufficient medical evidence of a phobia against the wearing of a seat belt, contributory negligence maybe avoided (see *Condon* (above)).

Where there is a statutory exemption from fitting or wearing a seat belt, it has been held to be a question of fact and not of law whether a person has failed to take proper care of his own safety in failing to have a seat belt fitted or worn. Thus, in *Hoadley* v *Dartford District Council* (1979) CLY 2367, the owner/driver of an exempt van avoided a finding of contributory negligence. Even where a person under 18 years of age may be found liable for contributory negligence in not wearing a fitted seat belt, that reduction may be limited where the adult driver ought to have instructed the young person accordingly, or insured that the seat belt was worn.

In *Eastman* v *South West Thames Health Authority* (1990) *The Times*, 4 May, a passenger in the back of an ambulance failed to use or see the fitted seat belts and also failed to see a notice stating: 'for your own safety use the seat belts provided'. It was held that the passenger was not contributorily negligent and that the defendants had failed in their duty adequately to alert her to the provision of seat belts.

In *Pasternack* v *Poulton* [1973] 2 All ER 74, an 18 year old undergraduate non-driver had her own contributory negligence in failing to wear a seat belt reduced to 5 per cent when the driver failed to demonstrate the need to wear a seat belt by wearing one himself, or at least to point out the existence of the seat belt and explain that it was for her use. (*Froom* v *Butcher* (above) probably overruled this case in respect of adult passengers failing to note the presence of a front seat belt, and in *Eastman* v *South West Thames Health Authority* (above), Judge J confirmed this view).

A back seat passenger should guard against tripping over a seat belt. The driver is under no duty to ensure that it remains taut or to provide a warning, at least to a regular passenger in his car (see *Donn* v *Schater* [1975] RTR 238.

Finally, it remains to be seen how many accidents are caused by drivers fitting their seat belts while driving, perhaps in an attempt to avoid any possible findings of contributory negligence or the commission of a criminal offence.

4   Coaches

There is no statutory requirement to have seat belts fitted to coaches. In June 1990 an English operated double decker coach careered off a French motorway, resulting in the death of 11 passengers. Parliamentary concern was expressed about the lack of fitted seat belts in coaches, and legislation may be contemplated in due course (despite the failure of the European Community to back this measure).

Chapter 13

Drivers and Vehicles

1   The drinking driver

By s 11 of the Road Traffic Act 1988, the maximum limit permitted for the driver by the criminal law is 80 mg of alcohol per 100 ml of blood, and 107 mg of alcohol per 100 ml of urine. By the Transport Act 1981, evidence from breath-testing machines became admissible and they largely replaced blood or urine in analysis in drink and driving cases. The statutory limit for breath alcohol concentration is 35 microgrammes per 100 ml of breath. However, if the breath analysis is between 35 and 50 microgrammes, the motorist is able to request a blood or urine test, although the final choice of which sample is taken rests with the police (s 8(2) of the Road Traffic Act 1988).

Smith v *Geraghty* [1986] RTR 222 confirms the admissibility of expert evidence to calculate the likely readings at the time of the driving from the interval of time that has passed between then and the taking of the relevant sample for analysis. There may be circumstances where not only the driver, but also the passenger is liable for a criminal offence; eg aiding and abetting the drunken driving.

For the purposes of civil proceedings and the passengers of the drunken driver, *Owens* v *Brimmell* [1976] 3 All ER 765 is a starting point in assessing the contributory negligence on the part of the passenger who knows his driver has been drinking. Eight pints or more of beer had been consumed by the driver between 8 pm and 2 am in a 'pub crawl'. The passenger's contributory negligence was assessed at 20 per cent, either because he knew that the driver had taken drink in such a quantity as to impair to a dangerous extent the driver's capacity to drive safely, or because he had accompanied the driver on a bout of drinking which, as well as diminishing the driver's capacity to drive safely, also had the effect of depriving the passenger of his own capacity to appreciate the danger. The defence of *volenti non fit injuria* (that the defendant knew of the risks involved and willingly accepted them) was ruled out (see also s 149(2) of the Road Traffic Act 1988).

If, however, the passenger actively encourages drunken and reckless driving and is then injured, his claim may fail on grounds of public policy (see *Pitt* v *Hunt* (1990) *The Independent*, 4 May).

2 The learner driver

An accident involving a learner driver may involve a prosecution of the driver and/or the instructor and/or the examiner (if during the driving test) or a Civil Claim for damages by or against any of them, or against any of them by another road user.

Regulation 8 of the Motor Vehicles (Driving Licences) Regulations 1981 makes it a condition of a Provisional Licence that the holder shall use it only when under the supervision of a holder of a full licence for a vehicle of the same class who is present in or on the vehicle (save for motor-cycles and invalid carriages). The breach of this statutory duty does not in itself give rise to a cause of action for civil damages by an injured third party (*Verney* v *Wilkins* [1962] Crim LR 840). A breach of the Common Law duty of care is still required.

The standard of skill and care required of the learner driver is not merely to do his incompetent best, but is that of a competent and experienced driver (who does not make errors of judgment and is free from infirmity; see *Nettleship* v *Weston* [1971] 3 All ER 581 CA). The learner driver who causes or contributes to an accident cannot excuse himself by saying that he did the best that could be expected from a learner of his limited skill and experience.

It may be, of course, that some of the responsibility for the negligence of the pupil lies with the instructor. In the absence of any evidence enabling the court to draw a distinction between them, they will be held equally to blame—as happened in *Nettleship* v *Weston* (see above) although Megaw LJ, in a dissenting judgment, held that on the evidence the liability was the teacher's rather than the pupil's (who panicked during her third lesson and who was still having the gears, hand-brake and even the steering-wheel moved for her on some occasions).

(a) The driving instructor

The driving instructor may be in a difficult position as an injured party claiming for the negligence of the pupil's driving. Where the instructor knows that the pupil is not in fact of the standard of the competent and experienced driver and accepts the consequential risks as his, the pupil may successfully raise the complete defence of *volenti non fit injuria*. This defence failed in *Nettleship* v *Weston* on the basis that there was no evidence that the instructor accepted such a risk (despite his acceptance of being the inexperienced pupil's teacher) and the instructor's enquiry of whether there was fully comprehensive insurance was held by the majority of the court to be a positive indication to the contrary.

The instructor may also be in a difficult position with regard to his own liability once his pupil has been proved to be negligent at the time of the accident in question. It may be difficult to avoid a clear inference that there must have been something he could and should have done, whether by prior instruction or positive action at the onset of the accident. In *Rubie* v *Falkner* [1940] 1 All ER 285, the instructor unsuccessfully appealed his conviction for aiding and abetting careless driving by the driver in failing to tell the driver not to overtake when it was dangerous to do so.

Thus, passive inactivity could also amount to a criminal offence. However, in *Gibbons* v *Priestly* [1979] 4 RTR 4, the instructor did avoid any finding of liability against himself. The plaintiff pupil was aged 51, and had had 18 lessons at the time of the accident in a car without dual-controls. The accident occurred quickly and the instructor could do no more than he did in shouting 'Brake, brake', and applying the hand-brake.

The evidence for the defence of an instructor might be found in quantifying the time between an unexpected action by the driver and the time required by which the instructor could have remedied this. For example, at 30 mph a vehicle will travel 44 feet in one second. A quantified time and evidence of the lay out of the controls may show that the superviser could not reasonably have been expected to have corrected the learner's actions.

Since 1 September 1989 driving instructors are required to pass a written examination, (see the Motor Cars (Driving Instruction) (Amendment) Regulations 1989 (SI No 1373)).

(b)   The driving examiner

The driving examiner is in a relatively easier position concerning his potential liability. In *BSM* v *Simms* [1971] 1 All ER 317, it was held that the examiner was there to observe faults and to interfere only if it was essential in the interests of safety. Further, the action of the examiner in so acting in the agony of the moment is to be judged only by a test of reasonableness, and not in hindsight, even if his action made the situation worse (as in so many cases where someone is obliged to act in the agony of a moment created by another).

3   Motor Cycles

Motor cycle riders and their pillion-passengers are particularly vulnerable to injury if there is an accident, whether or not the rider is at fault. In measuring that fault consideration will have to be given to what training and experience the rider had, how in fact a motor cycle could be controlled and, where those controls are on it, and the relevance of the motor cycle helmet and visor.

(a) Training and testing

The Motor Vehicle (Driving Licences) (Amendment) No 2 Regulations were amended by the Driving Licences Regulations 1981 to provide for persons undergoing a test of competence on motor cycles to have the test in two parts, save that 16 year-olds may drive a 50 cc moped (ie maximum design speed of 30 mph and kerbside weight not exceeding 250 kg) and 17 year olds may drive a motor cycle up to 125 cc with no initial training.

Part one of the test examines the ability of the rider to execute seven basic manoeuvres, albeit at low speed and off the road. Learners must pass both tests (the second test being a road test) within two years or be forbidden from riding for one year. Preparation for these tests may be assisted by training schemes such as the nationally accepted 'Star Rider Scheme' (see Star Rider, Federation House, 2309 Coventry Road, Sheldon, Birmingham, B26; (021) 742 4296)).

In assessing the potential negligence of a motor cyclist, in addition to referring to the Highway Code, reference may also be made to a standard work such as 'Motor Cycle Road Craft' published by HMSO. A detailed description of the rider's actions will have to be obtained and may be compared with the advice given in such a training manual. 'Motor Cycle Road Craft' contains an important section dealing with good road observation, and every motor cyclist should be familiar with its general maxim: the rider must see in good time any road features which might endanger him. To do so he must concentrate at all times. He must think before acting, exercise restraint, and be prepared to hold back where necessary. He must use speed intelligently, ride fast only in the right places, and negotiate every corner with safety.

(b) The controls of the motor cycle

When a problem presents itself the motor cyclist must react quickly and correctly and within the capabilities of his machine. This may mean braking in an emergency, taking avoiding action or both.

Motor cycles are fitted with:

(1) a hand operated front brake control which is mounted upon the right side of the handlebar;

(2) a foot control for the rear brake which is operated by the right foot while the foot is upon the foot rest;

(3) a clutch control which is mounted on the left hand side of the handlebar; and

(4) a gear control, operated by the left foot.

The position and character of the controls is recommended by the Society of Automotive Engineers. To avoid an emergency situation, all of these controls may have to be operated in the correct sequence and without excessive force.

The following are guidelines from which some comparisons can be made to the rider's account of his actions:

(1) A rider should brake firmly only when travelling in a straight line. The front brake should be applied first (right hand on the lever) followed by the rear brake (right foot on the pedal) subject to surface conditions.

(2) Braking should never be fierce.

(3) Braking causes the weight to transfer on to the front wheel from the rear wheel. Therefore, during braking more force can be applied to the front brake and less to the rear, to reduce the chance of 'wheel locking'.

(4) The front brake should not be applied when the motor cycle is banked over or when on loose or slippery surfaces.

(5) The rear brake may be carefully applied when the motor cycle is in the banked position.

(6) On surfaces with a very low co-efficient of friction (eg when the road is wet or icy) the engagement of lower gears should be used to reduce the speed until it becomes safe enough to apply the rear brake.

(7) The rear brake should only be used at low speeds while manoeuvering or coming to rest.

(c) Motor cycle helmets

The relevant regulations are under s 16 of the Road Traffic Act 1988 and the Motor Cycles (Protective Helmets) Regulations 1980 (see also r 28 of the Highway Code).

The helmets which motor cyclists are required to wear must conform to one of the British Standards specified in reg 5 or the Schedule and be marked with the number of the British Standard and the certification mark of the British Standards Institution. If not, it must not only give a similar but greater degree of protection than a British Standard Helmet, but also be of a type manufactured for motor cyclists. If the helmet is worn with a chin cup it must be provided with an additional strap or other fastening under the jaw for securing the helmet. If the helmet is worn unfastened or improperly fastened, a criminal offence is committed under reg 4(3)(c).

Helmets must be worn by persons riding or driving a motor bicycle, whether with or without a side-car. Both the driver and the pillion-passengers are required to wear helmets, but not those riding in the side-car. Followers of the Sikh religion are exempted while wearing a turban (reg 4(2)(c)) as originally provided for by the Motor Cycle Crash Helmet (Religious Exemption) Act 1976 (and see s 16(2) of the Road Traffic Act 1988).

Since 13 August 1985 persons other than the actual offender are exempt from criminal liability in respect of the offence of driving or riding on a motor cycle in contravention of regulations requiring the wearing of crash helmets, unless the person actually committing the contravention is a child of 16 years (see s 14(4) of the Road Traffic Act 1988 and before that the Motor Cycle Crash Helmets (Restriction of Liability) Act 1985). The Court of Appeal reduced the damages awarded by 15 per cent for contributory negligence for the failure of a plaintiff to wear a crash helmet in *O'Connell* v *Jackson* [1972] 1 QB at p 277 (when the requirement to wear a helmet was provided for by the Highway Code but not then by statute). When in *Capps* v *Miller* [1989] 2 All ER 333 the motor cyclist wore a crash helmet but failed to fasten the chin strap, he suffered a more serious brain injury in consequence. Contributory negligence was assessed by the Court of Appeal at 10 per cent even though it was impossible to assess to what degree the brain damage had been made worse by this failure contrary to the statutory requirement.

If the motor cycle is being pushed by someone on foot, protective headgear does not have to be worn unless the motor-cycle is being used as a scooter with one foot on the pedal and one foot pushing on the ground (*Crank* v *Brookes* (1980) RTR and reg 4(2)(b)).

Under s 17 (2) of the 1988 Act, it is an offence for a person to sell or to offer for sale or to let or hire, a helmet which is not of a type prescribed by the Regulations. A person charged with this type of offence may himself summons the person actually responsible for the offence in the same proceedings, as may of course the prosecutor. An offence of selling an illegal helmet is committed even though the helmet is sold for off-road use only; see; *Losexis Limited* v *Clarke* (1984) RTR 174.

(d) Eye protectors (visors)

The statutory requirements with effect from 1 July 1987 are the Motor-Cycle (Eye Protectors) Regulations 1985, (as amended) by the Motor-Cycles (Eye Protectors) (Amendment) Regulations 1988 (SI No 1031) made under s 18 of the Road Traffic Act 1988).

Section 18(7) of the 1988 Act defines a 'head worn appliance' for use on a motor cycle as:

'an appliance designed or adapted for use with any headgear or by being attached to or placed upon the head by a person driving or riding a motor cycle and intended for the protection of the eyes'.

Anyone who drives or rides on a motor bicycle on the road (otherwise than in a side car) and uses eye protectors not as prescribed is guilty of an offence.

There are some exemptions to this requirement provided by reg 4 of the 1985 Regulations in respect of mowing machines (for the time being propelled by a person on foot) and for vehicles brought temporarily into Great Britain by persons resident outside the UK who have not remained in the UK for more than one year from the date the vehicle was last brought into the country. There are also exemptions for persons on duty in the Armed Forces of the Crown who wear an eye protector as part of their service equipment. There are also similar provisions for helmets in respect of the sale of non-prescribed eye protectors.

Some riders do not appreciate that a badly maintained visor can drastically reduce visibility, particularly at night or when it is raining. Scratches can seriously affect the rider's ability to see in detail. The preservation of the visor worn by a rider in an accident may provide good evidence of the kind of visibility he would have had at the time. Photographs of a view taken through a visor may illustrate scratches but are unlikely to show with any accuracy the actual visibility which would have been available to the wearer at the time.

(e) Restriction to the use of motor cycles

Motor cycle provisional driving licence holders are permitted by law to ride certain types of motor cycles only. These include motor cycles which were first used before 1 January 1982, where the capacity of the cylinders does not exceed 125 cc or motor cycles first used after 1 January 1982 where the cylinder capacity does not exceed 125 cc and the maximum power developed by the engine does not exceed 12 brake horse power (9 kilowatts).

Those motor cycles first used after 1 January 1982 must be fitted with a 'distinguishing plate' which gives information about both the capacity of the engine and its power. Usually such machines are fitted with a silencer and smaller carburettor jets, both of which can be changed after the rider passes the test, thus avoiding the necessity to exchange the motor cycle for a more powerful one. Unfortunately, it is not unknown for riders to change one or both of these restrictive devices before passing the test. In the modified form the power can be increased to about twice the legal limit, and with it an increase in speed. Consideration should be given to the possibility of alterations having been made when allegations (or the evidence) seem to indicate that a restricted motor cycle had been travelling at excessive speeds.

(f) Pillion passengers

In *Pitts* v *Hunt* (1990) *The Independent*, 4 May, the Court of Appeal dismissed a pillion passenger's claim for damages because he had actively encouraged his young driver to drive recklessly while both were under the influence of drink. The claim failed on the grounds of public policy (*ex turpi causa non oritur actis*).

4 Public service vehicles

This section refers specifically to buses and the road accidents associated with them. The full statutory definition of a public service vehicle is, however, very broad. For the purposes of the Public Passenger Vehicles Act 1981, a 'public service vehicle' means a motor vehicle used for carrying passengers for hire and reward which is either adapted to carry more than eight passengers, or being a vehicle not so adapted, is used for carrying passengers for hire or reward at separate fares in the course of a business.

(a) Vehicles

It is the duty of the holder of a PSV Operators' Licence, on the occurrence of any failure or damage of a nature calculated to affect the safety of the occupants of a public service vehicle or persons using the road, to report the matter as soon as practicable to the Secretary of State (s 20 of the Public Passenger Vehicles Act 1981). In the event of a road accident which might have been caused or contributed by the condition of the vehicle, litigation might well be assisted by discovery of the documents which are produced as a result of this statutory requirement, whether in respect of the accident in question or any previous similar accident involving the vehicle.

(b) Drivers and conductors

Drivers must wear their identity badge in a conspicuous position when on duty unless it has been lost, destroyed or defaced and notice has been given of this (reg 14 of the Public Service Vehicles (Drivers' and Conductors' Licence) Regulations 1934).

Up until June 1990, the standard of behaviour of drivers and conductors was provided for by regs 4 to 8 of the Public Service Vehicles (Conduct of Drivers, Conductors and Passengers) Regulations 1936 (as amended). Drivers and conductors must:

(1) behave in a civil and orderly manner;

(2) not smoke in or on a vehicle during a journey or when passengers are on board;

(3) take all precautions to ensure the safety of passengers in or on entering or alighting from the vehicle;

(4) not wilfully deceive or refuse to inform any passenger or intended passenger as to the destination or route of the vehicle or as to a fare of any journey;

(5) if requested by any Police Constable or other person having reasonable cause, give particulars of the name and address of the person by whom they are employed and in the case of the driver, of their licence;

(6) not at any reasonable time, obstruct or neglect to give all reasonable information and assistance to any person having authority to examine the vehicle.

Regulation 5 of these Regulations prohibited the driver speaking to the conductor or any other person when the bus was in motion unless the conversation was either with an authorised person on operational matters or it was necessary on the grounds of safety.

Regulation 6 prohibited a conductor from distracting the driver's attention without reasonable cause or to speak to him unless it was necessary to do so in order to give directions as to the stopping of the vehicle when the vehicle was in motion.

After 1 June 1990 the Public Service Vehicles (Conduct of Drivers, Inspectors, Conductors and Passengers) Regulations 1990 replaced the 1936 Regulations. The requirement that the driver and conductor behave in a civil and orderly manner is omitted on the grounds that such behaviour could constitute offences under the Public Order Act 1986.

The prohibition against smoking has been relaxed, for instance when the vehicle is hired and the operator and hirer agree to this. The requirements that drivers or conductors shall not obstruct or neglect to give information and assistance to persons having authority to examine the vehicle is omitted on the basis that the substance of this is an offence under s 8(2) of the Public Passenger Vehicles Act 1981 (an offence intentionally to obstruct certifying officers or public service vehicle examiners).

The limitations upon the driver speaking to others is also replaced by a new requirement that the driver shall not (when the vehicle is in motion) hold a microphone (unless it is necessary to speak into it in an emergency or on safety grounds) or speak directly or through a microphone to any other person. Speech which does not distract from driving is allowed to fellow employees about the operation of the vehicle or on a service bus, in respect of brief statements from time to time indicating the location of the vehicle. The wording is to be noted of the following parts of reg 5 of the 1990 Regulations:

Reg 5(1): A driver and a conductor shall take all reasonable precautions to ensure the safety of passengers who are on, or who are entering or leaving, the vehicle.

(2): A driver, inspector and conductor shall take all reasonable steps to ensure that the provisions of these regulations relating to the conduct of passengers are complied with.

(5): A driver shall, when picking up or setting down passengers, stop the vehicle as close as is reasonably practicable to the left or nearside of the road.

(6): A conductor shall not, while the vehicle is in motion and without reasonable cause, distract the driver's attention or obstruct his vision.

Previously decided cases have laid down certain principles by which negligence might be judged:

(1) The passengers must be firmly aboard before the bus sets off (*Wilkie* v *London Transport Board* [1947] 1 All ER 258).

(2) On the other hand, there is no duty for the driver to wait until able-bodied passengers are seated. *Fury* v *Council of the City of Cardiff* (1977) CLY 2031).

(3) The bus should not stop with a jerk so as to cause injury (see *Hatton* v *London Transport Executive* (1956) CLY 6032), nor come to an unreasonably fierce halt (*Glasgow Corporation* v *Sutherland* (1951) 95 SJ 204, HL). There may however be an emergency that causes an abrupt halt where the driver will not be found liable (see *Parkinson* v *Liverpool Corporation* [1950] All ER 367 where the driver sought to avoid a dog and reasonably thought he could do so without endangering his passengers).

(4) If passengers are standing, the duty of care naturally extends to them as well as seated passengers in considering the speed at which corners might safely be taken (*Western Scottish Motor Traction* v *Allam* [1943] 2 All ER 742, HL).

(c) Passengers

The contract of conveyance of passengers in a public service vehicle is void if it seeks to deny or limit liability in respect of the death of or bodily injury to a passenger while being carried in, or entering or alighting from the vehicle (s 29 of the Public Passenger Vehicles Act 1981). Up until 1 June 1990, the conduct of passengers was subject to regs 9–12 of the Public Service Vehicles (Conduct of Drivers, Conductors and Passengers) Regulations 1936. They must not:

(1) deliberately and unreasonably impede passengers seeking to enter the vehicle or alight therefrom when entering or attempting to enter;

(2) enter or remain in or on the vehicle when requested not to do so by an authorised person on the ground that a vehicle is carrying its full complement of passengers; or that the operater is debarred from picking up passengers at the place in question by reason of the conditions attached to

his road service licence;

(3) travel in or on an upper deck of the vehicle unless occupying a seat provided for that purpose, or in or on any part of the vehicle not provided for the conveyance of passengers;

(4) wilfully do or cause to be done in respect of any part of the vehicle or its equipment anything which is calculated to obstruct or interfere with the working of the vehicle or to cause injury or discomfort to any person;

(5) when the vehicle is in motion, distract the driver's attention without reasonable cause or speak to him unless it is necessary to do so in order to give directions as to the stopping of the vehicle;

(6) give any signal which might be interpreted by the driver as a signal from the conductor to start;

(7) when in or on the vehicle to the annoyance of the other persons use or operate a noisy instrument or make or combine with any other person or persons to make any exceptional noise by singing, shouting or otherwise;

(8) to throw out of the vehicle any bottle, liquid or litter or any article or thing likely to annoy persons or to cause danger or injury to any person or property;

(9) to throw any article from the vehicle or attach to or trail from the vehicle any streamer, balloon, or other article in such a manner as to overhang the road;

(10) wilfully obstruct or impede any authorised persons.

If a passenger contravened those regulations, he might be removed from the vehicle by the driver or the conductor or at their request by a police officer. If the driver or conductor reasonably suspected the passenger in or on the vehicle of having breached the regs, the passenger could be required on demand to give his name and address to the driver, conductor or the police officer (reg 12).

Since 1 June 1990, the Public Service Vehicles (Conduct of Drivers, Inspectors, Conductors and Passengers) Regulations 1990 replaced the 1936 Regulations. Behaviour by passengers that might constitute offences under the Public Order Act 1986 have resulted in deletions from the new regulations. The requirement that passengers shall not travel on the upper deck of the vehicle unless they are seated is omitted by reason of the provisions of the Public Service Vehicles (Carrying Capacity) Regulations 1984 which provide that no person shall stand on the upper deck of a double-decker public service vehicle. The requirement that passengers shall not use nor operate noisy instruments is replaced by a requirement that passengers shall not play or operate musical instruments or sound reproducing equipment to the annoyance of any person on the vehicle or in a manner likely to cause annoyance to such a person.

The 1990 Regulations provide new requirements for passengers as follows:

(1) A passenger shall not without reasonable cause, obstruct the driver's vision or give any signal which might reasonably be interpreted by the driver as a signal to stop the vehicle in an emergency.

(2) A passenger may not remain on the vehicle when directed to leave by the driver, inspector or conductor on the ground that he has been causing a nuisance.

When passengers fall and are injured while a bus is in motion, it is frequently pleaded against them that they were negligent in failing to hold onto a rail part of the bus furniture. In *Western Scottish Motor Traction Co v Allam* [1943] 2 All ER 742, HL, a standing passenger for whom there was no vacant seat was thrown through the open door of the bus because the driver took a sharp curve at a great speed. He was thrown out and killed. He was not holding onto any part of the vehicle at the time.

The House of Lords held that this did not amount to contributory negligence. However, not only is the report of this case exceptionally brief for a House of Lords' decision, in that particular vehicle no bar or strap had been provided for standing passengers. It does however seem reasonable to suggest that where a passenger is in a position of some vulnerability (standing or only half-seated), it would amount to contributory negligence to fail to hold onto whatever was available in anticipation of the ordinary speeding up, slowing down and turning of the bus in the course of its journey. On the other hand, in *Azzopardi* v *State Transport Authority* (1983) CLY 2515, the Supreme Court of Australia overruled a finding of 20 per cent contributory negligence on the part of the plaintiff who was walking down the aisle to a centre seat when the bus started suddenly and he failed to grip firmly one of several hand holds which were provided and were available for use in the bus.

Chapter 14

Crossing Traffic, Collisions at Junctions and Speeding

1   Junctions

A substantial proportion of road accidents occur at road junctions. Indeed, statisticians have been known to define the 'average road accident' at this point; and also, incidentally, at 25 mph in a built-up area, in daylight. So many and varied may be the circumstances in which a collision occurs that other sections of this book may more appropriately be referred to.

However, some types of collisions at junctions fall readily into a separate category of their own, and deserve special analysis here. They concern the impatient or otherwise frustrated driver crossing traffic, usually in a steady stream; where a reasoned judgment leads the driver to take some steps to emerge rather than, perhaps, to stay still for so long as to cause annoyance and risk-taking by others behind. Not infrequently, the driver emerges with some co-operation from other traffic, or a fortuitous event; and an accident then occurs. What of the apportionment of liability then, or indeed, a successful prosecution?

(a) Legal background

In the 1960s there appeared to be an understanding of a principle of law involved in sorting out two competing interests. On the one hand there was the oncoming driver on the main road passing a probably stationary, if not slow-moving, inside row of traffic, all travelling in the same direction while, at the same time, a driver without precedence proceeded at right angles through an apparent gap created by the inside line of traffic, of which the overtaking driver on the outside was unaware. The answer as to the duties of each is not so straightforward, where the emerging traffic from the minor road on the left exercises as much care as seems reasonable, and the overtaking driver on the main road proceeds in the belief that he is protected by his right of way.

The law now can generally be stated to be the sum of simplicity, but with no satisfaction: 'Each case depends upon its own facts'. Even so, there are considerations of law to be applied which depend upon those facts.

To gain any understanding of the law at present it may be helpful to refer to the following cases in chronological order by way of example, each

117

illustrating in its own way the nature of judicial determination between competing claims.

(1) *Powell* v *Moody* (1966) 110 SJ 215, CA. The defendant emerged across two stationary lines of traffic on the main road and collided with the plaintiff motor cyclist 'queue-jumping' by travelling on the outside. The plaintiff proved liability subject to 80 per cent contributory negligence. It was suggested that the defendant might have flashed his lights or sounded his horn or just put the nose of his car out a very short distance and then stopped, giving the plaintiff an opportunity (perhaps) to avoid the defendant. Although the defendant had received an indication from a bus driver on the nearside lane that it was safe to emerge, the finding of fact was that the motor cyclist was already in the course of passing the bus at that time. There was some suggestion that perhaps the defendant was not travelling very slowly when emerging as he did, but then the plaintiff was 'jumping the queue', which is expressly prohibited by what is now r 77(72) of Highway Code.

(2) *Clarke* v *Winchurch and Others* [1969] 1 All ER 275, CA. The first defendant car driver who had parked his car on the offside of the road in a parking strip, indicated left, and pulled out slightly from the parked cars. The oncoming bus driver (the second defendant) saw that the traffic ahead of himself was stationary. He checked in his mirror to see that all was clear, and flashed his headlights to let out the first defendant. The first defendant observed that the second defendant had checked his mirror and then flashed his headlights, and emerged slowly, by way of inching forwards. The plaintiff moped rider passed by on the outside lane of the stationary traffic on the main road and collided with the first defendant. The first defendant was held not to be negligent in inching out. The bus driver was not to blame, because the flashing of the headlights meant only that it was safe for the first defendant to emerge (as far as he was concerned). Therefore the only question that remained was the liability of the plaintiff moped driver, who failed for his own negligence in pressing on, being unaware of what was happening on the inside lane and who should only have driven on at such a speed as would have enabled him to deal with any emergency. The court distinguished *Powell* v *Moody* (above) on the findings of fact by the trial judge that the first defendant was moving so slowly that he could not have done more.

(3) *Worsfold* v *Howe* [1980] 1 All ER 1028, CA. The defendant wished to drive his car out of a minor road and turn right onto a major road. The oncoming traffic included a petrol tanker who stopped, leaving a gap in front of it. The defendant began to inch his way past the tanker when the plaintiff, riding a motor cycle in the outside lane of the main road, collided with the defendant. The Court of Appeal held that there was no principle of law that a driver was entitled to emerge blind from a minor road onto a major road by inching forward beyond the line of vision, so that if he did so very slowly, he was under no liability to other traffic on the main road. The trial judge would have held both parties equally to blame (the defendant for

proceeding as described and the oncoming plaintiff for travelling too fast), but for an understanding that *Clark* v *Winchurch* (see above) laid down a principle of law in favour of the defendant, so that the Court of Appeal found both parties equally liable.

(4) *Lancaster* v *HBH Transport* [1980] CLY 267. The defendant driver of a heavy goods vehicle on a foggy morning, in poor driving conditions, attempted to cross the A1 from one side to the other and in so doing collided with the plaintiff's husband who was killed. The appeal from Donaldson J (as he then was) was allowed because of the high duty of care owed by HGV drivers to other road users and the defendant was held liable.

(5) *Truscott* v *McLaren* [1982] RTR 34, CA. The plaintiff was sitting by the roadside. The second defendant was 50 yards from the crossroads and driving at 40 mph on the major road when he saw the first defendant 75 yards away approaching the crossroads on the minor road at about 50 mph. The second defendant drove steadily on without paying any attention to the first defendant. In the resulting collision, the plaintiff was injured and both defendants were held liable on the basis of 80 per cent for the first defendant and 20 per cent for the second defendant.

(6) *Crawford* v *Jennings* [1982] CLY 516. The defendant attempted to emerge from the minor road into the major road and turn right. The vehicle on the nearside lane of the main road flashed their lights indicating that the defendant should cross in front of him. The defendant very slowly edged out and stopped when the front of his car was some six inches to one foot outside of the stationary vehicle. The plaintiff, travelling at between 20 to 28 mph down the clear offside lane, collided with the defendant. The Court of Appeal dismissed an appeal by the defendant who was found wholly to blame for the accident.

(7) *Vulcano* v *Benitez* [1983] CLY 2561. The plaintiff rode his bicycle at 10 to 15 mph between slow moving cars and a line of parked cars, there being no parked cars for a distance of three car lengths before a junction with a minor road. While the plaintiff was passing on the inside available lane, the defendant turned from the minor road into the major road. The plaintiff succeeded but was held to be 25 per cent liable by the Supreme Court of British Columbia.

(b) Legal principles

Some statements of law ought nevertheless to be derived from these and similar cases, even starting from the principle that each case turns upon its own facts. For instance, the flashing of headlights has only one meaning— like sounding your horn, it lets another road user know you are there. Headlights should not be flashed for any other reason than this (see r 122 of the Highway Code). In *Clarke* v *Winchurch* (see above) publication of the intended change to the Highway Code was brought to the notice of the Court of Appeal (at p 282 H). Russell LJ commented: 'How the powers that be can suppose that this will override a practice that has in the course of a few years become universally recognised passes my comprehension'.

Another principle concerns traffic moving across the main stream of traffic. Rule 93 of the Highway Code still requires that the driver should only drive on when sure that it is safe to do so. It is respectfully submitted that even 'inching forwards' blindly, cannot overcome this duty of care, and that where there is (or ought to be) a doubt for the emerging motorist, he should not continue. Even so, the motorist on the outside lane of the stationary line of traffic, albeit on the main road, should still proceed with care, and r 84 of the Highway Code still requires that this should be done only when the overtaker is sure that this can be done without danger to others. Whenever there is a break in the traffic on the nearside from which anyone might reasonably be foreseen as likely to emerge, it is respectfully contended that the overtaker should drive at such a speed that he can stop in the distance he can see to be clear, (see r 50 of the Highway Code). In many cases, depending upon the circumstances of fact, there may be an equal apportionment of liability as between the emerging vehicles and the overtaking vehicle on the outside lane on the main road (see *Worsfold* v *Howe* above).

(c) Opposing vehicles

There is, however, an analogous situation where opposing vehicles are travelling on the same road in opposite directions and one vehicle is waiting to turn right at traffic-light controlled crossroads. In *Hopwood Homes Ltd* v *Kennerdine* [1975] RTR 82, CA, a lorry driver began to turn right from the intersection of crossroads when the lights had turned red against traffic coming in the opposite direction. He had seen a car approaching in the lane he was attempting to cross and assumed (it was held reasonably) that it would slow down and stop at the lights; it did not and there was a collision. The lorry driver was held to be not negligent. However, in *Smithers* v *H & N Transport (Oxford) Ltd* [1983] CLY 2527, the deceased was riding his motor cycle toward a crossroads controlled by traffic lights which turned amber as he crossed the 'stop' line. The defendant, who had been travelling in the opposite direction and who had been stationary at the junction waiting to turn right, turned across the deceased's path and killed him. It was held that the defendant was wholly liable and should not have emerged across the oncoming traffic while the traffic lights were in his favour.

(d) Vehicles emerging from the right

As an example of a collision between an overtaking vehicle with a vehicle emerging from the right see *Hardy* v *Walder* [1984] RTR 312, CA where the plaintiff motor cyclist overtook at excessive speed a car on a blind corner on the main road near the junction with a minor road from which the defendant's car emerged without stopping and while the defendant was looking the wrong way. The apportionment of the plaintiff's contributory negligence at two-thirds was upheld by the Court of Appeal.

Interestingly, that apportionment compares with a higher finding of contributory negligence in more straightforward circumstances in *Hannam* v *Mann* [1984] RTR 252 where the plaintiff motor cyclist collided with a car parked without lights just before a junction. The Court of Appeal (with some reluctance) upheld a finding of 75 per cent contributory negligence on the part of the motor cyclist.

If anything more can usefully be said upon this subject, it is surely this. For every case where a principle of law is at issue, 99 others will involve questions of fact only, and accordingly, the importance of establishing the facts as set out in the earlier parts of this work cannot be emphasised enough. Wherever reliance may be placed on old case law, greater assistance is likely to be found in the first place in the Highway Code. In some of those cases the Highway Code was not cited, and even where it was, there may have been subsequent important revisions to the Code.

2   Speed limits

The motoring public has come a long way from the imposition upon it of the first speed limits in 1865, which were simplicity itself for steam-driven vehicles—2 mph in towns (with the vehicle preceded by a man on foot with a red flag), and 4 mph in the country. Research suggests that for the population as a whole the transition speed for predominantly minor to predominantly major injuries occurs at about 18 mph; while the transition from predominantly survivable to non-survivable injuries occurs at about 35 mph (this does not necessarily mean that a non-survivable injury necessarily occurrs at a speed of or over 35 mph). Schedule 6 of the Road Traffic Regulation Act 1984 now lays down the speed limits, having regard to the different types of vehicle and road (see below).

(a) Vehicles

Vehicles being used for fire brigade, ambulance or police purposes are not subject to any statutory speed limit if observance of the limit would be likely to hinder their use for the purpose for which they are being used on that occasion (s 87 of the Road Traffic Regulation Act 1984). However, drivers of emergency vehicles must exercise a degree of care and skill proportionate to the speed at which the vehicle is travelling and in the knowledge that the ordinary road user in a built-up area may not expect vehicles to be driven at that speed. An audible warning of approach should be given where possible. In civil proceedings, the duty of care owed to the public to drive with due care and attention, without exposing members of the public to undue danger, remains unaffected (see *Gaynor* v *Allen* [1959] 2 All ER 644. Nevertheless in that case a pedestrian who was killed was still held to be one-third contributorily negligent. The deceased civilian driver in *Wardell-Yearburgh* v *Surrey County Council* [1973] RTR 462 was held to be two-thirds contributorily negligent.

Certain types of vehicle owned by the Secretary of State for Defence and used for naval, military or air force purposes, or which are so used whilst being driven by persons subject to the orders of a member of the Armed

Forces of the Crown, are exempted from criminal liability for breaking statutory speed limits, by the Motor Vehicles (Variation of Speed Limit) Regulations 1947 (as amended by SI 1954 No 943). A similar exemption applies to like vehicles in the service of a visiting force. Even a civilian car taking a casualty to hospital in an urgent case is within the Oxford Dictionary definition of using a vehicle for ambulance purposes, namely to convey the wounded.

(b) Roads

Where a speed limit relates to a 'restricted road', this term is defined (by s 82 of the 1984 Act) as a road where a system of street lighting is provided by means of lamps placed at not more than 200 yards apart, or a road concerning which the relevant authority has made a direction that it shall be a restricted road, notwithstanding the absence of such street lighting. Street lighting of the kind described may, however, be the subject of 'derestriction' signs on each lamp post.

The table below gives the maximum permissible speed limits for the different types of vehicles on the three main types of road (motorways, dual carriageways and other roads). Whatever the statutory provisions, in civil proceedings Rule 50 of the Highway Code nevertheless provides for the restriction of speed appropriate to the circumstances prevailing.

Travelling within the statutory permissible maximum speed will not of itself amount to a defence against civil liability; but nor will exceeding the limit automatically give rise to civil liability. Thus in *Quinn* v *Scott* [1965] 2 All ER 588, the plaintiff failed to prove negligence against one of the defendants although he had been overtaken at an illegal speed of 75 mph and crashed into a tree that fell into his immediate path.

NB: There is always the possibility that the speed of the vehicle has been recorded on the tachograph chart *if* the vehicle was fitted with a tachograph (see Chapter Two).

(c) Temporary speed limits

Both maximum and minimum speed limits may be provided for by temporary signs under s 88 of the Road Traffic Regulation Act 1984. Temporary speed restrictions for road works or works near the road, or because of the likelihood of danger to the public or because of serious damage to the highway, may be imposed by a highway authority under ss 14–16 of the Road Traffic Regulations Act 1984. These restrictions cannot remain in force for longer than three months without approval of the Secretary of State (unless made by the Secretary of State or the appropriate highway authority).

Type of vehicle	Motor-way	Dual Carriage-way	Other Roads
Passenger Vehicles (inc Private Cars)/ Motor Caravans/Dual Purpose Vehicles			
(1) Under 3050 kgs and not more than 8 passengers	70 mph	70 mph	60 mph
(2) Over 3050 kgs or adapted to carry more than 8 passengers and not longer than 12 metres	70 mph	60 mph	50 mph
(3) Over 3050 kgs or adapted to carry more than 8 passengers and longer than 12 metres	60 mph	60 mph	50 mph
(4) Drawing one trailer (in all cases)	60 mph	60 mph	50 mph
Goods Vehicles			
(1) Car-derived vans			
(a) Solo	70 mph	70 mph	60 mph
(b) Drawing a trailer	60 mph	60 mph	50 mph
NB If aggregate weight of vehicle and trailer exceeds 7.5 tonnes	60 mph	50 mph	40 mph
(2) Over 7.5 tonnes max. laden weight			
(a) Solo	60 mph	50 mph	40 mph
(b) Drawing a trailer	60 mph	50 mph	40 mph

Chapter 15

Lights

The importance of vehicles displaying the appropriate lights when necessary is obvious. But particular mention should be made of when lights are required by law, what those lights are, and the particular difficulties of vehicles parked at night.

1   Lighting-up times

Rule 111(b) of the Highway Code requires the driver of a vehicle to switch on lights at 'lighting-up time'. This is in addition to the requirement of Parliament since 1975 of the use of dipped headlamps whenever daytime visibility is seriously reduced by fog, snow, smoke, heavy rain or any other similar conditions.

'Lighting-up time' used to be defined as the time between half an hour after sunset to half an hour before sunrise. However, with the day divided into two periods of 'daytime hours' and 'hours of darkness' in the Road Vehicles Lighting Regulations 1989 (SI No 1796) these periods are replaced by the periods between 'sunrise and sunset' and 'sunset and sunrise.' The official times will vary from one area to another, in accordance with the regional differences of the times of sunrise and sunset.

The official times may be obtainable initially from the police force for the area in question, failing which enquiries should be made of HM Nautical Almanac Office, Royal Greenwich Observatory, Madingley Road, Cambridge, CB3 OE7. Telephone (0223) 374000 or Fax (0223) 374700.

2   Lighting on vehicles

Lights are fitted to vehicles for two reasons: to enable the vehicles to be seen and to enable the driver to see. Rule 119 of the Highway Code advises a driver to switch on his lamps both at lighting-up time and whenever daytime visibility is seriously reduced by fog, snow, smoke, heavy rain or any similar condition—to see and be seen.

The Road Vehicle Lighting Regulations 1988 have introduced a number of new concepts and terms into the rather complex provisions for the fitting and using of lamps and reflectors on motor vehicles and trailers. The

124

conditions of fog, snow, etc have been replaced by a comprehensive phrase 'seriously reduced visibility'.

Regulation 24 requires that when a vehicle is being used on a road between sunset and sunrise, or which is in motion during daytime hours of seriously reduced visibility, or is at rest on a road during the hours of darkness, then that vehicle must display those lights which are required by the Regulations. Regulation 27 sets out the restrictions on the use of certain lamps, for example front fog lamps and rear fog lamps must only be used when there are conditions of seriously reduced visibility.

Regulation 23 provides for the rear number plate, now called the rear registration plate lamp, to be a lamp included in the Lighting Regulations—as such it will be examined in annual tests. The terms 'side light' and 'rear lights' are made obsolete and the new terms 'front position lamp' and 'rear position lamp' are adopted. A thorough examination of the lamps and reflectors of any vehicle should be undertaken where there are any allegations of a failure to comply with the Regulations leading to doubt concerning conspicuousness of the whole or part of the vehicle or its load at the time of the accident. In most cases the expert should be able to distinguish between a defect caused by accident damage or a defect which had manifested itself before the accident.

3 Parking at night

By reg 101 of the Construction and Use Regulations 1986 it is a criminal offence to cause or permit a motor vehicle to stand on any road during the hours of darkness, other than with its nearside as close as possible to the edge of the carriageway. A number of exceptions apply, for instance for fire, police, defence and ambulance vehicles where compliance with the regulation would be likely to hinder the use of the vehicle for the purpose for which it was being used on that occasion; parking with leave of a policeman in uniform; car parks; taxi stands; bus stops; one-way streets; and vehicles on building/roads/repair works. Section 22 of the Road Traffic Act 1988 prohibits causing or permitting a vehicle or trailer to rest on the road so as to be likely to cause a danger to other persons using the road.

If a motorist collides with a parked vehicle that should have displayed obligatory lights, but did not, the Divisional Court of the Court of Appeal has been prepared to uphold the dismissal of a charge of driving without due care and attention. In *Webster* v *Wall* [1980] RTR 284, a motor cyclist travelling at no more than 30 mph (where the speed limit was 40 mph) with dipped headlights and poor visibility by reason of the night's torrential rain, collided with a car not showing obligatory lights, parked on the nearside of the road, 35 feet away from the nearest street light. The prosecution failed to prove the charge of driving without due care and attention both in the magistrates' court and the Court of Appeal (see also *Jones* v *Bristol Crown Court* (1986) 150 JP 93, DC).

The criminal law set out above may necessarily be relevant in civil cases in assessing the basic duty of care to be exercised by the person responsible for causing a vehicle to be parked at night. So numerous have been the reported cases of collisions with vehicles parked at night, where each case turns upon its own facts, no useful purpose is served here in setting out a detailed list of cases, other than to suggest reference should be made to standard text books. Regard may, however, be had to the following developments in case law:

(1) *Stewart* v *Hancock* [1940] 2 All ER 427. A motor cycle at night drove past a stationary car parked on the offside of the road which was displaying its headlights. On passing out of the beams of the headlights, the motor cyclist came upon an unlit stationary car on the nearside, braked, but could not avoid the collision. It was held (note, in 1940!) that on these facts the motor cyclist was not negligent and that there was no rule of law that a driver must drive at a speed slow enough to enable him to pull up within his range of vision.

(2) *Hill-Venning* v *Beszant* [1950] 2 All ER 1151, CA. A motor cycle stopped because the lighting system failed. While the motor cycle was left in order to do necessary repairs, a car ran into it. The motor cyclist was held one-third to blame and the car driver two-thirds to blame. Lord Denning held: 'The presence of an unlit vehicle in a road is *prima facie* evidence of negligence on the part of the driver, and it is for him to explain how it came to be there and why he could not move it out of the way or give warning to other traffic.'

(3) *Hill* v *Phillips* [1963] 107 SJ 890, CA. A driver using dipped headlights ran into an unlit trailer in the country road which had been left by the lorry driver while he went to get lights. Liability was apportioned equally.

(4) *Moore* v *Maxwells* [1968] 2 All ER 779, CA. The plaintiff driver failed to prove any liability by reason of not keeping a good lookout, when driving into collision with a parked trailer whose lights had just fused. The defendant lorry driver did not think it would take long to mend, and he had sent a mate to the rear to warn traffic. He had not got the lorry on to the verge because it was too soft for the load. He was unaware that 700 yards further on the road was lit.

(5) *Dymond* v *Pearce and Others* [1972] 1 All ER 1142, CA. The defendant long-distance lorry driver parked his employers' lorry at about 6 pm on an August bank holiday on the nearside of the northbound dual carriageway, intending to move it at about 4 am the next day. It was held that the parking of a large vehicle for many hours on this road resulted in the creation of a nuisance but that the driver and his employer were not liable in damages to the motor cyclist who had driven into collision with it, because the sole cause of the accident was the negligence of the motor cyclist and/or because the nuisance did not present a danger to those using the highway in the manner in which they could have been expected to use it.

(6) *Lee* v *Lever* [1974] RTR 35, CA. The plaintiff's lights failed so he pushed his car to the side of a well-lit clearway. While the plaintiff went to

the garage to re-charge the battery, some 20 minutes later the defendant collided with the car. Liability was apportioned equally by reason of the plaintiff failing to display a warning sign and the defendant failing to keep a good lookout.

(7) *Hannam* v *Mann* [1984] RTR 252. The plaintiff motor cyclist collided with a car parked without lights just before a junction. The Court of Appeal (with some reluctance) upheld a finding of 75 per cent contributory negligence on the part of the motor cyclist.

(8) *Schilling* v *Lenton* [1989] 6 CL 321 (Australia). The plaintiff who had been drinking and driving too fast on a wet road stopped at traffic lights. The pursuing police car failed to stop in time and collided with the plaintiff. The plaintiff's liability for wrongful behaviour was held to be relevant to the accident and assessed at one-third.

4 Conspicuity of the sides of vehicles, trailers and projecting loads

Accident data shows that there are about 600 injury accidents per year during the hours of darkness in which vehicles collide with the sides of goods vehicles. This is twice the rate of the same type of accident which occurs during daylight hours.

The 1989 Road Vehicle Lighting Regulations 1989 make provision for the fitting of lamps and reflectors to certain vehicles and trailers to improve their side conspicuity. If in the circumstances of an accident the conspicuity of a vehicle is alleged to have been a contributory factor, then the conditions of the lights and reflectors which ought to have been fitted should be examined. The responsibility for preserving such evidence will lie with the person or person who carry out the initial examination of the vehicle. The circumstances of the accident will differ as to whether or not the approaching vehicle collided with the front, rear, off-side or nearside of the emerging vehicle.

(a) Cars

There is no provision for the lamps of cars to be visible from the side although some progressive manufacturers have fitted front and rear position lamps which 'wrap' around the corners of the vehicle and which are visible from the side.

If headlamps are being used then they may display a pool of light on the area of the road in front of the vehicle which in turn gives advanced warning of the emerging vehicle, but street lamps tend to wash out this light.

(b) Side-retro reflectors

According to Schedule 17 Part I, reflectors must be fitted on goods vehicles first used before April 1986 and trailers manufactured before 1 October 1985 exceeding 8 metres in length. One reflector should be fitted within 1 metre from the rear of the vehicle and one toward the centre of the vehicle.

All goods vehicles first used after 1 April 1986 exceeding 6 metres in length and trailers manufactured from 1 October 1985 exceeding 5 metres must have one reflector fitted within 4 metres from the front of the vehicle, one within 1 metre from the rear of the vehicle and additional reflectors must be fitted so that the separation distance between them does not exceed 3 metres.

(c) Side marker lamps

By Schedule 9, trailers first manufactured before 1 October 1990 shall be fitted with a side marker lamp positioned within 1530 mm of the centre line of the overall length of the trailer.

Vehicles first used before 1 April 1991 and trailers manufactured after 1 October 1990 must have lamps positioned in similar positions to the reflectors in Schedule 17, ie, one not more than 4 metres from the front and one not more than 1 metre from the rear, with additional ones between if necessary.

(d) Long vehicles and vehicle combinations

Regulation 21 sets out the provisions for lighting these vehicles and their loads (see *Table 1*).

(e) Projecting and overhanding loads

There is always a potential danger arising from a vehicle colliding with part of a load which extends beyond the extremities of the carrying vehicle. The provisions for lighting these vehicles is set out by Regulation 21 (see *Table 2*).

(f) Use of marker boards

These are the triangular shaped boards which display red and white stripes and which must be fitted to some loads that project over the front or the rear of the vehicle. Forward projections must be fitted when the projection exceeds 2 metres but does not exceed 3.05 metres. When the projection exceeds 3.05 metres end and side marker boards must be fitted, an attendant must be carried and two days notice must be given to the police. Rearward projections between 1 and 2 metres must be made clearly visible (the means has not been specified) and between 2 and 3.05 metres, end marker boards must be fitted. For projections which exceed 3.05 metres end and side marker boards must be fitted, an attendant must be carried and the police must be given two clear days notice. Additional side markers must be fitted for any forward projection exceeding 4.5 metres or a rearward one exceeding 5 metres. All marker boards must be adequately illuminated at night.

TABLE 1

Item No.	Vehicle or combination of vehicles	Side marker lamps
1	A vehicle or a combination of vehicles the overall length of which (including any load) exceeds 18.3 m.	There shall be fitted– *(a)* one lamp no part of the light-emitting surface of which is more than 9.15 m from the foremost part of the vehicle or vehicles (in either case inclusive of any load); *(b)* one lamp no part of the light-emitting surface of which is more than 3.05 m from the rearmost part of the vehicle or vehicles (in either case inclusive of any load); and *(c)* such other lamps as are required to ensure that not more than 3.05 m separates any part of the light-emitting surface of one lamp and any part of the light-emitting surface of the next lamp.
2	A combination of vehicles the overall length of which (including any load) exceeds 12.2 m but does not exceed 18.3 m and carrying a load supported by any two of the vehicles but not including a load carried by an articulated vehicle.	There shall be fitted– *(a)* one lamp no part of the light-emitting surface of which is forward of, or more than 1530 mm rearward of, the rearmost part of the drawing vehicle; and *(b)* if the supported load extends more than 9.15 m rearward of the rearmost part of the drawing vehicle, one lamp no part of the light-emitting surface of which is forward of, or more than 1530 mm rearward of, the centre of the length of the load.

TABLE 2

Item No.	Conditions	Requirements
1	A trailer which is not fitted with front position lamps and which projects laterally on any side so that the distance from the outermost part of the projection to the outermost part of the illuminated area of the obligatory front position lamp on that side fitted to any preceding vehicle in the combination exceeds 400 mm.	A lamp showing white light to the front shall be fitted to the trailer so that the outermost part of the illuminated area is not more than 400 mm from the outermost projection of the trailer. The installation and performance requirements relating to front position lamps do not apply to any such lamp.
2	A trailer which is not fitted with front position lamps and which carries a load or equipment which projects laterally on any side of the trailer so that the distance from the outermost projection of the load or equipment to the outermost part of the illuminated area of the obligatory front position lamp on that side fitted to any preceding vehicle in the combination exceeds 400 mm.	A lamp showing white light to the front shall be fitted to the trailer or the load or equipment so that the outermost part of the illuminated area is not more than 400 mm from the outermost projection of the load or equipment. The installation and performance requirements relating to front position lamps do not apply to any such lamp.
3	A vehicle which carries a load or equipment which projects laterally on any side of the vehicle so that the distance from the outermost part of the load or equipment to the outermost part of the illuminated area of the obligatory front or rear position lamp on that side exceeds 400 mm.	Either– *(a)* the obligatory front or rear position lamp shall be transferred from the vehicle to the load or equipment to which must also be attached a white front or a red rear reflecting device; or *(b)* an additional front or rear position lamp and a white front or a red rear reflecting device shall be fitted to the vehicle, load or equipment. All the installation, performance and maintenance requirements relating to front or rear position lamps shall in either case be complied with except that for the purpose of

determining the lateral position of such lamps and reflecting devices any reference to the vehicle shall be taken to include the load or equipment except special equipment on a vehicle fitted with a movable platform or the jib of any crane.

4	A vehicle which carries a load or equipment which projects beyond the rear of the vehicle or, in the case of a combination of vehicles, beyond the rear of the rearmost vehicle in the combination, more than– *(a)* 2 m in the case of an agricultural vehicle or a vehicle carrying a fire escape; or *(b)* 1 m in the case of any other vehicle.	An additional rear lamp capable of showing red light to the rear and a red reflecting device, both of which are visible from a reasonable distance, shall be fitted to the vehicle or the load in such a position that the distance between the lamp and the reflecting device, and the rearmost projection of the load or equipment does not exceed 2 m in the case mentioned in sub-paragraph *(a)* in column 2 of this item or 1 m in any other case. The installation and performance requirements relating to rear position lamps do not apply to any such additional lamp.
5	A vehicle which carries a load or equipment which projects beyond the front of the vehicle more than– *(a)* 2 m in the case of an agricultural vehicle or a vehicle carrying a fire escape; or *(b)* 1 m in the case of any other vehicle.	An additional front lamp capable of showing white light to the front and a white reflecting device, both visible from a reasonable distance, shall be fitted to the vehicle or the load in such a position that the distance between the lamp and the reflecting device, and the foremost projection of the load or equipment, does not exceed 2 m in the case mentioned in sub-paragraph *(a)* in column 2 of this item or 1 m in any other case. The installation and performance requirements relating to front position lamps and front retro reflectors do not apply to any such additional lamp and reflecting device.

6	A vehicle which carries a load or equipment which obscures any obligatory lamp, reflector or rear marking.	Either–
		(a) the obligatory lamp, reflector or rear marking shall be transferred to a position on the vehicle, load or equipment where it is not obscured; or
		(b) an additional lamp, reflector or rear marking shall be fitted to the vehicle, load or equipment. All the installation, performance and maintenance requirements relating to obligatory lamps, reflectors or rear markings shall in either case be complied with.

Chapter 16

Miscellaneous Hazards

1 Builders' skips

The lawful positioning of builders' skips is governed by statute and litigation arising from collision with skips is surprisingly frequent. Skips may pose a particular hazard. Usually constructed from steel plate, reinforced by steel-boxed sections, a loaded skip may have an inert mass of some ten tonnes. Their angular construction is of particular danger to anyone who has the misfortune to collide with one.

Their use became increasingly prevalent from the 1960's and expanded to include the collection of many kinds of waste as well as builders' rubble. Many were sited off the road, but it became common practice for them to be left on roads or footpaths to facilitate their positioning, loading, and subsequent removal. Legislation was therefore introduced to control the siting of skips and the steps to be taken to make them readily visible by markings and lights.

(a) The criminal law

Section 139 of the Highways Act 1980 makes provision for the depositing of builders' skips on the highway. A 'builder's skip' is defined as a container designed to be carried on a road vehicle and to be placed on the highway or other land for the storage of builder's materials, or for the removal and disposal of builder's rubble, waste, household and other rubbish or earth.

The hirer himself may fall within the definition of an 'owner' where the skip is hired for not less than one month or is hired under a hire purchase agreement. It is a criminal offence to be the owner of a builder's skip which has been deposited on the highway without permission in writing from the highways authority. Conditions may be imposed upon that written permission. The skip must then be:

(1) clearly and indelibly marked with the name, address and telephone number of the 'owner';

(2) marked with a specific warning mark;

(3) properly lit at night; and

(4) removed as soon as practicable after the skip has been filled.

The Builder's Skips (Markings) Regulations 1984 provide for skips to be fitted with the type of markings with which certain goods vehicles have had to be fitted, ie the diagonally broad striped plates of red fluorescent material and yellow reflecting material.

It is a defence to a criminal charge under s 139 if the commission of the offence was due to the act or default of another and that the defendant took all reasonable precautions and exercised all due diligence to avoid the commission of the offence (s 139(6) of the 1980 Act). For the defence to apply, notice must be given to the prosecutor seven clear days before the hearing, identifying or assisting in the identification of the other person, so far as it is possible so to do.

Under s 140 of the Highways Act 1980, a highways authority or a policeman in uniform may require the owner of a skip to remove or reposition it. Failure to comply with the request is a criminal offence and the highways authority or a policeman may remove the skip and recover the expenses from the owner. A request made by a telephone and not by a visit to remove or reposition the skip is insufficient: *R* v *Worthing Justices ex p Waste Management* (1989) RTR 131 DC.

(b) Civil litigation

Following upon *Dymond* v *Pearce* (see p 126) there have been three cases which serve to illustrate potential litigation risks.

(1) *Wills* v *Martin* [1972] RTR 368. It was suggested (*obiter dicta*) that a plaintiff driver could be liable for 100 per cent negligence, even if there was a badly lit skip at night.

(2) *Drury* v *Camden LBC* [1972] RTR 591. The skip was not lit at night, but by reason of the lack of care of the plaintiff the damages were reduced by 50 per cent for his negligence in colliding with it.

(3) *Saper* v *Hungate* [1972] RTR 380. On collision with an unlit skip the contributory negligence was assessed at 40 per cent.

Finally, *Photograph 15* (taken in January 1986) shows a skip deposited in the highway which has not been fitted with any reflective markings. Neither have the ends been coated with paint for the purpose of making it immediately visible to oncoming traffic. Where no provision is made to attach a red light to each corner during the hours of darkness these unlit obstructions are a potential hazard to other road users.

2   Negligent opening of vehicle doors

Regulation 105 of the Motor Vehicles (Construction and Use) Regulations 1986 makes it an offence to cause or permit any door of a motor vehicle or trailer to be opened on a road so as to cause injury or danger to any person (*Photograph 16*). It is open to a criminal court to find as a fact that the opening of a vehicle door did not cause danger, for instance if the driver of the stationary vehicle took all reasonable precautions and the danger was in fact occasioned by the overtaking vehicle (see *Sever* v *Duffy* [1977] RTR 429).

Rule 128 of the Highway Code provides: 'Before opening any door of a

Photograph 15

Photograph 16

vehicle make sure there is no one on the road, pavement or footpath close enough to be hit by the door. Be particularly careful about cyclists and motor cyclists. Get out on the side nearer the kerb whenever you can and make sure that your passengers (especially children) do so too.'

In civil cases the negligence of the opener of the door is usually self-evident. Where cases are contested, it is to be noted that reliance should be placed upon the Highway Code, for a breach of this type of statutory regulation (see Chapter 10) has been held not to give rise to a civil remedy (see *Barkway* v *South Wales Transport* [1950] 1 All ER 392, HL). Regulation 71 of the Motor Vehicles (Construction and Use) Regulations 1941 required all the tyres of a motor vehicle to be maintained in such a condition as to be free from any defect which might in any way cause danger. An accident occurred because the respondents' bus tyre burst. It was held that a breach of this regulation gave no right of action to persons injured by a breach of it (but the appellant succeeded by proving negligent tyre care).

3   Drivers in convoy

The convoy referred to here may be one formally constituted, for instance by the armed services, or informally arranged by way of a family or social agreement. The problems arising may stem from:

(1) the leader being expected to take the correct route so that the others following by arrangement do so to their detriment when the leader makes a mistaken turn; and

(2) from the vehicles driving too close together.

(a) The Correct route

The leader owes a duty of care to those whom he has agreed to lead to drive along the agreed or safe route. Where the leader deviates and leads the follower on to rough ground who then sustains injury, the leader will be liable (see *Sharp* v *Avery* [1938] 4 All ER 85, CA). A finding of contributory negligence may well arise, and in *Smith* v *Harris* [1939] 3 All ER 960, CA, the leader and the led were found equally at fault.

(b) Driving too close

Where the problem of driving too close arises, the 'convoy' may also include others who have joined a string of traffic other than by design, for instance because of fog or the nature of a narrow road. The risk of each vehicle in the convoy driving too close together is enhanced as each driver seeks to keep the next in proximity. Rule 50 of the Highway Code requires the driver to be able to stop within the distance he can see to be clear and to leave enough space so as to be able to pull up safely if the vehicle in front slows down or stops suddenly. These rules may, however, be the unrealistic counsel of perfection. In an extreme case, the driver obeying these rules might find other vehicles overtaking and filling the gap so carefully created that he drops back further to find the same result. Depending upon the particular facts, the Divisional Court has upheld acquittals of driving without due care and attention (see *Scott* v *Warren* [1974] RTR 104 and *Jarvis* v *Fuller* [1974] RTR 160), and the civil courts have dismissed plaintiffs' cases of negligence against drivers in breach of these two rules (see *Wooller* v *LTB* [1976] RTR 206, CA and *Parnell* v *MPDR* [1976] RTR 201).

The appropriate test to apply, whether in criminal cases of driving without due care or civil cases of negligence, may be found in the judgment of Lord Cooper in *Brown & Lynn* v *Western Scottish Motor Traction Co Ltd* 1945 SC 31, Ct of Sess (and adopted subsequently by English Courts):

'The distance which should separate two vehicles travelling one behind the other must depend upon many variable factors—their speed, the nature of the locality, the other traffic present or to be expected, the opportunity available to the following driver of commanding a view ahead of the leading vehicle, the distance within which the following vehicle can be pulled up, and many other things. The following driver is in my view bound, so far as reasonably possible, to take up such a position and to drive in such a fashion as will enable him to deal successfully with all traffic exigencies reasonably to be anticipated; but whether he has fulfilled this duty must in every case be a question of fact whether, on any emergency disclosing itself, the following driver acted with the alertness, skill and judgment reasonably to be expected in the circumstances.'

The following cases serve by way of example:

(1) *Jungnickel* v *Laing* (1966) 111 SJ 19, CA. The leading driver was not negligent for suddenly slowing down in the slow lane of the M1 at night and the following driver was wholly at fault when the two collided.

(2) *Thomson* v *Spedding* [1973] RTR 312, CA. The defendant stopped suddenly preparatory to turning right. The first vehicle behind stopped in time but the plaintiff following on a moped did not. The plaintiff and defendant were found equally to blame.

4 Horses and road accidents

Road accidents on the highway, may, of course be caused by all sorts of animals in addition to horses, but horses are singled out for particular reference here because of the high proportion of claims involving them, the likelihood of (usually expensive) claims concerning not only them but those accompanying them (unlike dogs, sheep or cattle), and the lack of any readily available work of reference that deals with them in relation to road traffic and related accidents.

Research by the British Horse Society has shown that on average every day there are eight road accidents involving horses and motor vehicles. This is nearly 3,000 accidents per year. This involves the instant death of at least a dozen riders and 100 horses. Perhaps contrary to expectation, the instance of such accidents is greatest in areas of denser population. Their riders may well do another job of work which means that weekends, early mornings and late evenings are frequently the only times that the riders are able to exercise their horses, and about which they have little choice. It is therefore no surprise that the British Horse Society identifies the autumn and winter, when nights are drawing in and visibility is often bad, as the worst seasons for accidents involving horses. Because a horse may weigh as much as a racing car, with a capacity for doing something as unexpected as a child in the street, but with a greater capacity of being frightened by moving objects passing close to it at speed, the duty of care of all concerned must be heightened.

(a) Horses and other traffic

When a horse is present upon the highway, the capacity for and opportunity of creating a danger is heightened. A bright colour, flashing lights, a sudden noise, waving passengers, the flapping of luggage-rack covers, or aerials with fluttering pennants may all cause a horse to act in panic. The sudden noise may only be a loud car radio or cassette, or even the acceleration of a vehicle which has slowed down on approach of the horse in consideration of it (and worse still, has the horn sounded to acknowledge consideration on the part of the rider). But it is also important to remember that a totally silent approach to a horse from behind can be dangerous, for instance when a cyclist or coasting vehicle suddenly appears within the field of perception of the horse. Even a road-user striving to strike a balance between too much and too little noise may discover that the pistol-shot sound of cracking ice, water splashing from a puddle, or the shot-gun effect of stones spraying from the tyres on a freshly gritted road causes a horse to precipitate an accident.

Rules 68 and 87 of the Highway Code require road users to go slowly when driving past animals, to give them plenty of room, and to be ready to stop if necessary (*Photograph 17*). The AA suggests the safest maximum passing speed is 15 mph. This is in addition to the Highway Code requiring them not to frighten animals by sounding the horn or revving the engine, to keep a watch out for animals being led on the side of the road, and to appreciate danger when approaching a left-hand bend.

A driver of a vehicle might find it tempting to argue that a horse should be kept off a carriageway wherever there is a pedestrian footpath on which it can be led or ridden. However, this is illegal and contrary to s 72 of the Highway Act 1835, which explains why Rule 149 of the Highway Code states '. . . you must not ride, lead or drive a horse on a footpath or pavement by the side of a road'. Of course, the position is different if there is a recognised bridle path or 'adequate grass or other margins' which the Highways Authority has a duty to provide (s 71 of the Highways Act 1980) '. . . where they consider the provision of margins necessary or desirable for the safety or accommodation of ridden horses and driven livestock . . .'.

If a horse is being led, should the leader walk on the righthand side of the road towards the oncoming traffic (as would be appropriate for an unaccompanied pedestrian and in accordance with Rule 2 of the Highway

Photograph 17

Code), or on the nearside, in the direction of the traffic (perhaps by analogy with Rule 5 of the Highway Code, which requires this for a group of people marching on the road)? Surprisingly, s 72 of the Highway Act 1835 makes it an offence not to lead or ride a horse on the nearside of the road. In *Phillips* v *Britannia Hygenic Laundry Co* [1923] 1 KB at p 548, it was held that a breach of this section did not necessarily give rise to civil liability (no doubt having regard to the increased prevalance of motorised traffic). The AA does, however, advise that horses being ridden or led should always travel on the lefthand side of the road (see 'Road Sense: About Horses on the Highway').

(b) Horses and their owners

Where horses (or other animals) stray from unfenced land onto the highway, their owners are protected from a claim in negligence by s 8(2) of the Animals Act 1971, if the animal had been placed onto and strayed from common land or land situated in an area where fencing is not customary or from a town or village green and the owner had a right to place the animal on that land. This is now all that is left from the common law principle confirmed by the House of Lords in *Searle* v *Wallbank* [1947] AC 341.

Where an animal strays in other circumstances, the person responsible for the horses must exercise a duty of care such as is reasonable to see that damage is not caused by animals straying onto the highway. Section 2(2) of the Animals Act 1971 provides for liability where:

(a) the damage is of a kind which the animal, unless restrained, was likely to cause, or which, if caused by the animal was likely to be severe; and
(b) the likelihood of the damage or of its being severe was due to characteristics of the animal which are not normally found in animals of the same species or are not normally to be found except at particular times or in particular circumstances; and
(c) those characteristics were known to that keeper or were at any time known to a person who at that time had charge of the animal as that keeper's servant or, where that keeper is the head of a household and were known to another keeper of the animal who is a member of that household and under the age of 16.

Negligence cannot be established merely by proof that the owner of a tame animal of mild disposition has failed to provide against the possibility that it will do something contrary to its ordinary nature. This statement of the law by Du Parq LJ in *Aldham* v *United Dairies (London) Ltd* [1941] K B at p 514, is still considered to be good law. However, in *Burns* v *Ellicott* (1969) 113 SJ 490, Paull J found the defendant vehicle driver negligent in attempting to pass a horse travelling in the same direction while a vehicle was travelling in the opposite direction on a narrow road. The duty of the driver was to slow down and give the horse a wide berth, and if he could not do that because the vehicle was coming in the other direction, his duty was to wait until the other car had passed. In *Haimes* v *Watson* [1981] RTR 90. The plaintiff was riding his horse along the nearside of a country road. As the defendant overtook, the horse moved across the road and collided with it broadside. While the fact of the horse moving as it did called for an explanation, in the absence of any evidence that the plaintiff knew that the horse might behave as it did, the explanation of the plaintiff sufficed that unexpectedly the horse had shied and control had been lost temporarily. Similarly, in *Carryfast* v *Hack* [1981] RTR 464. Gibson J held an overtaking motorist entirely to blame when a nervous part-thoroughbred horse ridden on the verge began to 'dance' in traffic, as it was wont to do. The rider was, however, an experienced and skilled horsewoman and considered that she could control it, as she had been able to do in the past. As the horse began to take fright, the motorist thought that the horse might veer into the road, so he braked hard and veered away from the nearside into an oncoming lorry. The horse rider was acquitted of any negligence on the basis that the sole cause of the accident was the overtaking motorist's failure initially to slow down and give clearance to the horse, and to stop if necessary. Per Ralph Gibson J:

'I would comment that in the ordinary experience of most people who use the road, both in a car or on a bicycle, there appears to be a wholly false belief held by many motorists that they are entitled to proceed without being required to slow down by slower traffic such as bicycles or horses. I would merely wish to emphasise that this is a wholly false belief since slow traffic on an ordinary road has a right to be there ... I would say that it is certainly not negligent of a rider to go on a highway on a horse simply because the rider knew that the horse did not like some traffic noises and may on occasion act as if unsettled and unhappy and in such a way that the rider must use proper skills of control to keep the horse in check . . . A rider is entitled to ample clearance from other vehicles just as is a bicycle on the road, and if there is no room by giving that clearance to overtake, then the driver must wait.'

Carryfast v *Hack* was not however cited in *Wallace* v *Newton* [1982] 2 All ER 106, on the question of liability arising on the part of the owner (albeit in different circumstances). The plaintiff groom was concerned with a horse (called 'Lord Justice') known by both parties to be unpredictable and unreliable during the period it was with this groom. The groom was injured when the horse suddenly leaped or lunged forward. Liability was proved on the facts before the court on the basis that the horse did what it did by reason of a characteristic not normally found in horses (see s 2(2)(*b*) of the 1971 Act, above). These two cases are no doubt reconcilable on the evidence that was called in each case, but one can well see that given other (perhaps expert) evidence, the result in either case might have been very different.

(c) Horses and their riders

Riders themselves have their own duty of care to other road users. However, it should be noted that the code for horses is sometimes different from that required for vehicles. For instance, horse riders wishing to turn right are advised that, having signalled, they should approach and keep to the nearside of the road, up and beyond the centre of a junction, before turning right. Wherever possible, horse riders should make a wide right turn into the nearside of the intended route and they should keep to the outside of roundabouts rather than take an inside course.

Generally, horse riders should have regard to rr 149–151 of the Highway Code; the rider must make sure that the horse can be controlled in traffic and is kept to the nearside, and that a rider's hard hat is worn. The leader of a horse should not only keep to the left, but also keep the horse to his left. After sunset, light-coloured or reflective clothing should be worn, and lights should be carried (eg by stirrup-lights) showing white to the front and red to the rear. Reflective legbands are available, with other safety related items, through the British Horse Society.

While the Road Traffic Act 1988 makes no provision requiring equestrians to obey police signals (as motorists must) such a failure could obviously amount to negligence in a civil case (or perhaps as the result of a conviction of obstructing the police, contrary to common law). Section 12 of the Licensing Act 1872 makes it an offence to be in charge of any carriage, horse or cattle on any highway or other public place when drunk (but not merely under the influence of drink).

There is a horse riding and road safety test organised by the British Horse Society for riders aged between ten and 65. The test is in three parts and usually takes place on a farm or at a riding school. Part one (a) is a theory test on the knowledge of the Highway Code, and of the generally accepted rules for riding on a highway. Part one (b) is a track and turn-out inspection with an emphasis on safety. Part two involves all candidates in simulated road conditions which includes hazards to test the horse such as a man shovelling gravel into a barrow, a parked car complete with blaring radio, dogs, and an open door, a person with a pram or an umbrella, children playing with a ball, a pedestrian crossing, a junction, crossroads and those circumstances which will test a rider's awareness and ability both to give clear and concise arm signals and to control the horse. Part three is the road test which is only taken by those who have passed Parts one and two.

(d) Publications

The British Horse Society (British Equestrian Centre, Stoneleigh, Kenilworth, Warwickshire CV8 2LR) has produced a number of excellent publications, including: 'Code of Safe Practice for Rider's, 'A Manual of Riding and Roadcraft', A Riding and Road Safety Syllabus and their 'Recommended Procedure in the Event of an Accident; (see also 'About Horses on the Highway' published by the Public Affairs Division of the Automobile Association, Farnum House, Basingstoke, Hampshire).

Part Four

Motor Vehicle Loss or Damage

Chapter 17

Damage or Loss of the Vehicle

This book would be incomplete without some reference to the formulation of the claim for special damages arising from the loss of or damage to the vehicle involved. Unlike other aspects of special damages (being specific losses which can be quantified to the date of trial), or general damages (being the other losses claimed), both of which may very likely require reference to more specialised publications, these losses are almost an inevitable consequence of every road accident claim. This will be so for both parties if the defendant makes any allegation of contributory negligence and has suffered damage to his vehicle for which he makes any counterclaim in civil proceedings brought by the plaintiff.

Such losses arise at the same time as the question of liability and may frequently be investigated at the same time, to advantage. They may give rise to difficult legal problems, and an awareness of them at the earliest opportunity is important. Although there is a tendency to leave the preparation of this aspect of the claim to the last, especially if liability appears to be in issue, experience suggests that the sooner regard is had to these aspects of any claim, the better.

1   Compensation from criminal courts

Civil claims may be preceded by criminal prosecution arising from the accident in question. In criminal cases the court is empowered to consider claims for criminal compensation under s 35 of the Powers of Criminal Courts Act 1973 (as amended by s 104 of the Criminal Justice Act 1988). There are however substantial restrictions in relation to compensation being ordered by the court in respect of road accidents. Compensation is limited to damage which can be treated as arising out of an offence against the Theft Act 1968, such as theft or taking a vehicle without consent of the owner or damage for which the offender is uninsured and in respect of which compensation is not payable under the Motor Insurer's Bureau, (see Chapter 18).

The financial limits of the MIB scheme are such that criminal compensation may be ordered where the offender is uninsured in respect of the use of a vehicle for the first £175 worth of any damage and for any damage in excess of £250,000. Compensation may also be ordered where the offender is uninsured in respect of the use of the vehicle and the victim himself is not insured, and further, where the offender is uninsured and the victim was being carried in the vehicle at a time when he knew or ought to have known that the vehicle had been stolen or unlawfully taken or that a required insurance policy was not in force.

There are two further financial limitations on any award of compensation, namely in respect of the offender's means to pay (by reason of s 25(4) of the 1973 Act) and in the Magistrates' Court compensation may not be awarded of more than £2,000 in respect of any one offence (there is no such limit on the Crown Court's power).

Where compensation is awardable by criminal courts, the policy of the Act is that an award should be made 'as a convenient and rapid means of avoiding the expense of resorting to civil litigation when the criminal clearly has the means which would enable the compensation to be paid' (see Scarman LJ in *R* v *Inwood* [1973] 1 WLR 647).

(a) Loss of Value as a 'write-off'

Where the vehicle is not reasonably repairable, damages will be claimed for its loss of value. This will not, of course, be assessed on its replacement value, but rather its market value at the time of the accident. The insurer will almost certainly obtain a report of its value both as it was before the accident (not least to know that it should be treated as an insurance write-off) and as scrap. Either value may be contested and its owner may need to obtain a separate report. If there are records of its regular and/or recent repair or maintenance, or photographs of its pre-accident condition, these should be sought out. A separate statement may be desirable from its keeper as to its condition. If the scrap value is contested, quotations may have to be obtained. Whether the vehicle is a write-off depends upon its market value as compared with the costs of repair (being the reasonable value of parts and labour involved).

A not unusual problem arises where the written-off vehicle is the subject of an outstanding consumer credit agreement: the vehicle is no longer usable but payments are still having to be paid to the finance company. Those payments are not, however, claimable as such, for they do not relate to the market value of the vehicle and the payments due arise as a result of the credit agreement and not because of the negligence complained of. On the other hand, the victim does have an additional claim for its loss of use (whether or not the vehicle was subject to a credit agreement). The valuation of 'loss of use' is claimable as general damages (and will have to be pleaded as such), in a sum to be assessed by the court, if not by prior agreement.

For the victim whose vehicle is the subject of a credit agreement, the value of the loss of use might be pleaded on the basis of the value of the instalments due (unless that loss can be mitigated by payment of an earlier lump sum to the finance company (see p 152, the Australian case relating to this, *Millar* v *Candy* (1984) CLY 1035, and also *Murray* v *Doherty* (1986) CLY 2331) in which a car on hire purchase was damaged and a loss of use was awarded as equivalent to the hire purchase charges. Similarly, in *McKay* v *Jackson* (1987) CLY 1128 a nine week loss of use was assessed at £60 per week in respect of a car used for a 12 mile round journey to and from work and social activities. In *Hatch* v *Platt* (1988) CLY 1073, £60 per week was awarded in November 1987 for an eight week period of loss of use in respect of a motor cycle. In this case *McKay* v *Jackson* was relied upon in addition to the evidence that the hire of an alternative would have cost about £60 per week. In *Luyke-Roskott* v *Cupocci* (1989) CLY 122 £300 was awarded in August 1988 for the 12 day loss of the use of a Porsche used for part of a journey to work, (being an average of £175 per week) and in *Chidgey* v *Crow* (1989) CLY 1168, a nine week period of loss of use by a housewife of her car was assessed at £35 per week in March 1989.

2 Calculating the loss of use

Whether the claim is based upon the loss of use of a vehicle in private use, a commercial vehicle, or a public service vehicle, the method of assessing loss of use is somewhat similar (see above, if the vehicle is on 'hire purchase'). In the first place, it must be established for how many days the use of the vehicle was lost to the plaintiff. Second, the 'standing charge' for the vehicle must be either calculated or estimated. The calculation will be made from known figures derived from records, while the estimated charges can be based upon those incurred by similar vehicles. Usually private individuals do not keep accurate records of standing charges, whereas company controlled vehicles should have detailed costs for planning and taxation purposes. Where estimates have to be used, the AA Technical Services, PO Box 50, Basingstoke, Hampshire, compile a 'Schedule of Estimated Standing and Running Costs' for cars up to 4,500 cubic centimetres, diesel cars, and mopeds, motorcycles and scooters (see below, pp 148–150).

'The Commercial Motor', published by IPC Transport Press Limited, Quadrant House, The Quadrant, Sutton, Surrey, SM2 5AS, contains up-to-date cost tables for the whole range of goods vehicles from the small van to the 38 tonne articulated lorry. Costs are broken down into two main categories:

(1) *running costs*, which are expressed in pence per mile; these include petrol, oil, tyres, servicing and repairs but since these are not incurred while the vehicle is not being used, they cannot form part of the claim; and

(2) *standing charges*, which include an excise licence, insurance, depreciation, interest on capital, garage or parking and also any subscriptions, ie for breakdown or recovery services and other licence fees (these charges are incurred regardless of mileage travelled).

The pleading of a claim for damages for the loss of use of a vehicle will begin by calculating the standing charges for the year and dividing by 365 (less an allowance for days of non-use eg, Christmas Day) to determine the cost per day; then multipying by the number of days in the period of the claim. Some caution must be exercised if the plaintiff is to follow the principle of taking reasonable steps to mitigate his losses. This must be taken into account when any of the standing charges are subject to refunds, for instance insurance and excise licences. Thus, for example, a 38 tonne articulated goods vehicle may attract an excise licence duty of some £2,730 per annum.

The plaintiff has the burden of proving the loss claimed. Some losses will be the kind of which judicial notice will be taken, eg in respect of depreciation, Glass's guide may be a starting point. It may not, however, be specific enough for certain vehicles, in which case the value of the vehicle may have to be assessed by an expert and his evidence served upon the defence. Any photographs of the vehicle before the incident may well corroborate claims of its particular condition.

Petrol Cars

	Engine Capacity (cc)				
	Up to 1000	1001 to 1400	1401 to 2000	2001 to 3000	3001 to 4500
Standing Charges per annum (£)					
Car Licence	100.00	100.00	100.00	100.00	100.00
Insurance	449.44	550.88	647.79	1045.98	1176.33
Depreciation (based on 10,000 miles (per annum)	771.06	1118.44	1441.02	2818.44	3771.12
Subscription	51.00	51.00	51.00	51.00	51.00
	1371.50	1820.32	2239.81	4015.42	5098.45
Cost per mile (in pence)					
5,000	27.430	36.406	44.796	80.308	101.968
10,000	13.715	18.203	22.398	40.154	50.984
15,000	10.171	13.627	16.853	30.527	39.018
20,000	9.171	12.457	15.522	28.532	36.806
25,000	8.570	11.755	14.723	27.335	35.478
30,000	7.142	9.796	12.269	22.779	29.565
Running Cost per mile (in pence)					
Petrol*	4.600	5.257	6.134	8.364	9.200
	(4.925)	(5.628)	(6.567)	(8.954)	(9.850)
Oil	0.457	0.457	0.487	0.537	0.878
Tyres	0.467	0.600	0.725	1.403	1.819
Servicing	0.969	0.969	0.969	1.264	1.887
Repairs & Replacements	4.946	5.236	6.119	9.259	11.507
Pence	11.439	12.519	14.434	20.827	25.291
	(11.764)	(12.890)	(14.867)	(21.417)	(25.941)

* Unleaded Petrol at £1.84 per gallon—40.5 pence per litre.
Figures in brackets for Leaded Petrol at £1.97 per gallon—43.3 pence per litre.
For every penny more or less add or subtract:

	0.025	0.028	0.033	0.045	0.050

Diesel Cars

	Up to 2000	Engine Capacity (cc) Over 2000 cc (Please see notes overleaf)	
Standing Charges per annum (£)		A	B
Car Licence	100.00	100.00	100.00
Insurance	599.33	647.79	1045.98
Depreciation (based on 10,000 miles per annum)	1148.19	1505.52	2471.48
Subscription	51.00	51.00	51.00
	1898.52	2304.31	3668.46
Cost per mile (in pence)			
5,000	37.970	46.086	73.370
10,000	18.985	23.043	36.685
15,000	14.188	17.369	27.752
20,000	10.641	13.027	20.814
25,000	10.350	12.830	20.605
30,000	8.625	10.692	17.171
Running Cost per mile (in pence)			
Diesel*	3.956	5.086	5.934
Oil	0.623	0.686	0.686
Tyres	0.662	0.725	1.403
Servicing	0.934	1.006	1.006
Repairs & Replacements	5.678	6.119	9.259
Pence	11.853	13.622	18.288
At £1.78 per gallon (39.2 pence per litre) For every penny more or less add or subtract	0.022	0.028	0.033

Mopeds, Motorcyles and Scooters

	50*	50*	125	Engine Capacity 250	500	750	1000+
Standing Charges per annum (£)							
Road Tax	10.00	10.00	10.00	20.00	40.00	40.00	40.00
Insurance	60.00	121.00	307.00	507.00	683.00	786.00	1046.00
Depreciation	105.56	159.12	254.00	408.64	523.44	805.39	946.28
Helmet/Clothing	40.00	40.00	85.00	85.00	85.00	85.00	85.00
Subscription	29.00	29.00	29.00	29.00	29.00	29.00	29.00
	244.56	359.12	685.00	1049.64	1360.44	1745.39	2146.28
Cost per mile (in pence)							
5,000	4.892	7.182	13.700	20.992	27.208	34.908	42.926
10,000	2.446	3.591	6.850	10.496	13.604	17.454	21.463
15,000	1.631	2.394	4.567	6.997	9.069	11.636	14.309
20,000	1.223	1.795	3.425	5.248	6.802	8.727	10.731

Running Cost per mile (in pence)								
Petrol**		1.840	2.044	2.453	3.067	3.680	4.089	4.600
Oil		0.265	0.344	0.477	0.503	0.530	0.662	0.662
Tyres		0.388	0.444	0.767	1.122	1.506	1.833	2.072
Servicing		0.975	1.286	1.656	1.656	1.861	2.103	2.103
Repairs		0.496	0.619	0.742	0.929	1.238	1.858	2.478
	Pence	3.964	4.737	6.095	7.277	8.815	10.545	11.915

**Unleaded Petrol at £1.84 per gallon (40.5 pence per litre)
For every penny more or less add or subtract

		0.010	0.011	0.013	0.017	0.020	0.022	0.025

Total Cost per mile—based on 10,000 miles per annum

Standing Charges		2.446	3.591	6.850	10.496	13.604	17.454	21.463
Running Costs		3.964	4.737	6.095	7.277	8.815	10.545	11.915
	Pence	6.410	8.328	12.945	17.773	22.419	27.999	33.378

*50cc Class: The two figures represent, respectively, the lowest priced commuter mopeds and the more sophisticated motorcycles and mopeds up to 50cc.

3   Repairs

Particular reference should be made here to three not uncommon problems, the first of which may be apparent from the start and two which can only be judged when the repairs are complete. First the cost of repairs exceeding the value of the vehicles, second the repairs resulting in a reduction of the vehicle's pre-accident value, however well they are carried out; and third, betterment.

(a) Repairs exceeding the vehicle's value

In applying the legal principle that damages are to restore the plaintiff to his position before the loss occurred each case must depend upon its own facts. The pre-accident value of the vehicle is generally (although not always) a guide to the value of the loss sustained when a reasonably similar vehicle can be obtained. Where the repair costs exceed those of a replacement, damages may be limited to the lesser amount. Even where the damaged vehicle may be something of a rarity and not easy to replace, courts have refused to award damages for more expensive repairs in the absence of evidence of an attempt to find a replacement of the type of vehicle in question which would cost less. In *Darbishire* v *Warran* [1963] 3 All ER 310, only the market value of a Lea Francis 1951 shooting brake was awarded to the plaintiff (who made no attempt to find a replacement which although difficult was possible). The report of the case leaves open the question of how difficult it was to obtain a replacement and indeed how far he should have gone in seeking it. It may generally be stated that in the light of some attempt made to find an alternative, the court will be sympathetic (see *Moore* v *DER* [1971] 3 All ER 517).

Where the damaged vehicle has something about it that is unique or otherwise so special as to make a replacement by the owner unreasonable, and evidence to this effect is put before the court, then damages will be recoverable for the vehicle's pre-accident value even if it exceeds the cost of repairs (see *O'Grady* v *Westminster Scaffolding Ltd* [1962] 2 Lloyd's Rep 238). The fact that the plaintiff has not at the time of trial undertaken the repairs is not necessarily fatal to such a claim (see *Jones* v *Stroud* [1988] 1 All ER 5).

(b) Repairs resulting in loss of value

However expertly repairs may be carried out, it is not difficult to imagine circumstances where the repaired vehicle nevertheless is still worth less than the pre-accident value; there may be some part of the structure not repaired that on closer examination reveals that it is slightly buckled, or some repaired part that cannot conceal the fact of its involvement in a collision that reduces the value, such as a re-sprayed new part not fully matching the rest of the paintwork. In principle, there is no reason why the diminution in value of the vehicle because of repairs should not be claimed. But this must be assessed objectively (for few owners will feel so themselves) and this assessment must be supported by expert evidence (for otherwise the court will have no basis upon which to award extra damages, at least in other than the plainest of cases. In *Payton* v *Brooks* [1974] RTR 169, CA, the principle of recovery of these damages was upheld but the appellant failed for want of evidence of the loss of value).

(c) Betterment

On occasion, repairs may cause an increase in the value of the vehicle, or at least some betterment or other advantage. Where this is the incidental result of the repairs, which would otherwise require unreasonable steps to be taken such as exposing the plaintiff to some loss or burden, there is to be no reduction of the damages (see *The Gazelle* [1844] 2 W Rob (Adm) 279). Thus, some poor paintwork on a wing that has to be replaced and therefore improves upon the old paintwork because of successful re-spraying, will not reduce the damages awarded. Where, however, a new engine replaces an old one and there is evidence that a suitable second-hand or reconditioned engine might suitably and conveniently have been used, it is not to be expected that the greater expense will be recovered.

Where a new part replaces an old one it might seem attractive for the defendant to call evidence of the average life of that part and apportion its value at the time of loss to its remaining 'life-span'. However, this argument failed in *Bacon* v *Cooper* [1982] 1 All ER 397 where a rotor was damaged and replaced by a new one. It was accepted that the part was just over half-way through its average life of seven years, but the full cost was recoverable because future wasting was held to be too uncertain. Had the part more obviously reached the end of its days, the result might have been otherwise (the plaintiff in this case also recovered the extra financial charges of the purchase—see below).

Similarly, a victim may take advantage of the period of repair of the damage done wrongfully to have other, non-urgent, damage repaired and still recover full damages for loss of use (see *Elpidoforos Shipping Corporation* v *Furness Withy (Australia) Pty Ltd* (1986) *The Times*, 28 November and *The Ferdinand Retzlaff* [1972] 2 Lloyd's Rep 120, cp *The Hassel* [1962] 2 Lloyd's Rep 139).

4   Hire charges for the replacement

The vehicle may be damaged and require repair, or it may be damaged beyond repair. In either case, an alternative vehicle may have to be hired pending replacement, resulting in expense which is to be claimed. What loss is recoverable in law will have to be subject to reasonableness and the duty upon the claimant to mitigate his losses. The claim for hire charges may therefore raise questions concerning both the nature of the replacement vehicle and the period of hire.

(a) The replacement vehicle

It should be stated as a warning that it has been held that the claimant's duty to mitigate his loss may extend to hiring a less prestigious vehicle. In *Watson Norrie* v *Shaw and Nelson* [1967] 1 Lloyd's Rep 515, CA, the managing director's Jensen motor car was damaged. The costs of hiring as temporary replacements a Rover and then a Jaguar were reduced by the court to the cost of hiring a cheaper, less prestigious and reasonable alternative: namely a Zephyr. The Court of Appeal upheld the county court judge's decision on the ground that in that particular case there was evidence upon which he could properly have come to that decision.

However, it is now generally accepted that like may be replaced with like, although each case must turn upon its own facts. In *Moore* v *DER* [1971] 3 All ER 517, a dentist who required a reliable car recovered 18 weeks' hire charges while awaiting a new Rover 2000, although an equivalent 18 month old Rover would have been available in about two weeks. It was held that the distance to be travelled by car to his practice and his custom of buying a new car every two years justified the longer period of hire of a temporary replacement. The justification for 25 weeks hire in *Daily Office Cleaning Contractors* v *Shefford* [1977] RTR 361 was on the even broader ground that there was no requirement to shop around to hire a cheaper car from someone with whom they did not normally deal. Certainly, where the plaintiff sustains damage to a vehicle owned by another, for instance during a test run by the repairers, the costs of the hire of an equivalent replacement will be compensated (as was the hire of a Rolls Royce involved in *HL Motorworks* v *Alwahli* [1977] RTR 276 CA).

The conclusion therefore appears to be that if an expensive vehicle is to be, or has been, hired with some evidence before the court of its justification, the hire costs incurred in replacing the damaged vehicle with a temporary equivalent will eventually be allowed. But in practice, the defendant may well put this to the test in court. Because all litigation is to be avoided where possible (with its unavoidable uncertainties, delays and expense), putting a premium on a settlement beforehand wherever possible, the sensible course will be to hire as cheap a replacement as is commensurate with its purpose.

(b) The hire period

The hire period may be delayed by the difficulty in obtaining parts. This may be no fault of the claimant if the instruction to effect the repairs was given as soon as was reasonably possible. However, the instruction to carry out repairs may well itself be the subject of delay.

In the first instance delay will be justified where approval of the repairs is sought from the other party (or, of course, the insurers, as is more likely). There may even be justifiable delay in awaiting agreement that repairs should be undertaken at all, rather than the vehicle being regarded as a 'write-off'. If the claimant acts upon his own expert advice (say from the repairers themselves) and prevents delay by having the repairs done immediately, the court is unlikely to penalise the claimant for not giving the other side an opportunity to inspect the damage. Nevertheless, such a lack of consideration may impede any out-of-court settlement and/or give rise later to an otherwise avoidable dispute as to what repairs should or should not have been undertaken. It is better by far, therefore, to invite prior inspection and agreement as to what should happen to the damaged vehicle, and hire a replacement meanwhile, even if the period of hire is thereby extended.

Where the hire period is due in any part to the culpable delay of the claimant the hire costs for that period will not, of course, be recoverable. But is delay on the part of the claimant by reason of lack of funds to effect repair or a permanent replacement culpable? It is submitted that it is not, at least where the court is not in doubt that the repair or replacement would otherwise have taken place. (Such doubt would not be relevant on the issue of the value of the damaged goods but may be relevant to the question of the hire period, see *Dodd Properties* v *Canterbury County Council* [1979] 2 All ER 118 at p 125 b–c, although the Court of Appeal ([1980] 1 All ER 928) subsequently assessed damages in that case as at the date of trial.) It has been argued that *Liesbosch Dredger* v *Edison* [1933] AC 449 prevents regard by the court to the means of the claimant in such cases as these, but it is now well established that this is not so when assessing the impecuniosity of the complainant in mitigating his loss in these circumstances (see *Clippens Oil Co* v *Edinburgh & District Trustees* [1907] AC 271 at p 471, cited in *The Liesbosch* (above); *Martindale* v *Duncan* [1973] 2 All ER 355 (a hire period of 22 weeks when during part of that time the authority of the insurers of the other side was awaited) and a more recent case, *Stone* v *Fulleylove* [1985] CLY 929, in which a hire period of 17 weeks was proved justified).

Part Five

Litigation

Chapter 18

Finance

Having gathered all of the material facts concerning the accident, obtained whatever expert evidence and disclosable report is needed, assessed liability, and engaged in correspondence with the other side (or the representatives dealing with the claim), the prospect of litigation may be unavoidable. Liability may be denied, or contributory negligence may be alleged, and/or the quantum (value) of the claim may still be in issue.

The prospect of litigation ought not to cause too much anxiety in itself. It should never result in any undue pause in the conduct of the claim, although it frequently does, not least because of the worry of what a commitment to actual court proceedings involves. Sometimes the delay is caused by the simple fear of ceasing negotiations (although there is no reason why attempts to settle the case should not continue during the course of litigation); or an unwillingness to discuss the financing of litigation (see hereafter); or anxiety about what is involved in court proceedings (which is explained in broad detail at the end of this chapter).

At all stages of litigation, delay is to be avoided. Indeed, if civil proceedings are not commenced within three years for personal injuries (or six years for other loss or damage), the claim will be at risk of being struck out as being statute barred under the Limitation Act 1980. Further, once litigation has started, the case must be brought to court with expedition if it is not to be at risk of being struck out for want of prosecution (unless the defendant has condoned the delay or cannot establish some prejudice as a result of the delay).

So litigation is not unavoidable. We turn to finance and pleadings.

1 Financial arrangements

Ideally, the problem of finance will have been sorted out by this stage. However, even if tentative arrangements have been made by the commencement of litigation, the question of finance should be reviewed with realism by all concerned.

(a) The client

Many a wise solicitor will already have said that the first rule of litigation is to get the money in first. The client should be prepared for this. The temptation for the solicitor is frequently to hope that the claim will be successful and that the bulk of the costs will be recovered from the other side. A solicitor may well baulk at the prospect of adding to the client's worries by talking about costs and what may happen if the action is not successful. However, this is a temptation of kindness to be strongly resisted, for in the end it may be no kindness at all. The question of the client's responsibilities for costs, whether successful or otherwise, is of course a sensitive area and one where the professional trusting relationship may appear to be under threat when there is talk of the possibility of losing and a liability for the costs of all parties. The best course to be taken will necessarily vary from one case to the next, but advice should never be withheld on the issue of finance and the risk of costs that might be incurred.

Finance may be available to assist the client (see below), but there may be delays involved in securing it. However, there are some enquiries that can be made to assist a successful outcome in litigation that should not be postponed in the interim. Any delay may prejudice the prospects of obtaining vital evidence (see Chapter One) and urgent enquiries may involve a modest financial outlay before other funds can be secured. The client should at least be given advice about this and the option of finding the small sums required to complete these vital enquiries before the evidence is lost or fades away. For the protection of the professional adviser, the giving of this advice should be recorded upon the file and confirmed to the client in writing along with the consequent instructions received.

In Chapter 10 reference has already been made to litigation being an investment in which either a modest outlay reaps substantial rewards or good money is thrown after bad. There may be dispute as to what kind of sum is modest. However, if the result is successful litigation, all well and good; if the likely result may be failure, it could well be that the relatively small sum expended in early days reveals the inherent weaknesses and prevents greater sums being spent later to no good effect.

(b) Legal aid

It may be that a trade union, an insurance scheme, a motoring organisation, or the Legal Aid Scheme will assist in financing litigation. The general basis upon which legal aid assistance is currently given is set out below.

The fixed fee interview The Law Society advises that many solicitors are prepared to give up half an hour's legal advice for £5 or less, whether or not the applicant's financial means fall within the limits that apply to other aspects of legal aid. The names of solicitors' firms who give the fixed fee interview are in the Solicitors Regional Directory, copies of which are available in libraries, town halls and most advice centres.

The 'Green Form' scheme This scheme entitles a potential litigant to advice and assistance by a solicitor free of charge (subject to a possible financial contribution depending upon the client's disposable income and capital, the levels of which are kept under review, and about which the solicitor will be able to advise or a fact sheet will be obtainable from the

Citizens' Advice Bureau, county courts, a solicitor's office or the local Legal Aid Board itself). The initial limit is assistance up to two hours' worth of work at the prevailing indexed rate (presently £83.50 in London and £78.50 in the provinces), which may be extended upon application.

The procedure for obtaining the advice under the 'Green Form' scheme is relatively quick and simple. The solicitor from whom help is sought will complete the form, which the client signs and which is then sent to the Legal Aid Office by the solicitor for his payment by the scheme.

Legal Aid Certificate A more comprehensive Legal Aid Certificate is obtainable on application to the Director of the Legal Aid Area Office, by the completion of Form CLA 1 by the client or solicitor (or Form CLA 3 where an emergency certificate is required). The Area Director may grant or refuse an application in the first instance, but there is a right to appeal to the Area Committee against a refusal of legal aid.

The Legal Aid Board administers legal advice and assistance (including assistance by way of representation) and legal aid for civil proceedings under the general guidance of the Lord Chancellor. For this purpose, England and Wales are divided into a number of areas. Each has a Legal Aid Office and an Area Committee made up of practising solicitors and barristers. Civil Legal Aid is not available for proceedings before a Coroner's Court or in a foreign jurisdiction, although advice can be obtained.

Emergency legal aid can be granted once, upon application. It lasts only until a decision has been taken on the full application for Civil Legal Aid. The applicant will have to cooperate fully with the assessment officer's enquiry into the financial means and pay any contribution that is then assessed. If it is found that the applicant does not in fact qualify for Civil Legal Aid, or if the subsequent offer of legal aid is refused, the applicant will have to pay the full costs of the case.

Many other countries have legal aid schemes and information about foreign legal aid can be obtained from the Legal Aid Board, Newspaper House, 8–16 Great New Street, London, EC4A 3BN (071) 353 7411.

The decision of whether or not legal aid is granted here will depend not only upon financial eligibility (as in the case of 'Green Form' applications), but also upon the merits of the case which may involve consideration of whether the value of the claim makes the award of legal aid worthwhile (usually the claim must be for more than £500). The procedure involved in applying for this more extensive certificate may take several months. Once granted, the certificate may require a further application for an extension beyond any stated limit such as 'up to but not including the commencement of pleadings' or 'up to the close of pleadings'. The certificate granted may not, however, only be limited to any express limitation such as is set out above and it will in any event only cover costs incurred while the certificate is in force; it will not cover any costs arising before it was granted.

Once a Legal Aid Certificate has been granted, notice of this must be sent to the other side to provide any protection from costs being awarded against the legally-aided party. Once that notice has been received by the other party, even if he is successful in the litigation, his prospects of recovering costs in the litigation may be: (a) nil; (b) limited to the value of the contribution made by the legally-aided party; or (c) in a rare case, limited to an application for costs against the Legal Aid Board as the current administrator of the scheme (since the Legal Aid Act 1988).

A legally-aided party may therefore have an advantage in persuading the other side, which is not legally-aided, to make an *ex-gratia* or 'nuisance' payment to the value of the likely costs involved so as to settle the case for the legal costs which the non-legally aided party will face in any event. The party with Legal Aid does not, however, have carte blanche to proceed on this hope alone. Having proceeded with the case and even proven the claim, the Legal Aid Board still has first charge ('the statutory charge') upon the costs and damages received to pay off all the costs for which the board is liable, leaving the client only with the net sum remaining.

(c) Motor Insurers' Bureau

There are two particular types of road traffic accident where litigation (and therefore the costs of going to trial) may be avoidable or indeed pointless. First, where the other driver is traced but found to be uninsured (or not covered by an effective policy of insurance because the insurers are entitled to deny liability under the policy); or second, the other driver is not traced and therefore no insurance company can be looked to for compensation anyway). In such cases compensation for personal injury (but not for damage to property) may be sought under the agreements made between the MIB and the Secretary of State for the Environment, entitled:

(1) 'Compensation of Victims of Untraced Drivers', dated 22 November 1972, with a supplementary agreement of 7 December 1977 to deal with claims more speedily where a settlement can be arrived at within £20,000; and

(2) 'Compensation of Victims of Uninsured Drivers', dated 22 November 1972.

In each case, the particular terms of each agreement must be studied, for each agreement contains conditions to be fulfilled by the claimant.

Notice is required in all cases. In the case of untraced drivers, notice is required to the MIB (Aldermary House, Queen Street, London EC4N 1TR) within three years from the date of the accident (cl 1(1)(*f*)), and in the case of uninsured drivers, notice is required to the MIB or the insurer, where identifiable, before or within seven days after the start of any proceedings (cl 5(1)). Under this scheme, the insurers of the relevant vehicle(s) will be liable to pay as the 'insurer concerned'. If the MIB require the plaintiff to undertake litigation with a view to seeking an alternative remedy against another who is covered by effective insurance, the MIB should offer an indemnity against the reasonable costs incurred under cl 6(2) of the Untraced Driver Scheme, or cl 5(c) of the Uninsured Driver Scheme.

The MIB may seek to have itself added as an additional defendant where it has an interest to pursue during trial on behalf of an uninsured driver, or an unidentifiable driver and the defendant driver (who is sued and is covered by insurance) denies liability.

Interim damages pending a full trial may be ordered by a court in certain circumstances under RSC Ord 29, r 12(2). One of the conditions is that there is an insurer with a specific responsibility to pay damages. It has been held that the MIB is not to be regarded as an insurer under the agreements between the Secretary of State and the Motor Insurers' Bureau and an interim payment of damages cannot be made against the MIB (see *Powney* v *Coxage* (1988) *The Times*, 8 March).

The potential complexity of seeking a remedy through the MIB means that such applicants should always be legally represented, and a condition precedent to the liability of the MIB for costs is that the applicant must be legally represented. Under the agreement concerning untraced drivers the standard fee from 1 May 1990 will be £175, which an extra £75 for any additional applicant, on the basis that the solicitor's work should ordinarily be limited only to putting the client in touch with the MIB and advising on the time limit. Necessary disbursements will be repaid to cover expenses such as obtaining the police and medical reports.

(d) Interim damages

Once pleadings have been commenced the court may award an interim payment of damages having regard to the likely sum to be recovered at the end of the trial, taking into account any relevant claims of contributory negligence, set-off and counterclaim (see RSC Ord 29, r 11; in the High Court and in the County Court, where the sum claimed exceeds £500, Ord 12, r 1 of the County Court Rules 1981). It is not unknown for such sums to be put to use by a party for the conduct of litigation where an individual does not have the benefit of legal aid. Such a prospect is obviously not welcomed by the insurers who can be expected to oppose such applications, but this in itself is not a good ground for opposing speedy relief if the claim for interim damages is otherwise well-founded. The applicant must, of course, be able to establish reasonable grounds that some damages will be recovered at the end of a trial.

An interim payment can only be made against a person who is insured in respect of the claim (and in this respect, a claim which will be paid for by the Motor Insurers' Bureau is not covered) a public authority, or a person whose means and resources are such as to make the interim payment.

In *O'Driscoll* v *Sleigh* (1985) CLY 136 the insurers sought to avoid an order for interim payment against the defendant driver on the grounds that although they had statutory liability to indemnify the driver, they would be seeking to recover any damages that they had to pay to the plaintiff from the defendant on the grounds that the defendant had breached conditions of the policy of insurance. It was held by the Court of Appeal that interim payments could be made whenever there was a policy in existence which obliged an insurer to meet liability, even though there had been breaches by the defendant of the policy of insurance.

An interim payment may be made in one sum or by such instalments as the court thinks fit. However, the plaintiff applying for an interim payment is not required to establish either any particular financial need for an interim payment or that he would suffer predjudice if he did not obtain it (*Schott Kem Limited* v *Bentley and Others*, CA (1990) *The Independent*, 6 March). To prove an entitlement to interim damages, the standard of proof required is only the civil standard of 'on the balance of probabilities' that the Plaintiff will recover significant damages at trial, and not any higher standard (*Gibbons* v *Wall*, (1988) *The Times*, 24 February).

Chapter 19

Pleadings

1 Procedure

Recent court statistics show that some 20,000 cases were started annually in the Queen's Bench Division of the High Court (where civil litigation would start in the more serious road traffic accident claims) and that this figure rises to over 2 million cases claiming smaller amounts which are started in the county court.

Unfortunately, it is not possible for us to state with accuracy how many of these court cases involve road traffic accident claims, nor how many such accidents give rise to disputes that result in pleadings. It can, however, be stated with some confidence that a significant proportion of road traffic accidents that necessarily involve lawyers will have to result in formal pleadings; and once pleadings have to be started, there can rarely be any confidence that an out-of-court settlement will be achieved (however likely this may seem), and that a trial will necessarily be avoidable.

Upon the first professional instructions to investigate any such claim, consideration should always be given to the prospects that formal court pleadings might one day be required (whatever the prospects of a satisfactory settlement) and the prospects thereafter that a trial may not be avoidable. Because there are so many pitfalls to trap the unwary at all stages of these pleadings, they ought usually to be left to counsel to settle. Wherever counsel is or may be instructed to represent the client at trial, where counsel will have to argue the case upon those pleadings, their drafting should always be left to counsel with the necessary expertise (and, if not, then the wrong counsel may have been instructed). Nevertheless, the following considerations apply to all concerned whose case may have to involve pleadings.

(a) Parties

The parties to a court case may be more than appear at first sight. The obvious parties will be the victim actually involved in the accident (or appropriate representative in the case of death, infancy or mental incapacity), and the person who caused the accident and/or who is vicariously liable for it, such as the employer of the servant who was driving in the course of his employment, or the owner of the vehicle whose agent was driving at the time.

If the victim requires the services of another in consequence of the accident, that other person will not be a party to the proceedings; the injured person must claim on behalf of the other person, for that other person will be unlikely to be within the scope of the duty of care owned by the defendant. Beyond the individual claimant involved in the accident, there may however be other beneficiaries from the litigation who should be made plaintiffs. This category may involve those who have a direct interest in an insured loss. Equally, litigation may be instigated by the insurers and they will be duty bound to have regard to other uninsured losses of those whom they insure. Because the principle is that only one action should arise from a given cause of action, anyone acting on behalf of a plaintiff's insurers to recover an insured loss must have regard also to the plaintiff's possible interest in claiming for his uninsured losses.

In respect of proceedings against any defendant:

(1) It may be attractive to bring proceedings against the original tor-feasor (wrong-doer), in person. Indeed, an admission by a driver of his liability for a collision is not admissible against his employer, unless he had the express authority to make admissions (or the admissions were part of what lawyers call the *res gestae*, see *Tustin* v *Arnold* [1915] 84 LJKB 2214, *Burr* v *Ware RDC* [1959] 2 All ER 688, CA (and subsequent cases)).

(2) It may be attractive to sue the employer as the insured party, against whom damages are to be claimed. Yet the conviction may be against the employee only, thereby reversing the burden of proof of negligence against him only. If the conviction of an employee (but not the employer) is to be relied upon (as in most cases), both the employer and the employee (as the directly involved party) may have to be sued as first and second defendants.

(3) It may be that any claim has to be brought against the insurer himself (as the party most likely and able to pay the damages awarded), for instance under s 1 of the Third Party's (Rights Against Insurers) Act 1930, where the employer is bankrupt, or under s 151 of the RTA 1988 (see Chapter 18).

(4) It may be that if the claim is within the MIB's scheme, undue delay or prevarication may mean that the proceedings should be brought against the relevant insurers under their statutory liability provided for by s 151 of the Road Traffic Act 1988.

(5) Even if the MIB are involved but have an interest in arguing their liability, it may be that they themselves will wish to be joined as an interested party, as a further defendant.

(6) The decision as to the appropriate party to be joined may have to be considered before counsel is, or can be, consulted (eg because of financial limitations). So the above should be considered by all concerned as a possible checklist.

(b) Forum

In some circumstances it may be necessary to consider whether there is an arbitration scheme which does not involve the court under which a claim should be made (see the Arbitration Act 1980 and RSC Ord 73). For the ordinary case brought within the subject of this work, the disadvantages of perhaps having to pay for the arbitrator (as opposed to the free services of a judge), and the inability of any tribunal to provide for an effective and enforceable time scale for all aspects of litigation, may necessarily mean that cases will be brought within the traditional court proceedings.

If cases are to be brought within the traditional court proceedings, then consideration must be given as to whether they should be brought within the High Court or the County Court. The decision as to whether proceedings should be brought in the High Court or the county court must be dependent upon the likely value of the damages to be awarded. If they are not likely to exceed £3,000 (at present), excluding any award of interest, then proceedings should be brought in the county court; if they may reasonably be expected to exceed that sum, then they should be brought in the High Court.

If they are brought in the County Court, then damages will ordinarily be limited to £5,000 for personal injuries (unless there is an agreement otherwise, whether initially or thereafter), failing which, damages should be limited to '£5,000' as a maximum award of the county court for personal injury (less interest and costs), or '£3,000' which is Scale 2, or '£500', being Scale 1 (below which the jurisdiction of the 'small claims court' should be considered). It is not the purpose of this work to set out these matters extensively, in respect of which the current County Court Rules should be consulted, but it is important to comment that the scale upon which costs are recovered by the successful plaintiff depends upon the scale within which damages are awarded, and the scale of costs recovered by the successful defendant depends upon the amount of damages pleaded by the unsuccessful plaintiff.

2 Pleaded cases

(a) Plaintiff's pleadings

The pleaded case must state material facts, and therefore details of the identification of the time, place and direction of the vehicles and people involved, and the road/weather hazards, where relevant. There are certain standard allegations of negligence which will almost certainly arise, and preferably they should be pleaded with reference to the Highway Code (with the benefit of s 38(7) of the Road Traffic Act 1988, which makes breaches of the Highway Code relevant to liability). If any conviction arose upon which any party relies, there must be pleaded the conviction and the date thereof, the court which convicted, and the issue to which the conviction is relevant, RSC Ord 18, r 7A.

The material injuries must be pleaded by way of general damages which generally are not subject to a request for further and better particulars, but the pleading must include the plaintiff's date of birth and ought to include, where relevant, whether the plaintiff is left or right-handed, has any relevant pre-existing disability, or has any unusual aspect relevant to the question of damages upon which the other party should be put on notice.

Special damages (ie those capable of calculation to date), must be pleaded, and sufficiently so to comply with the *Practice Direction* [1984] 3 All ER 165. If provisional damages are claimed in the High Court under s 32A of the Supreme Court Act 1981 (as amended) then the basis of this claim should be made plain. In the county court, s 51 of the County Courts Act 1984 applies. Interest on damages should always be claimed, with details where any 'commercial' or other specific rate is to be claimed.

(b) Defendant's pleadings

Consideration must always be given as to what to admit, what to deny (or at least, not specifically to admit and therefore to put in issue) and what to counter-allege, so that no other party is taken by surprise at trial, and either have ruled out what is not pleaded or cause an adjournment with costs.

When dealing with convictions, the particulars which must be pleaded are as set out at RSC Ord 18, r 7A(3) namely, as to whether the conviction is denied, that the conviction is erroneous, or that the conviction is not relevant. Any contributory negligence on the part of the plaintiff must be pleaded, whether about the accident, or that the injuries have been contributed to by the plaintiff's failure to wear a fitted seat belt, or the failure to take sufficient treatment and care, or otherwise by way of mitigation of damages (for instance a supervening act (*novus actus interveniens*)). If damages are alleged by the defendant to be reduced by a supervening act, this should be pleaded.

(c) Third party proceedings

The choice of whether third party proceedings are taken may depend in the first place on whether the plaintiff can be enticed into joining a further alleged tort-feasor as second defendant. If so, contribution may be sought as a matter of course. If not, third party proceedings may have to be taken to ensure the involvement of any other party. If the defendant relies upon a separate cause of action, such as the breach of a contract made between himself and another, third party proceedings against the other will be unavoidable.

(d) Requests for further particulars and interrogatories

The importance of tying down a party to a specific and detailed allegation is paramount both to prevent surprise at trial and to show that a party may have changed its story. Frequently, pleadings will usefully be the subject of a request for further and better particulars, and/or interrogatories (and in respect of either, a court order may well have to be obtained). However, in all cases there is a risk of enabling the other party to put its case in order or to gather together evidence not previously thought of or to become aware of some aspect of the case which should have been considered but has not.

The considerations for and against enquiring further about the opposing case are manifold. The important matter for appreciation is that a decision may need to be taken about this, and that if in doubt, counsel should always be instructed accordingly, both to consider the question of what further proceedings are necessary, and to draft what further pleadings may be needed.

Appendix One

Conversion Table of Equivalent Speeds

Speedometers are calibrated in miles per hour with a secondary scale in kilometres per hour, but their odometers are calibrated in miles. Tachographs have a primary scale in kilometres per hour and a secondary one in miles per hour, while their odometers record in kilometres.

Kilometres per hour	Metres per second	Miles per hour	Feet per second
5	1.4	3.1	4.6
10	2.8	6.2	9.1
15	4.2	9.3	13.7
20	5.6	12.4	18.2
25	6.9	15.5	22.8
30	8.3	18.6	27.3
35	9.7	21.7	31.9
40	11.1	24.8	36.5
45	12.5	27.9	41.0
50	13.9	31.0	45.6
55	15.3	34.1	50.1
60	16.7	37.3	54.7
65	18.0	40.4	59.2
70	19.4	43.5	63.8
75	20.8	46.6	68.4
80	22.2	49.7	72.9
85	23.6	52.8	77.5
90	25.0	55.9	82.0
95	26.4	59.0	86.6
100	27.8	62.1	91.1
105	29.2	65.2	95.7
110	30.6	68.3	100.2
115	31.9	71.5	104.8
120	33.3	74.6	109.4
125	34.7	77.7	114.0
130	36.1	80.8	118.5

1 km = 0.6214 mile.
1 m = 3.28084 ft.

Appendix Two

Distance to Stop in Feet

Brake Efficiency per cent	From 20 mph	From 30 mph	From 40 mph	From 50 mph	From 60 mph
2	670	1510	2680	4170	6000
4	335	754	1340	2085	3000
6	224	503	894	1390	2000
8	168	337	670	1040	1500
10	134	302	536	833	1200
12	112	251	447	694	1000
14	96	215	383	595	857
16	84	189	336	521	750
18	74.5	167	298	463	667
20	67	151	268	417	600
22	61	137	244	379	545
24	56	126	224	347	500
26	51.5	116	206	321	462
28	48	108	192	298	428
30	44.7	100	178	278	400
32	41.8	94	168	261	375
34	39.4	88.5	158	245	353
36	37.2	83.6	149	231	334
38	35.3	79.5	141	219	316
40	33.5	75.4	134	208	300
42	31.9	71.8	128	198	286
44	30.5	68.5	122	190	273
46	29.2	65.6	117	181	261
48	28	62.8	112	173	250
50	26.8	60.3	107	167	240
52	25.8	58	103	160	231
54	24.8	55.8	99	154	222
56	24	53.8	96	149	214
58	23.1	52	92.4	144	207
60	22.4	50.2	89.3	139	200
62	21.6	48.6	86.4	134	194
64	21	47.2	83.7	130	188

66	20.3	45.7	81.2	126		182
68	19.7	44.4	78.8	123	.	176
70	19.2	43	76.6	119		171
72	18.6	41.9	74.4	116		167
74	18.1	40.7	72.4	113		162
76	17.7	39.7	70.6	110		158
78	17.2	38.7	68.7	107		154
80	16.8	37.7	67	104		150
82	16.3	36.8	65.3	102		146
84	16	35.9	63.7	99		143
86	15.6	35.1	62.3	97		139
88	15.2	34.3	60.8	95		136
90	14.9	33.5	59.6	93		133

Notes for guidance to Appendices Two and Three

Please note that in Appendices Two and Three, many of the figures have been rounded up or down for simplicity, and should be used only as a rough guide. Any figures to be offered in evidence should always be calculated from the data available for that particular set of circumstances.

When giving evidence, an expert witness will often offer stopping distances from the Highway Code; a typical statement might read as follows:

'The plaintiff was travelling at 30 mph when the emerging vehicle was sighted. At that time the plaintiff was 80 feet from the point of impact. The Highway Code advises that a vehicle can be brought to a stop from 30 mph within 75 feet. Therefore we are of the opinion that the plaintiff should have stopped before colliding with the emerging vehicle.'

However, although it may appear that there is little to offer in the way of rebuttal to such evidence, Appendices Two and Three show how the stopping time should be broken into 'thinking distance' and 'braking distance', following the guidance of the Highway Code.

In the Highway Code, 'thinking distance' has been assessed as follows: the average perception time of a driver is 0.68 seconds; thus if a driver is travelling at 30 mph then the vehicle he is driving will travel for 30 feet while the driver is deciding what action to take; 40 feet at 40 mph, and pro rata.

'Braking distance' has been assessed in the Highway Code as follows: the coefficient of friction between the tyre and the road will be 0.68 and therefore likely to sustain a brake efficiency of about 68 per cent. (The coefficient varies, depending on road surface conditions. For example, a very low coefficient of say 0.15 might occur if the road surface was very icy or wet; the maximum brake efficiency would then be 15 per cent. Thus, according to Appendix Two, a vehicle will brake to a stop within 44.4 feet from 30 mph; plus the thinking distance of 30 feet, the shortest stopping distance will be about 75 feet.

A cross reference to Appendix Three will show that with a braking efficiency of 68 per cent a vehicle will take two seconds to stop from 30 mph; added to the average perception time, this gives a time of 2.68 seconds between the driver's first awareness of the emergency and the vehicle coming to a stop. If therefore, the thinking time is increased for any reason, such as shock, surprise or a complex decision as to the appropriate action to be taken, then clearly the overall stopping time will be increased.

Although the majority of drivers react to an emergency with a panic application of the brakes (and to a great extent the provisions of the driving test require a driver to act in this way and no other when faced with an emergency) a very careful analysis should be made of the driver's actions before attributing negligence to him because he failed to halt the vehicle within the guideline distances set out in the Highway Code.

Time to Stop in Seconds

Rate of Retardation

From 20 mph	From 30 mph	From 40 mph	From 50 mph	From 60 mph	Feet per sec	Brake Efficiency per cent
45.7	68.5	91.4	114	136	.64	2
22.8	34.2	45.6	57	68	1.29	4
15.3	23	30.6	38	46	1.93	6
11.4	17.2	22.9	28	34	2.57	8
9.1	13.7	18.3	23	27	3.22	10
7.6	11.5	15.3	19	23	3.86	12
6.6	9.8	13.1	16	20	4.5	14
5.7	8.6	11.5	14	17	5.15	16
5.1	7.6	10.2	13	15	5.8	18
4.6	6.8	9.1	11	14	6.44	20
4.2	6.2	8.3	10	12	7.08	22
3.8	5.7	7.6	9.5	11	7.72	24
3.5	5.3	7	8.8	11	8.36	26
3.3	4.9	6.5	8.1	9.8	9	28
3	4.6	6	7.6	9.1	9.65	30
2.9	4.3	5.7	7.1	8.5	10.3	32
2.7	4	5.4	6.7	8	10.9	34
2.5	3.8	5.1	6.3	7.6	11.6	36
2.4	3.6	4.8	6	7.2	12.2	38
2.3	3.4	4.6	5.7	6.8	12.9	40
2.2	3.3	4.4	5.4	6.5	13.5	42
2.1	3.1	4.2	5.2	6.2	14.2	44
2	3	4	4.9	5.9	14.8	46
1.9	2.9	3.8	4.7	5.7	15.5	48
1.8	2.7	3.7	4.6	5.5	16.1	50
1.8	2.6	3.5	4.4	5.3	16.8	52
1.7	2.5	3.4	4.2	5.1	17.4	54
1.6	2.5	3.3	4.1	4.9	18	56
1.6	2.4	3.2	3.9	4.7	18.7	58
1.5	2.3	3.1	3.8	4.6	19.3	60

1.5	2.2	3	3.7	4.4	20	62
1.4	2.1	2.9	3.6	4.3	20.6	64
1.4	2.1	2.8	3.5	4.1	21.2	66
1.3	2	2.7	3.3	4	21.9	68
1.3	2	2.6	3.2	3.9	22.5	70
1.3	1.9	2.5	3.2	3.8	23.2	72
1.2	1.9	2.5	3.1	3.7	23.8	74
1.2	1.8	2.4	3	3.6	24.4	76
1.2	1.8	2.3	2.9	3.5	25.1	78
1.1	1.7	2.3	2.8	3.4	25.7	80
1.1	1.7	2.2	2.8	3.3	26.4	82
1.1	1.6	2.2	2.7	3.2	27.1	84
1.1	1.6	2.1	2.6	3.2	27.7	86
1.1	1.6	2.1	2.6	3.1	28.3	88
1.1	1.5	2	2.5	3	29	90

Appendix Four

Record of Interview

Name of Investigating Agency

PLACE OF INTERVIEW _____   DATE _____
TIMES OF INTERVIEW: Commenced _____   Terminated _____
DEPONENT _____
ADDRESS _____
_____

INTERVIEWED BY _____
OTHER PERSONS PRESENT _____

The interview should begin with a statement which sets out to establish the circumstances of the incident, (road traffic accident).

Q1: At about 5 pm on Thursday 8 March 1990, you were in High Street, Barchester, when an accident occurred between a Nissan Micra, registered number _____ and a Bedford motor lorry, registered number _____. You later gave a statement to Police Officer _____. Would you please read a copy of that statement?

(PRODUCED)

Is that a true account of your recollection of the accident?

The opportunity to read what might have been recorded weeks, months or even longer before the interview, will serve to refresh the mind of the deponent.

A1: ...

Q2: With reference to this plan and these photographs (PRODUCED), I wish to go through your evidence to determine if it is possible for you to be more precise with respect to certain parts of your evidence, particularly in relation to distances speeds and positions. This may assist in a more accurate reconstruction of the accident. Do you believe that you could help towards this aim?

A2: . . .

The opportunity to have sight of the locus in the photographs and with further assistance of the plan should be of enormous assistance to a witness who is being asked to recollect an event which might have occurred a considerable time before. The questioning which follows should attempt to quantify wherever a quantity can be expressed. Remember that it is equally important to record the deponent's inability to offer a quantity as it is to record whatever quantities that can be expressed. This will prevent any turnabout in an interview with the other side or during examination in the court.

Further to the essential establishment of quantities, the questions should be put in a sequence which seeks to follow the same sequence of the events of the accident. It is best to try and imagine the accident recorded on an 8mm movie camera. Under astute questioning the deponent will describe what was seen in a sequence of separate frames. The interviewer should ideally finish with a statement which records each and every one of those frames in a correct order.

If a witness cannot remember the whole sequence, the missing frames may be completed by another witness. However, apart from loss of recall there are other reasons why a witness cannot provide a complete account of an incident.

For example, the deponent may not have been in a position to see all of the event. Care must be taken with the type of witness who simply does not realise that in some circumstances it would have been impossible for the whole incident to have been witnessed. Their account does not distinguish between what they could actually have seen and what they believe they should have seen. It falls to the interviewer to separate fact from honest but inaccurate belief.

In one such case, a witness offered a description of an accident, in which she described a pedestrian crossing a road from one kerb to the next, without a break in the sequence. At least two sources of enquiry accepted and recorded this and their conclusions relied on this for support. However, a more diligent enquiry revealed that the incident had occurred behind her back and what she had seen was part of the sequence over her right shoulder followed by a gap of some seconds followed by another part of the sequence from over her left shoulder. The missing 'frames' between the two views, were therefore found to be critical to the analysis. She could not offer any evidence, but in fact, other witnesses could.

In other instances, the deponent may wish to offer evidence which is more biased than truthful. The most difficult part of conducting an interview is to realise that the deponent is deliberately offering a false account of the incident. Again, there are many reasons as to why a deponent should think fit to do this and none more so than the 'birds of a feather syndrome.' In such situations a motor cyclist will tend to support a fellow motor cyclist as will a lorry driver support a lorry driver and a taxi driver a taxi driver.

However, if the deponent is insistent that his account is an accurate one there is little that the interviewer can do about it at this stage. Even where an interviewer knows that a statement is contrary to the weight of other evidence he should record the response as it is given. This at least ties down the witness to an account. In such cases, a note of the interviewer's opinion upon the credibility of the deponent will be very helpful to those instructing him. Should a deponent offer an opinion, then every attempt must be made to establish if such an opinion can be supported by expertise. Proof of such expertise must be submitted with the statement.

The record of interview should end with a signed declaration to the effect that the statement has either been read to the deponent or by the deponent. The record should also be signed at the bottom of each page in such a way as to prevent the insertion of any unauthorised additions. The preparation of a question and answer style record of an interview will certainly save time and should provide a better quality response than one obtained at an ad hoc meeting. While there is always the problem that something which has not been anticipated will come to light, this can be easily accommodated by the provision of space at the end of the pro forma upon which the unexpected responses can be recorded.

Appendix 5

Exemptions from Tachographs

There are a number of exemptions to the fitting of tachographs for vehicles used on both national and international journeys. They include:

(1) Goods vehicles not exceeding 3.5 tonnes maximum permissible weight, (including any trailer or semi-trailer).

(2) Vehicles used for the carriage of passengers constructed or equipped to carry not more than nine persons including the driver.
NB: For national use only, the limit is 17 passengers including the driver.

(3) Vehicles with a maximum authorised speed not exceeding 30 kph.

(4) Vehicles used by the armed services, for maintaining public order or fire services.

(5) Vehicles used in connection with sewerage, flood protection water, gas, electricity, refuse collection and disposal, highway maintenance, carriage of postal articles etc.
NB: From 1 January 1990 vehicles used by local authorities for certain commercial operations are required to be fitted with tachographs. Vehicles used to provide public services which are not in competition with professional road hauliers remain exempt. Similarly vehicles having a maximum permissible weight exceeding 3.5 tonnes but under 7.5 tonnes and used for the carriage of postal articles (except Post Office vehicles carrying letters on national journeys) must have a tachograph fitted from 1 January 1990).

(6) Vehicles used in emergency or rescue operations.

(7) Specialised vehicles used for medical purposes.

(8) Specialised breakdown vehicles.
NB: These are defined as a motor vehicle which is either permanently equipped with apparatus designed for raising a disabled vehicle partly from the ground and for drawing that vehicle when so raised, or which is not equipped to carry any load other than articles required for the operation of, or in connection with, that apparatus or for repairing disabled vehicles. This exemption is provided by Regulation (EEC) 3820/85, Art 4, para 10. It

is only applicable by reference to the type of vehicle: the particular use to which it may be put on a particular occasion is irrelevant for this purpose (*Hamilton* v *Whitelock* (1987) *The Times*, 10 June). It should be noted however, that this decision relates to the particular Community legislation and is not, for example, referable to the use of a breakdown vehicle under trade licences in accordance with English law, where the use to which a vehicle actually put is material (cf Road Vehicles [Registration and Licensing] Regulations 1971, reg 35 (4) (1)).

(9) Vehicles carrying circus and fun fair equipment.

(10) Vehicles undergoing road tests and development maintenance and repairs.

(11) Vehicles used for personal use or non-commercial purposes.

(12) Vehicles used for milk collection from farms and the return to farms of milk containers or milk products for animal feed.

Exemptions which apply to national operations only include:

(13) Vehicles being used by agriculture etc, carrying goods within a 50 kilometre radius from where they are normally based.

(14) Vehicles carrying live animals between farm and market etc.

(15) Vehicles carrying animal waste or carcases not intended for human consumption.

(16) Vehicles used as shops at a local market, mobile banking, door to door selling, exchange or savings transactions, for exhibitions or cultural events or for lending books or for the purposes of worship.
NB: Such vehicles must be specially constructed/fitted for the use to which they are being put.

(17) Vehicles carrying goods having a permissible maximum weight not exceeding 7.5 tonnes, and is carrying material or equipment for the drivers use in the course of his work within a 50 kilometre radius of the place where the vehicle is normally based (providing that the driving of the vehicle is not the driver's main activity).

(18) Vehicles operating on an island not exceeding 2,300 square kilometres in area and which is not connected to the rest of Great Britain by a bridge, ford or tunnel.

(19) A vehicle propelled by gas produced on the vehicle or a vehicle propelled by electricity, having a permissible maximum weight not exceeding 7.5 tonnes.

(20) A vehicle which is being used for driving instruction for the purpose of obtaining a driving licence.
NB: This does not apply if the vehicle or any trailer or semi-trailer attached

to it is carrying goods on a journey for hire or reward, or for or in the connection with any trade or business.

(21) Tractors used exclusively for forestry and agricultural work.

(22) A vehicle propelled by steam.

(23) Vehicles used for the collection of sea coal.
NB: The exemption applies to the fitting and use of tachographs only.

(24) Vehicles used for hauling RNLI lifeboats.

(25) Any vehicle manufactured before 1 January 1947.

Index

Accident–
  animal, involving, 32
  driver's report of, 32–3
  employer's duties, 33
  horses, and, 137–42, *see also* Horses
  insurance, information concerning, 34
  junctions, at, *see* Junctions
  place, identification of, 8
  police reports, 29–31
  public service vehicles, involving 112
  vehicles, *see* Vehicles
Aerial photographs, 45
Animal—
  accident involving, 32
  horses, *see* Horses
Armed forces—
  speed limits for vehicles, 121–2
Automobile Association—
  horses, guidance on, 138–9

Betterment, 151
Brake fade, 73
Braking efficiency, 62
Braking systems, 71–2
Breath tests, 106
British Horse Society publications, 142
Builders' skips, 133–4
Buses, *see* Public service vehicles

Case law, 85–6
Causation, 84
Children—
  pedestrians, as, 92–3
  seat belts, 102–3
Coaches, seat belts in, 105
Code de la Route, 85
Commercial Motor, The, 147
Compensation—
  criminal courts, from, 145–7
  victims of uninsured drivers, for, 160
  victims of untraced drivers, for, 160
Controlled crossings, 96–7
Convoy, drivers in, 136–7

Corrosion, 73–4
Costs tables, 147–50
County court—
  fees recoverable in, 79–80
  proceedings in, 165
Credit agreement—
  loss of vehicle subject to, 146–7
Crossings—
  controlled, 96–7
  level, 99–100
  pelican, 96–7
  school, 97, 99
  zebra, 94–6

Damages—
  interim, 161–2
  loss of use, calculating, 147–50
  loss of value, for, 146–7
  repairs, *see* Repairs
  replacement vehicle, hire charges for, 152–3
Digital maps, 40
Doors, negligent opening of, 134–36
Drinking and driving, 106
Drivers—
  accident reports, 32–3
  convoy, in 136–7
  drinking, 106
  insurance, information concerning, 34
  learner, 107–8
  offence, details provided on, 34
  public service vehicles, of, 112–14
Driving examiners, 108
Driving instructors, 107–8
Driving too close, 136

Emergency vehicles—
  speed limits, 121
Employers—
  accident reports, 33
Evidence—
  disclosure of, 77
  expert, *see* Expert evidence

Evidence—*contd*
 judicial notice, 57
 negligence, of, 85
Expert evidence—
 braking efficiency, as to, 62
 choice of expert, 57
 corrosion, as to, 73
 county court, fees recoverable in, 79–80
 facts on which based, 58
 formulae, use of, 58, 62
  conspicuity of pedestrians, 70
  emerging vehicle collision, in, 63–7
  pedestrian, collision with 66–8
  speed, calculating, 68–70
 need for, 57
 professional independence, 58–9
 proof of, 77–9
 qualifications, 58
 report, 77–9
 skid marks, on, 61–2
 tyres, on, 73–7
 vehicle damage related to speed on
  impact, as to, 60
 vehicle design and construction, as to,
  70–3
Eye protectors, motor cycle, 111

Finance—
 client, from, 158
 interim damages, 161–2
 legal aid, 158–60
 Motor Insurers' Bureau, 160–1
 review, keeping under, 11
Forensic Science Society, 57, 76
Formulae, 62–70

Gassing, reporting, 33
Glass's Guide, 148
Goods vehicles—
 individual control books, 16
 inspection card, 26–7
 lighting, *see* Lighting
 test certificate, 24–5
 tests, 23–9
Green Cross Code, 91–2

Helmets, motor cycle, 110
High Court, proceedings in, 165
Highway Authority—
 changes suggested to, 8
Highway Code—
 braking efficiency, 62
 breach of, 85
 crossings, 94
 driving too close, 136
 horses, driving past, 138–9
 ice cream vans, 100
 level crossings, 99–100

Highway Code—*contd*
 motor cycles, 109
 pedestrian road use, application to, 91
 pedestrians, conspicuity of, 70
 queue jumping, 118
 seat belts, 101
 speed limits, 122
 stream of traffic, moving across, 120
 vehicle doors, negligent opening of,
  134–6
 zebra crossings, 95
Hire charges for replacement vehicle,
 152–3
Horses—
 accidents caused by, 137–8
 other traffic, and, 138–9
 owners, liability of, 139–41
 passing, 138–9
 publications, 142
 riders, duty of care of, 141–2

Ice cream vans, 100
Institute of Road Transport Engineers,
 58, 77
Insurance, obtaining details of, 34

Judgment, alterations to, 90
Judicial notice, 57
Junctions, accidents at—
 legal background, 117–19
 legal principles, 119–20
 opposing vehicles turning right, 120
 queue-jumping, 118
 right, vehicles emerging from, 120–1

Learner drivers, 107–8
 motor cycle, 111
Legal aid, 158–60
Legislation, breach of, 84–5
Lessons for Life, 92
Letter before action, 52–3
Level crossings, 99–100
Liability—
 apportionment between the parties, 88
 assessment of, 83
 breach of legislation, 84–5
 case law, 85–6
 contributory negligence, 86–8
 Highway Code, breach of, 85
 judicial approach to, 88–90
 previous finding of, 90
Lights—
 conditions at time of accident, 45
 lighting up time, 124
 parking at night, 125–7
 sides of vehicles, conspicuity of—
  cars, 127
  long vehicles and vehicle

Lights—*contd*
    combinations, 128–9
    marker lamps, use of, 131–2
    projecting and overhanging loads,
        129–31
    side marker lamps, 128
    side-retro reflectors, 127
    vehicles, on, 124–5
Limitation periods, 157
Litigation—
    delay, avoiding, 157
    financial arrangements for—
        client, from, 158
        interim damages, 161–2
        legal aid, 158–60
        Motor Insurers' Bureau, 160–1
    forum for, 164–5
    limitation, 157
    parties, 163–4
    pleadings, *see* Pleadings
    procedure, 163–5
    third party proceedings, 166
Local authority—
    road safety programmes, 29
London Map Centre, 40

Marker boards, 131–2
MOT tests—
    certificate, 18–20
    general mechanical condition,
        exclusion of, 21
    pass or fail, limited to, 21
    regulations, 18
    requirements of, 18
    time limitation, 21
    VT30, 21–2
Motor Cycle Road Craft, 109
Motor cycles—
    controls of, 109
    distinguishing plates, 111–12
    eye protectors, 111
    helmets, 110
    pillion passengers, 112
    restrictions on use of, 111–12
    training and testing, 108–9
    visors, 111
Motor Insurers' Bureau, 11, 145, 160

Negligence—
    contributory, 86–8, 103–5
    evidence of, 85
    horse owners, of, 139–41
    pedestrians, of, 91
    vehicle doors, opening, 134–6

Ordnance survey scale plans, 40
"Over three-day" injuries, reporting, 33

Parking at night, 125–7
Passengers—
    drunken driving, encouraging, 106
    public service vehicle, 114–16
Pedestrians—
    children as, 92–3
    collision with, 66–8
    conspicuity of, 70
    crossings, 94–100, *see also* Crossings
    drunken, 94
    hazards for, 100
    negligence, assessing, 91
    two vehicles, run over by, 89
Pelican crossings, 96–7
Photographs—
    aerial, 45
    background to, 47
    camera positions, 45, 47
    distances—
        factors influencing, 44
        road markings assisting, 48–51
    lighting conditions, 45–6
    place of accident, of, 8
    sunlight, 47
Pillion passengers, 112
Pleadings—
    defendant's, 166
    further particulars, requests for, 166–7
    interrogatories, 166
    plaintiff's, 165–6
Police accident reports, 29–31, 39, 95
Projecting loads, 129–31
Provisional licences, 107
Public service vehicles—
    accident reports, 112
    drivers and conductors, 112–14
    passengers, 114–16
    statutory definition, 112

Queue-jumping, 118

Railways—
    level crossings, 99–100
Records—
    keeping, duration of time for, 10–11
    tachograph, 15
Repairs—
    betterment, 151
    loss of value, resulting in, 151
    vehicle's value, exceeding, 150–1
Road markings, 48–51
Road safety—
    local authority programmes, 29

Scale plans—
    costs of, 44
    digital, 40
    examples of, 41–3

Scale plans—*contd*
  ordnance survey, 40
  surveyors, 39
  units of measurement, 44
School crossings, 97, 99
Seat belts—
  child under 14, responsibility for, 102–3
  coaches, in, 105
  contributory negligence, failure to wear
    as, 103–5
  exceptions from regulations, 102
  front seats, for, 101–2
  rear seats, for, 102–3
  requirement for, 101
Sketches, 39
Skid marks, 61–2
Speed limits—
  emergency vehicles, 121
  exempt vehicles, 121–2
  first imposition of, 121
  restricted roads, on, 122
  table of, 123
  temporary, 122
Star Rider Scheme, 108
Statutory duty, breach of, 84
Surveyors' scale plans, 39
Suspension, jacked up, 72

Tachographs—
  breaks from driving, 14
  day, meaning, 14
  EEC regulations, 14–15
  installation and operation, liability for,
    15
  maximum tolerances, 16
  preservation of charts, 15
  speed recording, 15–16
  terms, definition of, 14
  vehicles on which fitted, 14

Tachographs—*contd*
  working of, 12–14
Trailer—
  inspection card, 27
Type approval, 70–1
Tyres—
  defects, 75
  loads and speed rating, 73, 75
  repaired, 75–6
  wheel detachment, 77

Vehicles—
  accidents, in, 9–10
  design and construction, alteration
    to—
    brake fade, 73
    braking systems, 71–2
    fitness, 70–1
    jacked up suspension, 72
    type approval, 70–1
  doors, negligent opening of, 134–6
  lighting, *see* Lighting
  loss or damage, compensation for, *see*
    Compensation; Damages
  replacement, hire charges for, 152–3
  tachographs, *see* Tachographs
  written off, 146–7

Witness—
  tracing, 8
  written statement of, 7–8, *see also*
    Witness statement
Witness statement—
  checklist for, 35–7
  court powers, 37
  examples of, 37–8
  importance of, 35

Zebra crossings, 94–6

A big thank you...

Thank you to the following individuals who have helped make this book a reality:

- Carrie Smith (Little Robins Owner and Manager), Fliss Dundon-Smith and all the staff from Little Robins Pre-School
- Lucy Cooper for developing the book with great support from Hannah Louka, Anna Thwaites and the other Little Robins parents
- Gill Compton for her recipe style guide and layout
- Holly Chambers for her beautiful front cover and illustrations
- Selina Glauert for her colourful book design
- And of course, all the children at Little Robins Pre-School who provided the inspiration for creating the book!

Contents

Introduction: Small beginnings   5

Chapter 1: Getting started   9
- Deciding what to grow   11
- Working with the space you have   12
- What equipment do you need?   15

Chapter 2: Growing our plants   17
- Herbs   23
- Vegetables   26
- Fruit   44
- Flowers   50

Chapter 3: Cooking with the children   53
- Herb inspired recipes   56
- Vegetable inspired recipes   62
- Fruit inspired recipes   70

Index   91

Introduction:
Small beginnings

"From a small seed, a mighty trunk may grow."

A 14th Century saying

Or in our case, from a small tomato plant, a pre-school play area overflowing with crunchy courgettes, gorgeous cabbages and edible flowers grew! I'm so pleased to be able to share our **Grow, Eat, Learn** book with you to show how a small, city centre pre-school transformed it's concrete, rectangular play area into a thriving and blossoming space for our pre-school children to grow, cook and eat their own wide array of fruits, vegetables, herbs... and even pineapples!

Back in September 2020 after the summer break, we returned to the Little Robins Pre-School, an educational setting for 2 to 5 year olds based in St Albans city centre, and discovered a few juicy cherry tomatoes had flourished in their pots during the holidays. When I asked our children "who wants to try one?", all of them, even our most fussy eaters, gave it a try and came forward to pick their own fruit from the vine. Most of the children gave us a large thumbs up and I was delighted to see them go back to pick more.

This made me think...could we extend this into something bigger? ...something our 2 to 5 years olds could benefit from after the Covid lockdown? If we could grow a few small tomato plants, why couldn't we extend our space to grow more fruit and vegetables and even get the children involved in the planting process? What about actually cooking up some dishes with some of our home grown ingredients? At this stage, further lockdowns were still possible - could our children benefit from growing things at home even if they didn't have any outdoor space? The tasty tomato tasting session had shown how keen the children were to try new things, and so in September 2020, we officially kicked off our **Grow, Eat, Learn** project to develop a food garden on site, that also provided the ingredients for our children to cook with.

The Grow, Eat, Learn Project:
Making a difference for all of our children

Through our garden and our cooking we wanted to ensure that ALL of our children had the opportunity to:

- try new things and explore the world around them
- experience the same opportunities regardless of their background
- extend their learning and development in the 7 key areas of the Early Years Foundation Stage (EYFS):

1. **Personal, social and emotional development**
2. **Communication and language development**
3. **Physical development**
4. **Literacy**
5. **Mathematics**
6. **Understanding the world**
7. **Expressive arts and design**

In the space of one year, with fantastic support from our parents and carers, the Little Robins Pre-School staff and children realised some amazing achievements especially in light of all the problems that Covid threw at us. Even with the pandemic, and being one of the coldest, wettest years for a while, I am amazed how everything has come together. I'm proud to say we have a group of children who have been inspired to grow, touch, smell, nurture, discover, measure, recycle, cook, eat... and learn new things! I hope you enjoy looking through this book to see what you and your children can grow, eat and learn.

Carrie

Little Robins Pre-School Owner and Manager

Our Growing Project

Garlic

Beetroot

We are growing potatoes we can make chips and mashed potatoes. - Skyler

We are growing melons at home they are growing very slowly. - Charlie

We are growing tomatoes.

and outside same size.

e of our wberries might hite.

Peas

Plums

Peppers

Chapter 1:
Getting started

Deciding what to grow

After running the idea of a pre-school garden past my team and a little bit of research on the internet, we immediately went to the key decision makers - the children! It was January 2021 during one of our daily Circle Time sessions that we mentioned the idea of creating a small garden to the children and were amazed by the list of ideas they came up with - a pond and a pineapple to name just two!

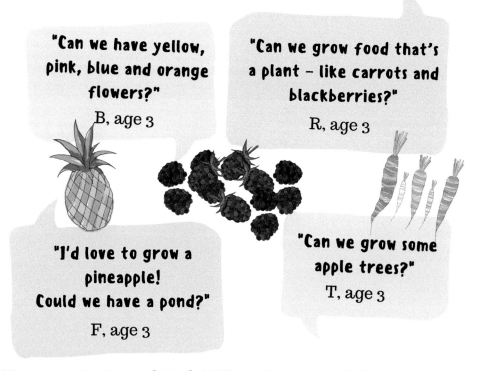

"Can we have yellow, pink, blue and orange flowers?"
B, age 3

"Can we grow food that's a plant – like carrots and blackberries?"
R, age 3

"I'd love to grow a pineapple! Could we have a pond?"
F, age 3

"Can we grow some apple trees?"
T, age 3

With a pre-school now full of children all very excited about growing their own garden, and a list of plants they wanted to grow, we had to get a bit of preparation work underway before we could begin. I wrote out a month-by-month plan in order to achieve our initial list and all of my team took on different tasks and activities such as sourcing containers, equipment and ideas for fun activities with the children. Writing this down on paper, I realised it wasn't quite as easy as it sounded but our project to grow fruits and vegetables did seem to grow quite naturally with input from the children and support from the parents and team.

Working with the space you have

It's amazing where a garden can grow! Our outdoor area is just concrete and the main square only measures 9.45m x 9.75m, so we had to be inventive on where we could plant and be aware of where the sun was throughout the day. We adapted our space as we went along - as the children came up with ideas, we developed redundant spaces for growing. The great news is that you can grow most of the plants almost anywhere - either inside in seed trays and small pots, outside in larger pots or even in outdoor beds if you have the space.

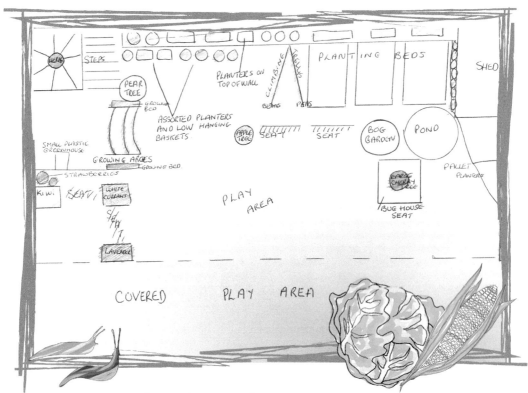

A sketch of our Little Robins Pre-School outdoor space

Every home or pre-school setting is different in terms of dimensions and layout but below are a few ideas we came up with:-

- **Top of cupboard units** - we cleared the top units to position our seed trays at a height that was easy for children to view.

- **Walls** - on the pathway to our pre-school entrance, we used the walls to grow tomatoes against. We also fixed some hanging baskets and brackets at child height for our trailing blackberries.

- **Raised beds** - if you need to create extra space, like we did, it's easy to buy raised beds very cheaply these days from the large supermarkets. These were a great height for the children to peer into and we did most of our vegetable planting in these.

- **Grass Banks** – an unused grass bank has now been transformed into a fragrant herb garden edged with pebbles which could be collected by children, or bought online!

- **Bench Seating** – the pre-existing bench seating had some planters attached where we grew white currants, lavender, and climbers.

- **On the floor** – our floor is now covered with a variety of pots, tubs, troughs and even welly boots that ended up filled with all sorts of plants, herbs and vegetables that the children can wander around during playtime.

- **Arches** – if you don't already have any arches in your space, you can buy cheap arches for climbers like honeysuckle. We hope in time that this entrance to our pre-school will turn into a thriving tunnel of plants to awaken the senses each morning.

What equipment do you need to get started?

- Pots and containers - you can collect all shapes and sizes for indoor and outdoor use as well as biodegradable pots that you can plant straight into the soil (or make from newspaper)
- Seed trays
- Compost - lots of it and peat-free
- Digging tools like trowels, spades and forks – both adult and children size
- Easy access to water - we had an outside tap and garden hose which was very useful
- Watering cans - both adult and children size
- Netting
- Canes or trellis
- Plant ties
- ....and a healthy dose of sunshine!

In summary, although we don't have a large outdoor area, you can see from the photos that by being inventive with space and creative with recycling, we managed to develop enough space to grow plants whilst still having enough space for our children to learn and play.

Chapter 2: Growing our plants

Growing our plants

One year after the children created their list of 'things we want to grow', we now have over 30 different fruits and vegetables, numerous herbs and a plentiful supply of flowers. I would love to say that we planned this all out meticulously, but in reality the children expressed their ideas of what they would like to see and we selected depending on the space available to us.

This chapter looks at what we grew and how we grew it - but also highlights some of the Early Years Foundation Stage (EYFS) learning opportunities made available to the children whilst growing these ingredients. These include mathematical skills such as counting and measuring as well as developing an understanding of the world around them such as exploring the impact of sun and rain on plants. Most of our plants were quite simple to grow and maintain, which meant the children could easily get involved in nurturing them. We have detailed some of the more complex growing processes, but you will quickly get the idea and should be able to easily grow other vegetables, fruits, herbs and flowers.

Keep an eye out for these coloured icons on the following pages as they highlight when and where to grow your plants:

 Look out for what space you need to plant.

 Look out for the best time to grow your plants.

Some plants have grown more successfully than others, but most importantly the children have had fun with the messy stuff while learning - digging, watering, planting, measuring, talking, counting, weighing, weeding, snipping and picking off the slugs!

Activity: Quirky Planters!

We quickly learned that you don't need to purchase lots of new plastic pots for your garden. The children helped turn many unwanted items into planters. These are just a few of our ideas - you can be as creative as you like!

Fizzy Bottles

We asked parents to save large fizzy drink bottles. We used a sharp knife to cut these, and the children filled them with soil before planting all sorts of things they had grown from seed.

Old Food Tins

The school kitchen saved all their large tins and every child planted sunflower seeds in their own named tin. They took these home at the end of term. We also used tins to grow tomato plants. Other free useful resources include old yoghurt pots, old wellies and even strong plastic bags for growing potatoes.

Tip: Don't forget to put drainage holes in the bottom of your container plus broken crockery or stones to stop the holes getting blocked and the compost getting waterlogged.

What will you find in our garden?

Herbs

Basil
Mint
Lavender
Thyme
Chives
Sage
Curry plant
Rosemary
Chocolate mint
Flat leaf parsley
Lemonade basil

Vegetables

Potatoes
Carrots
Broad beans
Runner beans
French beans
Peas
Spring cabbage
Lettuce
Red onion
Leek
Spring onion
Garlic
Courgettes
Pumpkins
Radish
Celery
Sweetcorn

Fruit

Raspberries
Strawberries
Blueberries
White currants
Blackberries
Grapes
Apples
Pears
Plums
Red kiwis
Rhubarb
Tomatoes
Avocados
...and a pineapple!

Flowers

Viola, cornflowers, nasturtiums, lavender, echinacea spider plants, angelica, lilies, fuchsia, oxeye daisies, african violets, sunflowers, geranium, pansies and roses

Activity: Herby Playdough

A really simple but fun activity was making smelly playdough using herbs from the garden. The children enjoyed taking it in turns to name and smell each herb. They were then able to help make the dough and choose what herbs they wanted to mix in before taking it home.

Ingredients:

- 2 cups of flour
- 1 cup of salt
- 1 cup of water
- Herbs of your choice

Method:

- Mix the flour, salt and water together.

- Knead mixture with your hands - you may need more flour to stop it sticking.

- Once in a nice dough, use scissors to chop your herbs and then knead the herbs into your dough.

"E pointed at lavender on his way home – lovely to see them making the connections."

E's Mum

Herbs

This was one of the first areas we planted as it was easy to do and also provided the children with a wonderful sensory experience. They enjoyed touching, feeling and smelling the wonderful variety of aromatic herbs.

How to grow

- Check the individual seed packets to see the optimal time for growing various herbs outside.

- Place two to five seeds per pot or distribute evenly in your herb bed.

- Cover sparsely with soil.

- Water gently to stop the seeds from washing away.

- Indoors, you could cover seed-starting cells with plastic to retain moisture. Outdoors, place a plastic water bottle with the bottom removed over the seeds. Remove plastic coverings once the seeds sprout.

- Ensure planters have drainage holes and provide your seeds with plenty of light.

What you need

- Herb seeds or young plants from the supermarket
- Pots or beds
- Compost
- Water
- Full sunshine and a sheltered position

Inside or Outside

All Year Round

Ways to eat

Pebble Mix pg.57
Sand Salad pg.58
Minty Blueberry Water pg.61
Tomato and Basil Sauce pg.77
Minty Strawberry Jam pg.83

What's in our herb garden?

Chives

Mint

Garlic

Rosemary

Oregano

Sage

Sorrel

Marjoram

Thyme

Lavender

During the course of the year we also grew:
- **Lemon balm** which as its name suggests, is lemon scented and should be grown separately.
- **Curry plant** which has a very strong smell.
- **Basil.** There are lots of different flavoured types to grow, which are perfect for adding to salads, pizzas and pasta dishes. We experimented with a lemonade basil which had a mild, lemony scent and flavour.

Flat Leaf Parsley

Unlike most herbs, it's best to grow parsley in partial shade, where it's less likely to burst into flower.

Mint and Spearmint

Grow mints separately as they are rampant - or plant in a pot! It's also very easy to pick stems of mint and root in water.

Pineapple Mint

Lemon Thyme

Chocolate Mint

Although it has a chocolate aroma, it resembles a citrus flavour when used in cooking.

Sage

The children may enjoy looking at the blue and purplish flowers.

Rosemary

Cut this back each Spring.

Activity:
Potato Printing

A really fun, easy activity that the children can also do at home! Our potato growing was a great success so we used some of the spare vegetables for printing. The children asked us to cut out flower shapes like the ones they could see in their own garden. The children chose their own paint colours and got creative!

Method:

- Pat the potato stamp dry with a paper towel.

- Press into paint.

- Firmly press the stamp onto a piece of paper for about 3 seconds then slowly lift the potato from the paper.

- Repeat to make a pattern - the children can check out their awesome prints.

- You can also print with other vegetables like the celery pictures you can see!

Potato printing photos courtesy of UnSplash.com

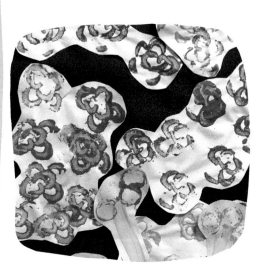

Potatoes

Growing potatoes was a great success on many levels - it provided fun times digging in the soil, plenty of ingredients for cooking as well as tools for craft activities.

How to grow

- Plant 2 or 3 seed potatoes in a bag - any strong plastic bag will do or you can buy specially made bags that can be reused.

- Plant with the shoots pointing upwards so that they can seek out the sunlight and water.

- Cover with compost until the bag is half full.

- Water well and put outside in a sheltered place away from frost.

- When the shoots are about 15 to 30 cm tall, add more compost until the bag is full. This is called 'earthing up'.

- When the potatoes are ready, the children will really enjoy digging them out with small trowels.

What you need

- Seed potatoes
- Strong plastic bags
- Compost
- Water
- Outside space - out of direct sunlight and away from frost
- Keep potatoes in a sheltered place as direct sunlight can make them go green and poisonous to eat.

Plant in Spring

Outside Space

Ways to eat

Potato and Leek Soup pg.63
Funky Frittata pg.65

"Potatoes are hiding in the plant - we can make mashed potatoes."
J, aged 3

Learning Area: Mathematics

Introduce mathematical language

Planting new items in the garden allows opportunities for introducing new mathematical words and phrases.

Shall we dig a 'deep' hole? How 'wide' is the planter? Can you put the seed 'under' the soil? Can you 'space out' the seeds?

Carrots

Once we planted our carrot seeds, we also gave some of the pots back to the children to continue growing at home, which both the children and their families enjoyed.

How to grow

- Make sure the soil in your pot or outdoor bed is damp.

- The children can then help mark a shallow line about 1cm deep.

- Space your seeds out or you will have to thin them out later and this may result in white fly!

- Cover with soil – again the children can help with this.

- Your carrots will take about three weeks to start to appear.

What you need

- Carrot seeds
- Pots or outdoor bed
- Compost
- Water

Outside Space

Plant in Spring

"We are growing carrots under the ground."

E, aged 3

" I grew carrots. I am making carrot soup at home."

E, aged 3

Leeks

Leeks are a tasty winter vegetable for the children to enjoy and we found them relatively easy to grow. If you sow seeds in Spring, the children will be able to enjoy them in the Autumn through to late Winter.

How to grow

- Sow in Spring for harvesting in Autumn through to late Winter.

- During March or April, sow leek seeds thinly, 1cm deep, in rows 15cm apart if outside.

- If you don't have space outdoors or only want a few leeks, you can sow in pots indoors, then transplant them outdoors later. Sow one seed per pot.

- The children can gently lift the leeks from the soil using a fork.

What you need

- Leek Seeds
- Compost
- Water
- Pots
- Inside space for germinating
- Outside space for planting out

Inside or Outside

Plant in Spring

Ways to eat

Potato and Leek Soup pg.66

Garlic

Planting in Autumn provides bigger bulbs than Spring and also gives an opportunity to plant outside of the busy Spring season. The children also enjoyed planting cloves rather than seeds as an alternative way to plant.

How to grow

- The children can break up the bulb into individual cloves. Only do this when you are ready to plant.

- Dig a hole in your pot or flower bed rather than just pushing it into the ground. Plant each clove just below the surface of the soil with the pointed end facing up.

- Remove the flower spike on the hard neck in the Spring.

What you need

- Garlic bought from the supermarket
- Compost
- Water
- Either pots or outside beds

Tip:
Soft neck garlic are slightly milder than the hard neck variety.

Inside or Outside

Plant in Autumn

Ways to eat

Add to a variety of dishes for additional flavour or make some simple garlic bread.

Describe what you have seen

With so much happening in a garden, the children can enjoy describing some of their observations.

Our children had great fun talking about Rainbow the tortoise and observing what she liked to eat from our garden - in her case, strawberries and celery!

Celery

Do give this a try - it was one of our most successful plants and really satisfying for the children to munch on as a snack. Our pre-school tortoise, Rainbow, also loved munching on the leaves.

How to grow

- Leave seed on the surface of the pot and water well – the children will need to learn a little patience as germination can take about 3 weeks.

- Plant out in May when the seedlings are large enough to handle. Plant about 25cm apart or work with the children to put single seedlings into 7.5cm pots.

- It's important to keep celery moist all the time so ask the children to help with the watering.

What you need

- Celery Seed
- Compost
- Water
- Pots or shallow trays
- Inside space for germinating
- Outside space for planting out

Inside and Outside

Plant in Spring

Ways to eat

We enjoyed munching on the fresh celery as a snack.

Talk about healthy food

Growing a variety of vegetables and fruit in the garden enables plenty of discussion about healthy foods and balanced diets.

When we picked our salad leaves and dug out our potatoes, we chatted to the children about how a variety of foods and a balanced meal can help them grow strong and healthy.

Salad Leaves

There are lots of different easy-to-grow salads – we grew assorted leaves but you could also try chicory, rocket and lamb's lettuce. We grew them inside on a window sill and outside near the back door so they were handy to pick.

How to grow

- Place compost in your pot and gently press down for a flat surface.

- Teach your children to use their pinchy fingers and sprinkle the seeds over the top of the compost.

- Gently cover the seeds with 1cm of compost and press down again.

- Gently water your containers with lukewarm water.

- With some varieties, the more you pick, the more leaves you will get and you will see results in a couple of weeks.

What you need

- Lettuce Seeds
- Compost
- Water
- Pots or containers

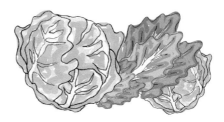

Inside or Outside

Plant in Spring

Ways to eat

Why not pick some tasty looking leaves and add to lunches?

Learning Area: Understanding the world

Explore other animals

The mini ecosystem that exists in the garden provides an opportunity to explore the natural environment and some of it's insects and animals.

The children had great fun looking for mini beasts and taking a closer look with our microscopes. Can you name them? Are they good or bad for the garden?

Spring Cabbage

Our cabbages provided the children with some excellent opportunities to spot some mini beasts as well a surprisingly tasty side dish for lunch.

How to grow

- Like the other vegetables grown from seeds, you can grow spring cabbage in seed trays in late September.

- Cover with a fleece until the end of October to keep the frost away.

What you need

- Cabbage seeds
- Compost
- Water
- Seed Trays
- Fleece – a protective cover
- Nets - optional

Inside and Outside

Plant in Autum

Mini Beast Alert

We've all heard of The Very Hungry Caterpillar - if you take a look at your cabbages, the children may very well see how hungry caterpillars can be! You can grow your cabbages under nets if you would like to avoid them.

Ways to eat

Cabbage Bites pg.69

Your garden will probably contain some beetles but the children will have to be very lucky to spot these as they mostly come out at night. However, if the children do spot them, you can tell this is good news - they eat the slugs and small insects who may eat your plants.

Learning Area: Personal, social and emotional development

Share equipment

Working together in the garden, the children will learn to share the equipment needed to tend to their plants.

We extended this learning as part of a group sharing exercise, where the children worked together to pick out beans and sweetcorn with our tweezers.

Beans

We grew beans, french beans, broad beans and peas. The children loved picking all the different varieties.... and eating them raw! Legumes are also great for increasing nitrogen in the soil.

How to grow

- Start off in seed trays or pots indoors, or sow directly outside.

- Plant outside at the end of May.

- Your beans will need support to grow up. You could use canes or a trellis. We grew ours up a trellis from some window boxes.

- Remember to tie in shoots as they grow and keep well watered.

What you need

- Seeds
- Compost
- Water
- Plant supports like canes or a trellis
- Indoor space for germinating
- Outside space for planting

Inside and Outside

Plant in Spring

Ways to eat

Bouncy Broad Bean Dip
pg.67
Or just eat raw, washed, straight from the garden - they taste yummy!

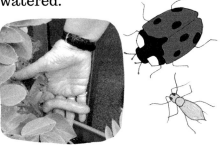

Mini Beast Alert

Our children loved discovering all the ladybirds and their larvae. These mini beasts are very greedy and love to eat greenfly which is beneficial for our gardens. Also keep an eye out for the slugs!

Courgettes

Courgettes are great as you don't need many plants to achieve a good crop. However, as it was so wet when we first put ours out, they rotted and we had to start again!

How to grow

- Sow 4 or 5 seeds in a 10cm pot about 2cm deep in multi-purpose compost.

- Leave on a sunny window sill to germinate until they are sturdy enough to withstand slug attacks.

- Split the seedlings once they fill the pot and put them into larger containers or pots, holding them by the leaves to avoid damage.

- When they are about 15cm, start putting them outside and bring them in at night for a couple of weeks.

- Plant out in beds or large containers in a sunny spot.

What you need

- Courgette seeds
- Multi-purpose compost
- Water
- Seed trays, small and larger pots
- Indoors with sunlight to start
- Outdoors in a sunny spot

Inside and Outside

Plant in Spring

Ways to eat

Funky Frittata pg.65

Mini Beast Alert

Watch out for slugs which eat seedlings and lots of plants. Our children had great fun picking them off!

Sweetcorn

This year our crop was not particularly successful - this may have been due to the wet spell we had earlier in the year and also the visit from our resident mini beasts! We agreed with the children that we will try again.

How to grow

- Plant plug plants of sweetcorn in a large tub with fertilised soil – plug plants are seedlings which have been germinated and grown in trays of small cells.

- Sweetcorn is best grown in groups not straight lines and in a sunny area of the garden.

- You may need to net them to stop the birds having a feast.

- They should ripen by mid to late summer.

- Once the tassels at the end of the cobs have turned brown, test for ripeness by pressing one of the kernels. The corn is ripe if the liquid that comes out is milky.

What you need

- Seeds
- Fertilised soil
- Water
- Netting
- Inside space for germinating
- Outside space in a sunny area for planting out

Inside and Outside

Plant in Spring

" We are growing carrots and sweetcorn because it is healthy and makes the garden beautiful."

L, aged 4

Ways to eat

Sweetcorn provides an easy side dish to munch on at lunchtime.

Activity:

Physical Development

The children had a great time banging golf tees into pumpkins with lightweight hammers. This was a really physical activity, which supported the children with their hand-eye co-ordination. This activity can go on for a long time as the children can pull the golf tees out, with a little bit of adult help, and repeat the activity – many of the children repeated it over and over again!

Pumpkin

As well as conjuring up exciting ideas of Halloween, the children also found the pumpkins visually appealing to watch with their speedy growth and colourful flowers.

How to grow

- Soak your seeds in water overnight to make them grow quicker.

- Fill your pots with compost.

- Plant a seed in each pot, on its edge (not flat), 1cm deep.

- Put your pots on a warm, light window sill and water to begin germination.

- Use compost or manure before planting out.

- Plant out about 2cm deep and 60 -90 cm apart.

- We grew ours in long planters and we tied them to the trellis. Keep well watered.

What you need

- Pumpkin Seeds
- Compost or manure
- Water
- Pots
- Trellis or ties
- Inside space for germinating
- Outside space in a sunny area for planting out

Inside and Outside

Plant in Spring

"We are growing pumpkins and going to use them for Halloween."
L, aged 4

Note: Pumpkin plants can grow very fast. You can trail them over the ground, a trellis or some strong arches. You should also focus on developing a few good pumpkins. You can do this by cutting off most of the flowers or removing the smaller, weaker pumpkins.

Learning Area: Mathematics

Count and weigh

The garden provides numerous items for counting. Children can use simple scales to discover how to balance the correct weight.

We counted out tomatoes from our garden, placed them on a simple set of balancing scales and used mathematical language such as 'more', 'less', 'heavy' and 'light'.

Tomatoes

Tomato fruits are so visual, recognisable and appealing to eat - which makes them a great plant to grow. We discovered children who wouldn't normally eat tomatoes were suddenly very keen to try out what they had grown.

How to grow

- Sow in seed trays or pots - the children can sprinkle seeds thinly across the surface. Cover with a dusting of compost and water lightly.

- Put in a propagator - or a warm area will also suffice.

- Move into the light when seeds start to grow. Once the first leaves show, the children can plant them into individual pots.

- Once roots have filled the pots, move into larger pots and move outside in May.

- Water well and support with canes. Remove side shoots , known as 'pinching out' to increase fruiting.

What you need

- Tomato seeds
- Compost
- Water
- Trays and pots (small and large)
- Canes
- Propagator or warm area in an inside space
- Outside space for planting out

Inside and Outside

Plant in Spring

Ways to eat

Italian Tomato Salad pg.71
Terrific Tomato Tart pg.73
Mini but Mighty Pizza pg.74
Tomato and Basil Sauce pg.77
Tangy Tomato Soup pg.79

Mini Beast Alert

The children enjoyed finding lacewings on our tomato plants - these pretty green insects with see-through wings benefit the garden as they eat green fly which suck out sap from plants, weakening them.

Learning Area: Expressive art and design

Paint what you see

The vibrant colours of a garden provides lots of inspiration for children's artwork. With a mixture of paint colours and brushes, the children can observe and paint a picture of their favourite plant.

We just loved all the different interpretations of a strawberry as seen in the artwork below.

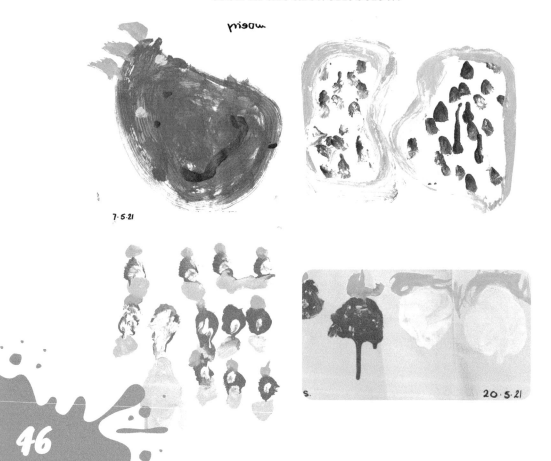

Strawberries

The children got really excited when we announced that we were growing both red and white strawberries as many hadn't seen white ones before.

How to grow

- Grow strawberry plants in different sized clay pots filled with soil and stacked on top of each other.

- Cover with a net to protect your plants.

- Leave in full sunshine and water well. The children will start to see their fruits grow.

What you need

- Strawberry plants
- Compost
- Water
- Clay pots - better for drainage but you can use plastic pots instead
- Netting
- Outside space

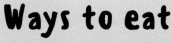

Outside Space

Plant in Spring

Ways to eat

Messy Meringues pg.81
Minty Strawberry Jam pg.83
Wibbly Wobbly Jelly pg.85
Fruity Pancakes pg.88

47

Other berries

Like the strawberries, we bought raspberry, blackberry and white currant plants ready to grow. They produced fruit at different times of the year which maintained the children's interest in the garden.

How to grow

Raspberries
- Plant in tubs - don't plant too deeply and water well.
- Cut back all growth to ground level in late Autumn.

White Currants
- You can grow these plants in any soil - we planted ours in tubs.
- Net them as soon as the fruit changes colour otherwise the birds will have a feast.
- Cut back young growth in Autumn/Winter as they fruit on old growth.

Blackberries
- We chose the Black Cascade variety - they have no thorns and trail down from hanging baskets.
- We hung the baskets low so the children could easily water them and pick fruit in late September.
- Cover with a net once fruit has formed.

What you need

- Small plants
- Acid soil e.g ericaceous compost available at garden centres
- Water
- Large containers with plenty of drainage
- Netting
- Outside space with full sunshine or dappled shade

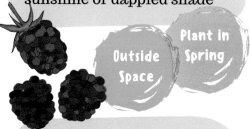

Outside Space

Plant in Spring

Ways to eat

Messy Meringues pg.81
Minty Strawberry Jam pg.83
Wibbly Wobbly Jelly pg.85
Fruity Pancakes pg.88

Note: Fruiting plants don't tend to produce fruit in the first year but do improve as time goes on.

Other fruits

We are experimenting with some other fruits, including some that wouldn't normally bear fruit in the UK climate. The children are waiting patiently as some of the fruit trees and vines grow.

Avocado: After tasting these fruits purchased from the shop, we dried the stones and planted them in pots of compost. The children are patiently keeping an eye on the small avocado tree now growing.

Grapes: Whether your grapevine produces fruit or not, the children will find the colourful foliage extremely interesting to look at in the autumn months.

Kiwis : Like grape vines, kiwi vines will take a few years to produce fruit. The children love watching the vine climb up to the sky, like Jack's beanstalk!
See Turtle Cake page 86.

Apple, pear and plum trees: While we are waiting for our trees to grow, we have also been experimenting with growing apples from pips! The children have been really excited to see how this turns out!

Pineapple: I still can't believe we are growing a pineapple in our pre-school! The children are keeping it watered and observing how it is getting bigger all the time with their care and attention.

Learning Area: Personal, social and emotional development

Care for the plants

There are plenty of positive personal development opportunities for children when they care for their bulbs and seeds. We used our noses for smelling, eyes for watching, our little hands for watering, and even our mouths for tasting our edible varieties - a new experience for many!

The children also responded positively when they received plants as presents to give to family and friends at Christmas, Easter and Mother's Day - or to take home and nuture themselves.

Flowers

Early on in the project, the children made it clear they wanted to grow flowers, so they chose from a variety of seed packets or plug plants donated by parents.

How to grow

- Plant seeds in seed trays inside and follow the individual instructions on the packets.

- Move them outside in late May after the frosts have finished and watch them bloom.

What you need

- Seed packets or plug plants
- Compost
- Water
- Seed trays

Inside and Outside

Plant in Spring

Mini Beast Alert

Brightly coloured and scented flowers attract the bees - and we need the bees! Without bees we would not have very much fruit or vegetables as they help to pollinate our flowers.

Describe what you see

Gardens provide many moments for discussing how and what plants we have grown. The children used the time to draw and paint what they had seen and how it had happened while exploring shapes and colours.

Chapter 3:
Cooking with the children

Cooking with the children

As our garden started to provide plentiful supplies, we decided to make the most of our plants and get cooking! Staff members, parents and the children provided ideas of what we might be able to cook, sharing easy-to-make recipes from different countries and cultures. The following chapter is a collection of some of the most popular recipes plus some straightforward ideas linked to the Early Years Foundation Stage.

We started off simply - making recipes that were easy for the children to participate in such as our Italian Tomato Salad. As our confidence grew, we tried out new kitchen skills like mashing strawberries for jam and peeling some freshly dug out potatoes for our Potato and Leek Soup. Obviously, you will have to determine how much adult supervision is required for some kitchen skills depending on the age and abilities of your children.

 Most of our recipes are relatively easy to make - even with children - but we have highlighted those that may take more time.

 All our recipes have been calculated for children's portions rather than adult sizes. These are estimations and will depend on individual appetites!

 An allergy icon has been placed next to any recipes that contain any of the 14 main allergens.

Use fine motor skills

Using children's scissors to cut herbs is a great way to involve children in food preparation and develop fine motor skills.

Pebble Mix

This fun and healthy recipe gives the children plenty of opportunities for fun with herbs - collecting them, snipping them up, and mixing them all in.

Ingredients:

- 400g tinned chickpeas, drained
- 100g tinned butter beans, drained
- 250g feta cheese
- 1 garlic clove, crushed
- 1 lemon, squeezed
- 5 tbsp olive oil
- A pinch of sea salt
- A handful of fresh chives, snipped
- A handful of fresh mint, stems removed, snipped
- A handful of fresh parsley, stems removed, snipped
- A handful of fresh coriander, stems removed, snipped
- A handful of fresh dill, stems removed, snipped

Serves 4-6

Easy to make

Dairy

Directions:

1. Rinse chickpeas and beans well under cold water and place in a mixing bowl.
2. Add the snipped herbs to the bowl, as well as lemon juice, garlic, oil, and feta cheese and mix.
3. Serve and enjoy.

Recipe created by Yulia Fisher, Little Robins Staff Member

Sand Salad

The children enjoyed the idea of eating 'sand' rather than couscous and got really involved with measuring, chopping, and snipping all the herbs.

Serves 4-6

Easy to make

Wheat and celery

Ingredients:

- 250g couscous
- 10 small tomatoes, roughly chopped
- 1 cucumber, sliced
- 4 radishes, sliced
- 5 celery stalks, tips removed
- 1 yellow pepper, sliced
- 120g peas
- 120g sweetcorn
- 1 lemon, squeezed
- 5 tbsp olive oil
- A small bunch of fresh mint
- A small bunch of fresh chives
- A small bunch of fresh basil
- A small bunch of fresh parsley

Directions:

1. Place couscous in a saucepan and cover with cold water.

2. Bring to the boil then reduce heat to simmer for 8 minutes or until soft. Use a fork to fluff the couscous.

3. Drain any excess water and allow to cool.

4. Place all the ingredients in a large bowl and mix with a wooden spoon.

5. Serve and enjoy!

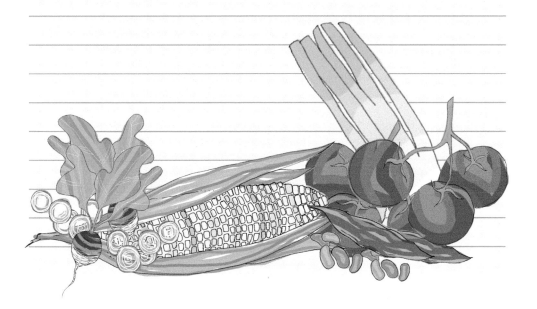

Recipe created by Yulia Fisher, Little Robins Staff Member

Learning Area: Mathematics

Use numbers in play

Cooking allows children to use the ingredients in front of them to practise their counting.

In this recipe, the children counted out the blueberries. We then cut the berries in half and the children could see that this created two.

Minty Blueberry Water

A fruity and refreshing way to enjoy water!

Ingredients:

- 1L still or sparkling water
- 20 blueberries, whole
- 5 mint leaves, remove stems

Serves 4-6

Easy to make

Directions:

1. In a glass jar or jug, add blueberries and mint leaves to still or sparkling water.

2. Stir and place in the fridge to infuse.

3. Best served chilled.

4. You can keep in the fridge for 1 day.

Note: Children should drink this fruit water with a straw to avoid any choking hazards.

What about making an alternative version of this with strawberries and basil? Delicious!

Recipe created by Carrie Smith, Little Robins Pre-School Owner and Manager

Learning Area: Communication and language development

Talk about your plans

Take some time to talk with your children about what you have done and what you plan to do with your ingredients.

When we prepared the Potato and Leek Soup we talked about where the potatoes had come from and what we were going to do with them next in order to create our soup.

Potato and Leek Soup

Under adult supervision, the children could help peeling the potatoes for this warming winter soup.

Ingredients:

- 1 large onion, diced
- 4 medium leeks, washed well, sliced
- 3 large potatoes, peeled, diced
- 1L vegetable stock
- A drizzle of oil (avocado oil recommended)

Serves 6-8

Takes a little time

Celery

Directions:

1. Heat a pan and add oil, onion, leeks, and potatoes.
2. Bring the pan up to sizzle on high heat, stir well. Reduce heat, cover with lid to sweat vegetables for 15 minutes.
3. Add vegetable stock and simmer for 15 minutes then let cool slightly.
4. Place ingredients into a blender and blend until smooth.
5. Reheat and serve.

Recipe created by Carrie Smith, Little Robins Pre-School Owner and Manager

Introduce new words

Cooking recipes from around the world provides a great opportunity to hear and use new words and phrases.

We had great fun sounding out the word 'f-r-i-tah-ta' as well as sounding out 'p' for potato. Maybe you can discover some words that rhyme with cheese or other ingredients?

Alphabet

Aa Bb Cc Dd Ee Ff Gg

Hh Ii Jj Kk Ll Mm Nn

Oo Pp Qq Rr Ss Tt Uu

Vv Ww Xx Yy Zz

Funky Frittata

The children can help peel, chop and slice the ingredients and even crack open the eggs to make this meal – with some adult supervision of course!

Ingredients:

- 500g new potatoes, skin on
- 50g butter
- 1 large onion, finely chopped
- 3 courgettes, thinly sliced
- 1tbsp fresh mint leaves, chopped
- 8 eggs
- 75g pecorino cheese, grated
- A pinch of ground black pepper

Serves 4-6

Takes a little time

Dairy and egg

Directions:

1. Cook the potatoes in boiling water until tender - this should take 15-20 minutes. Drain and let them cool down before slicing in half.
2. Melt the butter in a frying pan and add onion. Cook for a few minutes until soft. Add the courgettes and stir.
3. Stir in the potatoes and continue cooking for a further 5 minutes until the courgettes have softened.
4. Crack the eggs into a bowl and add pecorino and mint. Season with pepper and whisk together using a fork.
5. Pour the egg mixture into the pan on the lowest heat until it sets.
6. Place the pan under a preheated grill to brown the top. Remove from the grill.
7. Leave to cool slightly before you enjoy.

Recipe inspired by Courgette Frittata in
RHS Grow It, Eat It: Simple Gardening Projects and Delicious Recipes by DK

Bouncy Broad Bean Dip

Mashing, squeezing, crushing, stirring – this is a colourful dip for the children to help make.

Ingredients:

- 250g peas
- 250g broad beans
- 1 lime, squeezed
- 1 lemon, squeezed
- 1 garlic clove, crushed
- 200g cream cheese
- 3 chives
- 10 mint leaves

Serves 6-8

Easy to make

Dairy

Directions:

1. Steam peas and broad beans for 2-3 minutes until cooked.
2. Shell the beans and place into a mixing bowl along with the cooked peas.
3. Mash with a potato masher.
4. Add lemon, lime, garlic, cream cheese and herbs to the bowl and mix with a spatula.
5. Blend all the ingredients in a food processor until smooth.
6. Transfer onto a serving dish and enjoy with a side of carrots or flatbread.

Recipe created by Yulia Fisher, Little Robins Staff Member

" Waaaoooo! L ate mashed potato and cabbage – thanks Little Robins team"

L's Mum

3 Can play in the water

"Wow, I am impressed!"

V's mum on hearing he ate cabbage from the garden.

" Brilliant, I will add cabbage to next season's stash of seeds for our veggie patch."

E's mum on hearing that she ate her cabbage.

Cabbage Bites

Who knew cabbage would create such a positive response from our children!

Ingredients:

- 1 head of spring cabbage, shredded
- 3 tbsp unsalted butter
- Pinch of sea salt to taste

Serves 8-10

Easy to make

Directions:

1. Place the cabbage in a pot and cover with water.
2. Bring to boil for 3 minutes until the cabbage is slightly tender but not soggy!
3. Drain the cabbage and transfer to cold water.
4. Sautè in a pan with butter and season to taste with a pinch of salt.
5. Serve alongside a tasty piece of meat or fish for a delicious meal!

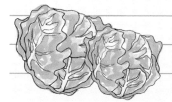

Recipe adapted from Basic Cabbage Stir-Fry recipe on bbcgoodfood.com

Practise hand-eye co-ordination

Food preparation is a great opportunity for children to practise their hand-eye co-ordination. Can you use a knife to cut the tomatoes? Or stir a mixture with a spoon?

Note: Children should use a sharp knife only under close adult supervision.

Italian Tomato Salad

You can delight in watching the children tear the basil leaves and mixing the flavours of Italy with this simple salad.

Ingredients:

- 4 large ripe tomatoes, chopped
- 4 tablespoons of olive oil
- 300g mozzarella cheese, sliced
- 8 large fresh basil leaves, stems removed, torn
- A pinch of sea salt to taste

Serves 4-6

Easy to make

Dairy

Directions:

1. Arrange the tomatoes and mozzarella on a plate in an alternating pattern.
2. Scatter the basil leaves over the plate.
3. Drizzle with a little olive oil.
4. Season with sea salt to taste and enjoy straight away.

Recipe by Lucy Cooper, Little Robins Parent

Learning Area: Expressive art and design

Manipulate materials to achieve a planned effect

Chiildren can learn to manipulate materials to achieve what they need to do.

We rolled out pastry with our children to help develop their fine motor skills when making our tomato tart.

Terrific Tomato Tart

This tasty tart will keep the children busy - slicing, rolling, pricking, spreading and then eating!

Ingredients:

- 350g puff pastry
- 4 tbsp pesto
- 4 tomatoes, chopped
- 1 small handful fresh basil leaves

Serves 4-6

Easy to make

Dairy and nuts

Directions:

1. Preheat the oven to 190°C/ Gas Mark 5 and line a tray with baking paper.
2. Roll out the pastry on the baking paper. Score 1cm from the edge. Use a fork to prick the middle of pastry.
3. Add the pesto to the middle of the pastry and spread out evenly.
4. Pop the tomatoes on top of the pesto, spaced out evenly.
5. Place the tart inside the oven and cook for 20 minutes.
6. Remove from oven once cooked and add fresh basil on top.
7. Slice up and serve warm.

Recipe adapted from Cheese, Tomato and Pesto Tart
from Good Food magazine, June 2006

Mini but Mighty Pizza

Whether it's kneading the dough or sprinkling out their toppings, children will love making their own pizzas, especially with vegetable toppings from the garden.

Ingredients:

Pizza dough

- 2 tsp dried yeast
- 1 tsp sugar
- 250ml warm water
- 350g strong plain flour
- 1 tsp salt
- 1 tbsp olive oil

Toppings

- 2 courgettes, grated
- 200g passata
- 4 ripe tomatoes, chopped
- 1 tbsp fresh mixed herbs
- 2 tbsp olive oil
- 300g sweetcorn

Makes 8 mini pizzas

Takes a little time

Wheat

Directions:

1. Mix the yeast and sugar with 4 tbsp of water. Leave in a warm place for up to 15 minutes or until frothy.

2. Mix flour and salt in a separate bowl. Create a well in the centre of the bowl with a wooden spoon. Add oil, yeast and remaining water, mixing to create a dough.

3. Place the dough on a flat, lightly floured surface and knead for 4-5 minutes or until smooth.

4 Return the dough to the bowl and cover with an oiled sheet of cling film. Leave in a warm place for 30 minutes or until the dough has doubled in size.

5. Place absorbent kitchen paper over the prepared vegetables for 5- 10 mins to soak up any excess moisture.

6. Preheat the oven to 200°C/ Gas Mark 6.

7. Divide dough into 8 parts and roll each one into thin circles. Place on an oiled baking tray, pushing out the edges until it's about 5mm thick- no more as it will rise during cooking.

8. Spread 2-3 tsp of passata over the pizza bases and add vegetable toppings. Add a sprinkling of mixed herbs to taste, then lightly drizzle olive oil over top.

9. Bake in the oven until crispy (about 15 mins) and serve hot.

Recipe adapted from Easy Tomato Pizzas by Jane Hornby on bbcgoodfood.com

Learning Area:
Personal, social and emotional development

Learn a new skill

Making pizza provides a number of opportunities for the children to learn new skills which build confidence. How about teaching the children how to crack an egg? Or how to knead the dough?

You can see from other recipes in this book, the children can also learn to peel potatoes and grate carrots under adult supervision.

Tomato and Basil Sauce

A lot of the preparation work for this sauce can be done with the children - they can challenge themselves to peel off the outer layers of the onions and garlic.

Ingredients:

- 1 small red onion, chopped finely
- 3 tbsp olive oil
- 2 garlic cloves, peeled, crushed
- 400g tinned chopped tomatoes
- 200g ripe plum tomatoes, chopped
- Pinch of salt and pepper
- A pinch of caster sugar
- A handful of fresh basil leaves, torn

Serves 6-8

Takes a little time

Directions:

1. Heat oil in a saucepan on a medium heat and add the garlic and onions. Sauté gently for 7-9 minutes, stirring occasionally, until the onions are soft and see-through.
2. Add the tinned and fresh tomatoes, a pinch of sugar and most of the basil leaves. Cook for 15 minutes, stirring occasionally. Remove from the heat.
3. This sauce is great served warm with pasta and a sprinkle of the remaining basil.

Explore mathematical terms

Simple food preparation allows children to build their knowledge of mathematical terms.

When chopping ingredients, you can talk about cutting into 'small' and 'large' pieces, or cutting in 'half' or leaving 'whole'.

Whole

Half

Tangy Tomato Soup

The children can help chop the tomatoes for this quick and easy meal.

Ingredients:

- 6 tomatoes, chopped
- 1 onion, peeled, chopped
- 2 tbsp tomato purée
- 500ml vegetable stock
- 2 tbsp oil (avocado recommended)

Serves
4 - 6

Easy to
make

Celery

Directions:

1. Heat oil in large pot over a medium heat. Add the onion and cook for 4 minutes or until soft. Sprinkle in enough flour to create a consistency you like and stir well.

2. Add tomatoes, vegetable stock and tomato purée to the pot. Bring to the boil whilst stirring well. Reduce heat and simmer for 10 minutes.

3. Let the soup cool slightly before blitzing in a food processor until smooth. Add water if you prefer a lighter texture.

4. Serve warm and enjoy!

"Great tomato soup – F couldn't stop telling everyone what he had made."

F's Mum

Recipe by Little Robins Parent

Describe the texture

Have fun with the children describing textures - how do some of your ingredients feel?

The meringue feels crunchy. The strawberries feel soft. What other textures can you discover and describe?

Messy Meringues

Have fun making this messy but simple dessert.
Encourage the children to crumble in the meringues and
chop up the strawberries.

Ingredients:

- 150ml double cream
- 300g plain greek yogurt
- 1 tbsp honey
- 75g meringues
- 300g strawberries, hulled, chopped

Serves
6-8

Easy to
make

Dairy and egg

Directions:

1. Whip the cream in a large mixing bowl with a whisk until thick.
2. Fold in the yoghurt and honey and mix with a spoon.
3. Crumble in pieces of meringue then add the chopped strawberries.
4. Serve immediately or keep in the fridge.

Healthy Touch: We added more yoghurt
than cream for a healthier touch.

Talk about changes

Cooking is a great opportunity to notice and talk about changes in your environment.

While making jam, you can explore how liquids can turn to solids. Or if baking a cake, discover what happens when a runny cake mix comes out of the oven? Why not see what happens to ice when it gets warm?

Minty Strawberry Jam

The children can have a great time mashing down the strawberries for this juicy jam.

Ingredients:

- 840g fresh strawberries, hulled
- 315g sugar
- 2 tsp fresh mint, finely chopped
- 1 lemon, grated zest
- 45g pectin

Makes 6 - 8 small jars

Easy to make

Directions:

1. In a mixing bowl, mash the strawberries with a potato masher.
2. Add sugar, mint, and lemon zest to the bowl, mix and let stand for 15 minutes.
3. Add pectin to the mixing bowl, stirring for 3 minutes. Let stand for 5 minutes.
4. Pour the mixture into glass jam jars and keep in fridge for up to 3 weeks.

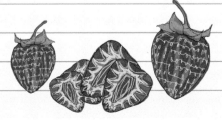

Recipe provided by Little Robins parent

Explore ways to move

Children love to explore all the different ways that they can move.

Take the opportunity to wobble like a jelly. Can your children roll like a sausage roll? What does it feel like to jump like a pancake flipping in the pan?

Wibbly Wobbly Jelly

The children will love adding the various fruits to give this classic jelly a splash more colour.

Ingredients:

- 250g fresh mixed summer fruit, washed, halved
- 1 packet of fruit flavoured jelly
- Cold water – check amount required on jelly packet
- Boiling water – check amount on jelly packet and keep away from children

Serves 4 -6

Takes a little time

Directions:

1. Separate the jelly into cubes and place in a large mixing bowl.
2. Add boiling water to the jelly cubes stirring gently until completely dissolved.
3. Stir in cold water.
4. Place the mixed summer fruit into the bowl and transfer into individual moulds.
5. Place in the fridge for 4 hours until the liquid turns into wibbly wobbly jelly.
6. Serve cold and enjoy.

Recipe created by Carrie Smith, Little Robins Pre-School Owner and Manager

Turtle Cake

Who doesn't like a reassuring slice of cake, especially when the children can decorate it with fresh kiwi to look like a turtle shell.

Ingredients:

For the Cake:

- 130g flour
- 1 tsp baking powder
- 2 eggs
- 150g caster sugar
- 1 tsp vanilla extract
- 4 kiwis, peeled, chopped

Serves 6-8

Takes a little time

Wheat, dairy and eggs

For the frosting:

- 225g cream cheese (room temperature)
- 60g unsalted butter (room temperature)
- 125g icing sugar
- 1 tbsp vanilla extract
- 2 kiwis, sliced for decoration

Directions:

1. Preheat the oven to 180°C/ Gas Mark 4 and lightly grease a 20cm cake tin.

2. Add eggs, vanilla extract, sugar and kiwi into a mixing bowl and stir with a spatula.

3. Sift in the flour and baking powder until it creates a smooth batter.

4. Place the batter into the greased cake tin, place in the oven and bake for 35-45 minutes until cooked through.

5. To make the frosting, add cream cheese, butter, icing sugar and vanilla extract to a bowl and mix until smooth.

6. Let the cake cool before using a spatula to spread the frosting evenly over the top.

7. Decorate with sliced kiwi and enjoy!

Fruity Pancakes

The children will be amused mashing and folding in the extra fruit for these juicy pancakes.

Ingredients:

- 2 ripe bananas
- 2 eggs
- 50g rolled oats
- 50g plain flour
- 25ml milk
- 150g mixed berries, chopped
- 1 tbsp coconut oil
- Pinch of cinnamon

Serves 4-6

Takes a little time

Wheat, dairy and eggs

Directions:

1. Mash the bananas in a bowl.
2. Add eggs, oats, flour, milk and cinnamon to the bowl. Mix well then fold in the berries.
3. Melt the coconut oil in a pan and spoon in a heap of your pancake mixture on a medium heat.
4. Fry your pancakes for about 3 minutes on each side until golden.
5. Serve warm with a dash of maple syrup and enjoy!

Recipe adapted from Fruity Pancakes in My Fussy Eater by Ciara Atwell

Other Recipes

We also tried out a number of other recipes with food from the Little Robins garden.
What ideas can you and the children come up with?

Baby Carrot Cakes

Fruit Kebabs

Frozen Yoghurt Bark

Cheesy Potato Bake

Index

AVOCADO - 49

ALLERGIES - 55

BEANS - 39
- Bouncy Broad Bean Dip - 67

BLACKBERRIES - 48

CABBAGE - 37
- Cabbage Bites - 69

CARROTS - 29

CELERY - 33

COURGETTES - 40
- Funky Frittata - 65

EARLY YEARS FOUNDATION STAGE (EYFS) - 7, 19, 55
- Communication and language development - 62, 64
- Expressive art and design - 46, 72, 80
- Mathematics - 28, 44, 60, 78
- Personal, social and emotional development - 38, 76
- Physical development - 34, 42, 56, 70, 84
- Understanding the world - 32, 36, 52, 82

EQUIPMENT - 15
  - Quirky Planters - 20

FLOWERS - 51

FRUIT TREES - 49

GARLIC - 31

GRAPES - 49

HERBS - 22 - 25
- Herby Playdough - 22
- Pebble Mix - 57
- Sand Salad - 58
- Minty Blueberry Water - 61

KIWI - 49
- Turtle Cake - 86

LEEKS - 30

MINI BEASTS
- Bees - 51
- Caterpillar - 37
- Lacewing - 45
- Ladybird - 39
- Slugs - 37, 40

PINEAPPLE - 49

POTATOES - 27
- Potato Printing - 26
- Potato and Leek Soup 63

PUMPKIN - 43

RASPBERRIES - 48

SALAD LEAVES - 35

SPACE - 12 - 14

STRAWBERRIES - 47
- Messy Meringues - 81
- Minty Strawberry Jam - 83
- Wibbly Woblly Jelly - 85
- Fruity Pancakes - 88

SWEETCORN - 41

TOMATO - 45
- Italian Tomato Salad - 71
- Terrific Tomato Tart - 73
- Mini but Mighty Pizza - 74
- Tomato and Basil Sauce - 77
- Tangy Tomato Soup 79

WHITE CURRANTS - 48